Commonsense Methods for Children with Special Educational Needs

Seventh edition

Peter Westwood

Routledge
Taylor & Francis Group

LONDON AND NEW YORK

Seventh edition published 2015
by Routledge
2 Park Square, Milton Park, Abingdon, Oxon OX14 4RN

and by Routledge
711 Third Avenue, New York, NY 10017

Routledge is an imprint of the Taylor & Francis Group, an informa business

© 2015 P. Westwood

First edition published by Routledge 1987
Sixth edition published by Routledge 2011

British Library Cataloguing in Publication Data
A catalogue record for this book is available from the British Library

Library of Congress Cataloging in Publication Data
Westwood, Peter S.
Commonsense methods for children with special educational needs / Peter Westwood. – Seventh edition.
    pages cm.
    1. Children with disabilities–Education. 2. Mainstreaming in education.
    3. Special education. I. Title.
    LC4015.W44 2015
    371.9–dc23   2014039081

ISBN: 978-1-138-02250-8 (hbk)
ISBN: 978-1-138-02252-2 (pbk)
ISBN: 978-1-315-71669-5 (ebk)

Typeset in Bembo
by Wearset Ltd, Boldon, Tyne and Wear

MIX
Paper from
responsible sources
FSC® C013056
www.fsc.org

Printed and bound in Great Britain by
TJ International Ltd, Padstow, Cornwall

Contents

Introduction   1

1   Special educational needs and learning difficulties   3

Disabilities and impairments   4
Meeting students' needs   5
Response to intervention model   6
Learning difficulties   7
Teaching children with general and specific learning difficulties   11
Online resources   12
Further reading   12

2   Students with intellectual disability and autism   13

Intellectual disability   13
Priorities in teaching students with intellectual disability   14
Learning characteristics of students with intellectual disability   15
Teaching approaches for students with intellectual disability   19
Preparation for work   20
Specific approaches for students with severe intellectual disability   20
Students with autism spectrum disorder (ASD)   21
Interventions for autism   23
Teaching, training and management: general principles   23
Specific programmes and methods   24
Online resources   26
Further reading   27

3   Students with physical disabilities or health issues   28

The impact of physical disability on learning and development   28
Cerebral palsy   29
Instructional needs of students with cerebral palsy   30
Epilepsy   31
Spina bifida   31
Traumatic brain injury   32

Augmentative and alternative communication 33
General points for mainstream teachers 33
Childhood obesity 34
Asthma and allergies 34
Online resources 35
Further reading 35

4   Students with sensory impairments   36

Vision impairment 36
Special educational needs of children with impaired vision 36
Accessing the curriculum and the environment 37
Teaching students with impaired vision 39
Transition to work or further study 41
Hearing impairment 41
Types and degrees of hearing loss 41
Impact of hearing loss on learning and development 43
Basic academic skills 44
Modes of communication 45
Assistive technology 46
Teaching students with impaired hearing 47
Online resources 48
Further reading 48

5   Gifted and talented students   49

Prevalence 49
Identifying gifted learners 49
Defining giftedness, talent and creativity 50
Underachievement 52
Meeting the needs of gifted and talented students 53
General principles of teaching gifted learners 56
Specific implementation models 57
Online resources 59
Further reading 60

6   Self-management and self-regulation   61

Definition of terms 61
Self-management in children 62
Teaching self-management 63
Locus of control 64
Attribution retraining 65
Strategy-based instruction 65
Maintenance and generalization 66
Metacognition 67

Cognitive behaviour modification 67
Online resources 68
Further reading 68

7 Managing classroom behaviour   69

The effects of misbehaviour 69
Preventing behaviour problems 70
Behaviour management policy 70
A three-tier model of intervention 71
Positive behaviour support 71
A team approach 72
Classroom behaviour 72
Identifying the problem 74
Modifying behaviour 74
Cognitive approaches for self-control 75
Strategies for reducing disruptive behaviour 76
Aggressive behaviour 79
Bullying 80
Attention deficit hyperactivity disorder 82
Online resources 83
Further reading 84

8 Social skills and peer group acceptance   85

Opportunities for social interaction 86
Creating a supportive environment 86
Facilitating social interaction 87
Importance of group work 88
Social skills training 89
Limitations of social training 91
Online resources 92
Further reading 92

9 The effective teaching of reading   93

A sound start 93
The simple view of reading 94
The role of phonemic awareness 95
Teaching letter-to-sound correspondences 96
Simple word-building experiences 98
Selecting early text materials 98
Moving beyond simple phonics 98
Building sight vocabulary 99
Comprehension 100
Teaching approaches 104

Reading aloud 106
Sustained Silent Reading 107
Online resources 107
Further reading 108

10   Intervention for reading difficulties   109

General principles for reading intervention (Tier 2) 109
Using tutors 110
Specific programmes for intervention (Tier 3) 111
Supplementary tutoring strategies and activities 115
Technology, ICT and reading 119
Online resources 120
Further reading 121

11   Problems with written language   122

Areas of difficulty 122
Losing confidence and motivation 123
Teaching approaches 124
Intervention for individuals and groups 127
Paving the way to success 128
Paired writing 129
Suggestions for reluctant writers 129
Word processors 132
Online resources 133
Further reading 133

12   Difficulties with spelling   134

Best practices in spelling instruction 134
Spelling as a complex behaviour 136
Teaching spelling 139
Spelling rules 141
Dictation 142
Spelling lists 142
Developing strategic spellers 143
Remedial strategies 143
Programming for individual students 145
Online resources 146
Further reading 146

13   Numeracy and basic mathematical skills   147

Contemporary perspectives on mathematics teaching 147
Whole-class teaching and group work 148
Learning difficulties in mathematics 149

Assisting students who struggle with mathematics 150
What should be taught? 151
A diagnostic approach 151
Learning at the concrete and semi-concrete levels 152
Teaching computational skills 154
Calculators 156
Developing problem-solving skills and strategies 157
Students with specific talents in mathematics 159
Online resources 159
Further reading 160

14 **Differentiating the curriculum and adapting instruction** 161

Keep it simple 162
Adapting curriculum content 163
Modifying activities and learning tasks 163
Instructional materials 164
Products from lessons 165
Homework assignments 165
Teaching strategies 165
Assessment 166
Starting points 167
Accommodations for students with disabilities 168
Universal Design for Learning 168
Online resources 169
Further reading 170

15 **Teaching methods for general and specific purposes** 171

Lesson study as a professional activity 171
Selecting teaching methods 172
Teacher-directed approaches 172
Student-centred approaches 176
Situated learning 180
Computer-based instruction (CBI) and computer-aided learning (CAL) 180
E-learning 182
Online resources 183
Further reading 183

References 185
Index 208

Introduction

This seventh edition of *Commonsense Methods for Children with Special Educational Needs* continues to be concerned with the practicalities of learning and teaching, rather than with the ideology of 'special needs education' and 'inclusion'. The material here comes partly from my own experiences as a classroom teacher, an educational psychologist and later a university lecturer; but I also draw extensively on the most recent international research related to children with special needs.

During the four years since the previous edition of the book appeared there has been growing concern in Britain, Australia and the US over the standard of teaching that is offered in many schools. Most recently, criticism has also focused on the quality of pre-service training and preparation that our teachers often receive – which has been described in the media as ranging from 'inadequate to appalling'. In particular, there seems to be reluctance on the part of teacher educators to expose our trainee teachers to research-based (evidence-based) methods of instruction. These are the teaching methods that studies have shown conclusively to be the most effective in raising students' attainment levels and lowering failure rates. I discuss this issue fully at the beginning of Chapter 15 – where I link poor quality teaching with the learning problems that some students exhibit.

In this edition I have continued to provide information and practical advice that has universal application. By drawing on sound research and practices in Britain, the US, Australia and New Zealand I have made it clear that all these countries tend to face similar challenges when meeting the needs of exceptional children. Countries have much to learn from one another. It is clear that children with special educational needs, no matter where they are in the world, display remarkably similar learning characteristics, and they all benefit from high-quality teaching.

All chapters have been revised to take account of recent research, policies and practices. I have given additional attention this time to issues associated with e-learning and computer-aided instruction, particularly in areas of language and literacy. The topic of lesson study, as an aid to professional development for teachers, has been addressed for the first time. And issues associated with transition from school to employment or to further study for students with disabilities have been discussed in more detail.

This seventh edition reflects changes in terminology and diagnosis introduced in the new edition of the *Diagnostic and Statistical Manual of Mental Disorders (DSM-5)*. I have also taken full account of recent important changes in the UK, such as the new *Children and Families Act*, the introduction of the *Education, Health and Care Plan (EHCP)* and the revised *National Curriculum*. In the US, a major important change has been the introduction of *Common Core State Standards*. Where appropriate, I have linked some of my practical advice to the Common Core. In Australia, a new *Australian Curriculum* was introduced in 2013, and I have endeavoured to show how students with disabilities can be helped to gain access to this curriculum.

I hope this new edition will continue to help all teachers increase their understanding of children's special educational needs, and at the same time increase their repertoire of teaching and management skills.

Peter Westwood

Chapter 1

Special educational needs and learning difficulties

It is appropriate to begin by delineating the population of students described as having 'special educational needs'. In most developed countries the term 'special needs' has legal significance, denoting a mandated responsibility for schools to identify students who are entitled to support and additional resources. It is necessary for children to be assessed by relevant professionals in order to be officially classified as having special learning needs. It is not a term that can simply be attached by teachers or school principals as a label to describe any student who fails to make normal progress.

There are other students who fall outside the official classification of 'disabled' or 'special needs' but still experience learning difficulties. In the past these students have been referred to by many labels – 'slow learners', 'the-hard-to-teach', 'under-achievers' and more recently, 'children who find school hard' (Booth, 2013, p. 20) and 'students who struggle to connect' (Wery & Thomson, 2013, p. 103). Taking all forms of disability and learning difficulties together, it is estimated in most countries that about 20 per cent of children of school age have some form of special educational need, short term or longer term (DfE, 2013a; NCES, 2013).

Educators in the US prefer the term 'exceptional children', rather than 'students with special needs'. Exceptional children are described as having differences that occur to such an extent that they require additional services and modification to school practices (Kirk *et al.*, 2012). Gifted students are included under the category 'exceptional', as well as students with disabilities.

In the UK, the term *special educational need* (SEN) was introduced many years ago in the Warnock Report (DES, 1978). It is still regarded as an appropriate general descriptor, and appears in the most recent legislation. For example, in the *Children and Families Act: Section 20.1* (House of Commons, 2014) it is stated that: 'A child or young person has special educational needs if he or she has a learning difficulty or disability which calls for special educational provision to be made for him or her.' The Act covers individuals in the age range from 0 to 25 years, and reflects the hopes and intentions expressed earlier in a government Green Paper titled *Support and Aspiration: A New Approach to Special Educational Needs and Disability* (DfE, 2011). More specifically, the Act explains that a learning difficulty refers to 'a significantly greater problem in learning than is experienced by the majority of others of the same age'. A disability is defined as 'a condition which prevents or significantly hinders a child from making use of facilities provided for others in mainstream schools'. These children have a right to special assistance when accessing the mainstream curriculum. Students with special needs in the UK are generally those with cognitive impairment, physical or sensory disability, health problems, attention deficits, reading and writing problems, or behaviour and social difficulties (Gov.UK, 2013a).

Similarly in Australia and New Zealand, students are described as having special educational needs if they cannot learn in the same way as other children (AngloInfo, 2014; New Zealand Government, 2014). According to the Australian Curriculum Assessment and Reporting Authority (ACARA, 2014a) children assessed as having special needs are those with disabilities, health-related conditions, or learning difficulties. ACARA also indicates that the national curriculum often needs to be modified to accommodate the needs and different rates of learning of these students.

In the US some 14 categories of disability or special need are covered by the *Individuals with Disabilities Education Act* (IDEA) (US Department of Education, 2014). Under IDEA, individuals with special needs identified by appropriate professionals are entitled to special support between the ages of three and 21 years. The categories under the Act refer to difficulties associated with intellectual, physical, sensory, personal, social, emotional and behavioural aspects of development (LDA, 2014). The US category that has seen most increase in number of students over the years is that of learning disability – for reasons that are explained later.

In an attempt to clarify definitions and descriptions of students with special needs applied in various countries, the OECD (2007) created three convenient categories. These categories are useful in that they embrace the increasingly diverse group of students with learning problems found in inclusive classrooms today:

- students with identifiable disabilities and impairments;
- students with behavioural and/or emotional disorders, or with specific difficulties in learning;
- students with difficulties arising from socio-economic, cultural or linguistic disadvantage (including those learning English as a second or additional language).

Other populations of students who may require additional support in schools are children who are intellectually gifted or specifically talented. In the US and Canada, gifted students are regarded as part of the population requiring additional provisions. In the UK and Australia these students are not covered under special education legislation but are regarded as definitely requiring support of a different nature.

Disabilities and impairments

As indicated above, some students have special educational needs because they have a disability. The abbreviation SEND (special educational needs and disability) has been introduced to refer to this population. Their disabilities may include: *intellectual disability* (previously referred to in some countries as 'mental retardation' or 'mental handicap'), *hearing impairment, vision impairment, physical disability, autism, language disorder* and *specific learning disability*. Associated with any of the above disabilities one may also find some degree of *emotional disturbance, behaviour problems* and *communication difficulties*. Physical handicaps, vision impairment and hearing impairment are all regarded as fairly low-incidence disabilities, together accounting for no more than 2–3 per cent of the school population. Significant emotional and behavioural difficulties are reported in approximately 9 per cent, with double that number of children judged to be at risk for developing such problems (Turnbull *et al.*, 2012). The number of children with social, emotional and behavioural problems has increased very significantly in recent years (ATL, 2014).

Intellectual disability is discussed fully in Chapter 2, covering all degrees of cognitive impairment from mild to profound. Intellectual disability is sometimes also referred to as a *developmental delay* or, as in the *Diagnostic and Statistical Manual of Mental Disorders (DSM-5)*, as *intellectual developmental disorder* (APA, 2013). The prevalence of intellectual disability among children has remained fairly stable over the past decade at 2–3 per cent. Some children with intellectual disability may have additional sensory, physical or communication impairments, and are described as having *complex multiple disabilities*. Chapter 2 also provides information about autism, a condition that may or may not accompany intellectual disability. Autism is sometimes classified as a *pervasive developmental disorder* (PDD).

Hearing impairment includes students who are deaf and others with some degree of hearing loss. Vision impaired students are those who are blind or with low vision (partial sight). The characteristics and special needs of these students with sensory impairments are described fully in Chapter 4. A very few individuals may have both hearing loss and blindness.

Physical disabilities are described in Chapter 3. The most common conditions include cerebral palsy, spina bifida, traumatic brain injury, epilepsy and chronic health problems such as asthma, cystic fibrosis, Type 1 diabetes and allergic reactions. Many of these students have normal ability to learn but may have problems attending school regularly or, in the case of physical disability, in accessing resources or activities in school, and in general mobility.

Specific learning disability (SpLD) refers to a severe learning problem experienced by some 3 per cent of students of average or high intelligence when acquiring the basic academic skills involved in reading, writing, spelling and mathematics. The most common form of SpLD is *dyslexia*. In the US, more than 50 per cent of children identified as having special educational needs are currently labelled 'learning disabled'. But it has been suggested that many of these students do not really meet the criterion of at least average intelligence – they are often categorized as learning disabled in order to attract funding and services for their schools and programmes.

An important difference between the UK and other countries – including the US – is in the use of the term *learning disability*. Unfortunately, the UK now applies this term to students with intellectual disability, not to average students with severe reading or mathematics difficulties. Under the UK definition learning disability (intellectual disability) involves impaired intelligence, a significantly reduced ability to understand complex information and to learn new skills, and an inability to cope independently and socially. Persons with learning disabilities in Britain are classified as having 'moderate learning difficulty', 'severe learning difficulty' or 'profound and multiple learning difficulties'. This inconsistency in terminology gives rise to much confusion when reading international research literature. In this book, the term *intellectual disability* will be used exclusively to refer to students whose learning problems and special needs are primarily due to significant cognitive impairment. Where the term 'learning disability' is used here it refers to a specific difficulty in learning basic skills in students of *normal intelligence*.

Meeting students' needs

It is now mandated in the UK that any child assessed as having special educational needs must be provided with an *Education, Health and Care Plan (EHCP)* specifying any special arrangements that need to be made and any additional services required. The EHCP replaces the previous 'statement of special needs' that had been in force for some years. The Code of Practice states that:

> A local authority must conduct an assessment of education, health and care needs and prepare an EHC plan when it considers that it may be necessary for special educational provision to be made for the child or young person through an EHC plan.
>
> (DfE, 2013b, Section 7.1, p. 92)

The aims of the EHCP are not only to increase accountability for designing effective programmes, but also to involve parents much more directly in the planning process. The EHCP also helps coordinate the various supplementary services more efficiently (e.g. medical, therapeutic, counselling). Students' special learning needs are also addressed by making adaptations to the mainstream curriculum, the teaching approach and the educational resources. These adjustments are often referred to as *differentiation* – the central topic of Chapter 14.

In the US, the *Individuals with Disabilities Education Improvement Act* (US Department of Education, 2004) states:

> Disability is a natural part of the human experience and in no way diminishes the right of individuals to participate in or contribute to society. Improving educational results for children with disabilities is an essential element of our national policy of ensuring equality of opportunity, full participation, independent living, and economic self-sufficiency for individuals with disabilities.
>
> (Section 682c)

To this end, children with special educational needs are provided with an *individual education plan* (IEP) that specifies in detail the modifications, accommodations and services they require. The use of an IEP is also common in Australian schools, although it may be called by a different name in some states. The value of an IEP is that it ensures all personnel involved in teaching and managing the child are clear about the objectives of the programme and the adaptations to curriculum that may be needed. Equally important, the IEP process keeps the child's parents fully informed and involved.

Response to intervention model

One of the more recent school-based approaches to meeting students' needs is known as *Response to Intervention* (RtI) (Barth *et al.*, 2013; NAEYC, 2014). Under this model all children beginning formal schooling receive high-quality instruction in basic literacy and numeracy using systematic evidence-based teaching. This is termed *Tier 1* or First Wave Teaching. During this period, any children who are not making adequate progress are immediately given additional, regular, intensive tutoring in small groups (*Tier 2* or Second Wave Teaching). Only those children who fail to respond within a reasonable period of time to this additional support are then considered to have a significant learning difficulty and are referred on to *Tier 3* (Third Wave Teaching) for in-depth assessment and for even more intensive one-to-one tuition (Barth *et al.*, 2013; Ludlow, 2014). According to Smith and Tyler (2010), the advantages of the RtI model include:

- a child does not have to accumulate many months of failure before being identified and receiving support;
- effective evidence-based teaching methods are used within each tier;
- learning disability is distinguished from general learning difficulties not by measuring IQ, but by the child's rate of response to additional support.

Learning difficulties

Children with learning difficulties tend to fall into one of three possible sub-groups – those with *general learning difficulties* but with no disability or impairment; those with a *language-based specific learning disability* (SpLD) which includes students whose difficulties are associated with receptive and expressive language weaknesses; and those with a *non-verbal learning disability* (NLD).

Children with *general* learning difficulties represent the largest group. There are far fewer children with specifically language-based learning difficulties, and fewer still with non-verbal difficulties. The learning characteristics of these three sub-groups are rather different, but they all share a common need for systematic and direct teaching. Students with learning difficulties frequently experience problems at the time of transition from primary to secondary school, not only in terms of increased academic demands but also in social adjustment (Hughes *et al.*, 2013).

General learning difficulties

The term *general learning difficulties* will be used in this book when discussing students of average or somewhat below average intelligence who are not in any way intellectually disabled or with sensory defects. The IQs for this sub-group are typically reported to be between 70 and 100. In the case of children from disadvantaged backgrounds or with emotional or behavioural problems, potential IQs can sometimes be well above 100. Often their difficulties in learning arise from social, emotional, motivational or behavioural problems, poor school attendance, or from the effects of socio-economic disadvantage (Abrams, 2010; Nowicki *et al.*, 2014). Poverty and social disadvantage in particular are known to be major causes of students' difficulties in school (Krashen, 2014). In some cases, their problems are exacerbated by inappropriate or insufficient teaching. Some authorities even suggest that many of these students would not have learning problems at all if schools focused more on improving the overall standards of teaching (Gov.UK, 2014a; OfSTED, 2010).

Children with general learning difficulties (many of whom are not formally identified and recorded in official statistics) and those with social, emotional and behavioural problems comprise the two largest sub-groups of children needing support. The overall prevalence of general learning difficulty among school-age children is estimated to be between 12 and 16 per cent, with great variation across schools.

The cause of general learning difficulty usually cannot be attributed to a single factor. Most learning problems arise from a complex interaction among variables such as the learners' prior knowledge and experience, learners' cognitive ability, learners' confidence and expectation of success, teachers' instructional method, complexity of teachers' language, the perceived relevance and value of the curriculum content or task, and suitability of resource materials. Until recently, teaching methods and instructional materials were rarely investigated as possible causes of a learning difficulty. Now it is readily acknowledged that inappropriate teaching and inaccessible curriculum materials can present major barriers to learning (DfES, 2004; Gov.UK, 2014a). Many additional factors also contribute to a failure to learn, such as distractions in the learning environment, the health or emotional state of the learner, the interpersonal relationship between teacher and learner, and social relationships within the peer group.

Many researchers have attempted to summarize characteristics of students with general learning difficulties, resulting in lists similar to the one below – often referred to as the 'deficit model' (Peterson & Hittie, 2010). This construct suggests that learning problems can be due to:

- below average intelligence;
- limited attention span and high degree of distractibility;
- difficulties understanding complex language, and limited vocabulary;
- weak motivation;
- poor recall of previous learning;
- inability to generalize learning to new contexts;
- lack of effective learning strategies;
- poor self-esteem;
- diminished beliefs concerning self-efficacy (learned helplessness);
- behavioural and emotional reactions to failure.

While these weaknesses do indeed exist in many children with learning difficulties, they should not be viewed as obstacles too difficult for teachers to overcome. They should be recognized as clear indications of the need for high-quality teaching that accommodates a student's learning characteristics. The deficit model does at least highlight specific areas of difficulty that must be taken into account when planning and implementing classroom programmes.

It is necessary also to examine factors beyond the child, such as quality and type of instruction, teacher's expectations, relevance of the curriculum, classroom environment, interpersonal dynamics within the class social group and rapport with the teacher. These factors are all amenable to modification. Teaching for these students with general difficulties should involve clear presentation of information and strategies by the teacher, direct explicit teaching, active engagement by the learners, guided practice with feedback, independent practice and frequent reviews or revision (Bellert, 2009; Hattie & Yates, 2014). Later chapters in this book deal with explicit instruction in more detail.

Specific learning disability

The Learning Disabilities Association of America (LDA, 2014) defines a learning disability as 'a neurological condition that interferes with an individual's ability to store, process or produce information'. The Association indicates that this disability can affect an individual's ability to read, write, speak, spell and compute mathematically. Some individuals also have problems with attention, memory, coordination, social skills and emotional control. The fifth edition of the *Diagnostic and Statistical Manual of Mental Disorders* (APA, 2013) now refers to a single classification *specific learning disorder*, instead of the various sub-categories used previously to cover difficulties in reading, writing and mathematics. There was concern that these subtypes were poorly differentiated and were difficult to use for diagnosis. A specific learning disorder is diagnosed through a clinical review of an individual's developmental, medical, educational history, family history, test scores, teachers' observations and the student's response to intervention.

It is often argued that children with specific learning difficulties are not identified early enough in school and are simply considered immature, lazy or unmotivated. Unless provided with effective teaching, some of these children may go on to develop serious social and emotional problems associated with constant failure in school, and some exhibit major behaviour problems. Early identification and effective intervention remain high priorities in improving the educational opportunities for these children (Booth, 2013).

Language-based learning disability

Language-based difficulties tend to seriously affect acquisition of literacy skills (phonic decoding, vocabulary, comprehension, writing and spelling). Students with this problem may also exhibit receptive and expressive oral communication weaknesses (Ebbles, 2014). Other forms of language-based learning disability include *dysgraphia* (problems with writing), *dysorthographia* (problems with spelling) and *dysnomia* (inability to retrieve words, names or symbols quickly from memory). However, the latest edition of *DSM-5* does not use these terms, nor does it refer to the category language-based disorders (APA, 2013). In this book, the term dyslexia is retained because it is widely understood within the teaching profession and by parents. However, it should be noted that the *educational value* of the term dyslexia has been seriously questioned (Elliott, 2014).

Reading disability is the most common form of SpLD. The oral reading performance of dyslexic students tends to be very slow and laboured, with maximum effort expended on identifying each individual word, leaving very little cognitive capacity for focusing on meaning. The student tires easily and avoids reading whenever possible. Rose (2009, p. 10) comments: 'Not surprisingly, young people with dyslexic difficulties generally do not read unless they have to; they are far less likely to read for pleasure or for information than other learners.' Lack of practice therefore exacerbates their problem.

Dyslexic students typically have great difficulty developing awareness of the phonological aspects of spoken language (understanding that words are composed of separate sounds), learning and applying phonic decoding skills; building a vocabulary of words recognized automatically by sight; and developing speed and fluency in reading.

Over many years, researchers have attempted to uncover the causes of language-based learning disability, and some attribute the problem to neurological deficits or developmental delay. However, the neurological perspective has failed to produce any useful treatment strategies or effective interventions. Others regard students with SpLD as 'non-strategic' learners (Smith & Tyler, 2010). Their lack of an effective learning strategy (they use a hit-or-miss approach) results in bewilderment, high error-rates and rapid frustration. This in turn causes the child to disengage and avoid participating productively in class. It is now widely accepted that the foundation of any literacy intervention for children with SpLD must include the teaching of effective learning strategies. Teaching objectives must also focus on improving the student's oral language skills (Nelson, 2013). Much more is said about intervention methods for literacy in Chapters 9 and 10.

One area in which students with SpLD also require well-targeted assistance is at the time of transition to further study beyond compulsory school years (Hamblet, 2014). Universities and colleges are beginning to realize the need to provide specific support for students who are intellectually capable but have problems with study skills. Such support may include accommodations made in the time allowed for assignments and assessments, note-taking assistance, supply of alternative study materials and additional guidance when beginning assignments.

Non-verbal learning disability

This category of learning difficulty was suggested as separate from other forms of learning disability in the late 1980s. However, the latest edition of *DSM-5* does not include the category 'nonverbal learning disorder' because its existence as a unique syndrome remains debatable (APA, 2013). But for purposes of teaching and intervention it is still important to identify the problems described below and to offer appropriate support.

To some extent, non-verbal learning disability shares some characteristics with a condition known as *dyspraxia*, although the two conditions are not the same. Non-verbal learning difficulties are associated most obviously with problems in gross and fine motor coordination and spatial awareness (McMurray *et al.*, 2009; Tanguay, 2010). The child may appear to be unusually clumsy or poorly balanced. Fine motor skills such as handwriting, setting down columns of figures or drawing diagrams are particularly problematic. The child may have difficulties applying visual perception effectively in tasks such as interpreting details in a picture, diagram or table, or attending closely to signs and symbols in arithmetic. The combined coordination and visual perception problems cause particular difficulties with many classroom activities including writing, assembling puzzles and models or handling equipment. Some children with these problems are now said to have a *developmental coordination disorder* (DCD) (Pooley, 2014).

The measured verbal IQ of children with non-verbal learning disability is usually very much higher that their non-verbal IQ. The child's oral verbal skills are usually within the normal range (or above) but he or she may have difficulty understanding non-verbal communication cues used by others (facial expression, stance, gesture). This difficulty can lead to problems interpreting social situations and interacting easily with other children and adults. In order to develop appropriate social behaviours these students often need help to interpret social situations more accurately. They are candidates for the social skills interventions described later in Chapter 8.

Children with NLD can be helped significantly once their problem is identified (Casey, 2012). Speaking and listening are their best channels for learning. For example, teachers can use much more verbal mediation (clear verbal explanations) when presenting visual materials and teaching physical skills. More time can be given for students to complete work, and more guidance and feedback can be provided. Often students with NLD will leave classroom tasks and bookwork unfinished. To overcome this tendency, they can be taught self-regulation strategies to enable them to approach classroom tasks systematically and to see them through to completion (see Chapter 6). The students with very poor handwriting can be helped to develop an easier and more legible style. More than the usual amount of guidance may be needed to help these students set out their bookwork appropriately.

It should be noted that even a few gifted students have non-verbal learning disabilities. These disabilities tend to prevent the individual from reaching his or her potential. This issue is discussed in Chapter 5.

Teaching children with general and specific learning difficulties

Research evidence indicates that students with learning problems usually do best in structured programmes, with methods that involve direct teaching, guided practice and feedback (Brown & Colmar, 2009; Hattie & Yates, 2014; Rowe, 2006). If one examines the vast literature on teaching methods for children with learning problems, one usually finds not a unique methodology applicable only to specific disabilities but a range of valuable teaching strategies that are helpful to all learners.

Swanson (2000) used meta-analyses of learning outcomes from different types of teaching approach to draw the conclusion that the most effective approach for teaching students with learning difficulties combines the following features:

- carefully controlling and sequencing the curriculum content to be studied;
- providing abundant opportunities for practice and application of newly acquired knowledge and skills;
- ensuring high levels of participation and responding by the children (for example, by asking questions; answering the teacher's questions; staying on task);
- providing frequent feedback, correction and reinforcement;
- giving clear demonstrations by the teacher of how best to attempt new learning tasks (direct strategy training);
- making appropriate use of technology (e.g. computer-assisted instruction; e-learning);
- providing supplementary assistance (e.g. homework; parental tutoring).

In other words, those who have difficulty learning to read, write and work with numbers are best served by intensive high-quality instruction, rather than informal approaches that lack direct guidance. The most effective lessons tend to have a clear structure, are carefully guided by the teacher, with optimum use made of the available time. Studies have shown that students who are receiving instruction directly from the teacher attend better to the content of the lesson than students who are expected to find out information independently (Rowe, 2006). The use of direct teaching methods in no way precludes a student from ultimately developing independence in learning; indeed, direct teaching in the early stages facilitates greater confidence and independence in later stages.

In response to concerns that in recent years informal methods have not been at all effective with some students there is now a call for 'evidence-based instruction' to be used in our schools (Masters, 2014). Demands are growing for schools to adopt teaching methods that have been carefully evaluated for their efficacy – rather than based purely on the latest 'fad', or teachers' idiosyncratic style or preference (Wendling & Mather, 2009). There is significant research consensus on what constitutes this high-quality instruction; and it is firmly believed now that the most effective teaching methods for developing basic skills are those that provide a balance between explicit instruction from the teacher coupled with abundant independent application and practice (Hattie & Yates, 2014).

In learning basic skills in literacy and numeracy, for example, effective teaching provides carefully sequenced steps, adjusts the level of task difficulty to match students' abilities, and incorporates principles of overlearning and frequent review. Effective teaching of this type at Tier 1 in the early years of primary school not only raises the attainment level of all students but also reduces significantly the prevalence of learning failure. Much more information on teaching methods is presented in later chapters on literacy and numeracy, and is also the main focus of Chapter 15.

Online resources

- The *About.com* website provides answers to the question: 'What is special education?' Available online at: http://specialed.about.com/od/idea/a/Special101.htm.
- The *Children and Families Act* in the UK (House of Commons, 2014) can be found online at: www.legislation.gov.uk/ukpga/2014/6/contents/enacted.
- Details of the *Individuals with Disabilities Education Improvement Act* (US Department of Education, 2004) can be located online at: http://idea.ed.gov/download/statute.html.
- In Australia, recent focus has been placed on the challenge of diversity in the classroom. Teachers are provided with examples of good practice in relation to the Australian Curriculum. Some video clips can be located at: www.australiancurriculum.edu.au/StudentDiversity/Illustrations-of-personalised-learning.
- The UK Government, through the National College for Teaching and Leadership, has produced online professional training modules and resources for teachers. The aim is to provide teachers in mainstream schools with knowledge about students with disabilities, and teachers in special schools with information about students with severe and complex disabilities. Details online at: www.gov.uk/government/publications/teaching-pupils-with-special-educational-needs-and-disabilities-send/training-modules-and-resources-for-teaching-send-pupils.
- The National Center for Learning Disabilities provides a useful overview of learning disability on the website at: www.ncld.org/types-learning-disabilities/what-is-ld/what-are-learning-disabilities.

Further reading

Ashman, A. (Ed.). (2015). *Education for inclusion and diversity* (5th edn). Frenchs Forest, NSW: Pearson Australia.

Cowne, E., Frankl, C. & Gerschel, L. (2015). *The SENCO handbook*. London: Routledge.

Elliott, J. & Grigorenko, E.L. (2014). *The dyslexia debate*. Cambridge: Cambridge University Press.

Farrell, M. (2012). *Educating special children*. London: Routledge.

Foreman, P. & Arthur-Kelly, M. (2014). *Inclusion in action* (4th edn). Melbourne: Cengage.

Hallahan, D., Kauffman, J. & Pullen, P. (2015). *Exceptional learners* (13th edn). Upper Saddle River, NJ: Pearson.

Heward, W.L. (2012). *Exceptional children: An introduction to special education* (10th edn). Upper Saddle River, NJ: Pearson.

Siegel, L. (2013). *Understanding dyslexia and other learning disabilities*. Vancouver: Pacific Educational Press.

Chapter 2

Students with intellectual disability and autism

It is often reported that the most challenging students to include effectively in mainstream programmes are those with intellectual disability and with autism. For this reason, all teachers need to have some knowledge of the effects of intellectual disability and autism on children's behaviour and capacity to learn. The increasing trend toward inclusion of these children in regular classes has made this an imperative.

Intellectual disability

In general terms, children with intellectual disability usually appear much less mature than their age peers. Their behaviour and self-control are typical of younger children, and are related more closely to their developmental stage than to their chronological age. These children are slower at acquiring the essential cognitive skills involved in interpreting information, reasoning and problem solving.

Intellectual disability was previously referred to as mental handicap or mental retardation. The fifth edition of the *Diagnostic and Statistical Manual of Mental Disorders* (*DSM-5*: APA, 2013) for the first time refers to 'intellectual disability' and 'intellectual developmental disability'. Until the publication of *DSM-5* it had always been estimated, based on the notion of a normal distribution of IQ, that individuals with intellectual disability comprise some 2–3 per cent of the general population. However, the interpretation in *DSM-5* now suggests a somewhat lower figure, based on diagnosis that relies more on assessing an individual's functional skills rather than simply relying on IQ (Reynolds *et al.*, 2014).

Intellectual disability impairs cognition in several areas – language, reasoning, attention, memory, reading, writing and number skills. Adaptive functioning is also affected in domains of interpersonal communication, social judgement and the ability to make and retain friendships. Persons with this disability may also have problems developing self-help skills, self-management and independence (APA, 2013). The most obvious characteristic of individuals with intellectual disability is that they usually experience significant difficulty learning almost everything that others can learn with ease. From a practical viewpoint, intellectual disability presents itself as an inability to think as quickly, reason as deeply, remember as easily or adapt as rapidly to new situations, when compared with so-called normal children.

Intellectual disability produces different degrees of impairment, ranging from mild to severe and profound. Children with mild difficulties form the majority (87 per cent of this group), and their learning problems are such that they can usually be educated in mainstream schools if provided with additional support. According to the National

Dissemination Center for Children with Disabilities (US) (2010) children with mild intellectual disability will only be a little slower than average in learning new information and skills. However, children with more severe impairments may be low-functioning in all areas, and require almost complete and continuous care and management. Their education is still provided mainly in special schools or centres, although a few mainstream schools have made efforts to accommodate them. Many individuals with moderate to severe intellectual disability may also have additional physical or sensory impairments and are frequently described as having 'high support needs'. Some students with intellectual disability also have attention deficit hyperactivity disorder (ADHD), a condition discussed fully in Chapter 7.

Priorities in teaching students with intellectual disability

Mild intellectual disability

The current view of educators is that children with intellectual disability can learn if provided with an appropriate instructional programme, teaching methods oriented to their individual needs and if given adequate support (Heward, 2012). In this regard, Peterson and Hittie (2010, p. 86) have remarked: 'When we use good teaching strategies, students with intellectual disabilities learn much more than anyone thought possible.'

When students with mild intellectual disability are included in mainstream classrooms, the intention is that they will follow the normal curriculum as far as possible (ACARA, 2013a; Westwood, 2013). This arrangement is preferable to providing an alternative programme because it includes these students more effectively in the total classroom experiences. However, these students may need to work at a slower pace, and possibly use different learning materials (e.g. simpler text with more illustrations; easier worksheets; different ways of producing written work) (Jimenez et al., 2014). Any necessary adaptations are usually specified in the student's IEP. Chapter 14 describes a number of strategies for adapting teaching methods and curricula. Students with mild intellectual disability will also need more frequent direct guidance from the teacher, classroom assistant and peers.

Moderate to severe disability

In the case of students with moderate to severe intellectual disability many other adaptations are required. Their disability often results in significant limitations of development in the following areas (Rosenberg et al., 2013), and these represent priorities for teaching:

- language and communication;
- attention;
- self-care and daily living skills;
- social skills;
- self-regulation and self-direction;
- basic academic skills (literacy and numeracy);
- transition to employment or sheltered work;
- independent functioning in the community.

The great dilemma facing those who wish to educate children with severe disabilities in the mainstream is how to meet their basic needs for training in self-care, daily living skills and communication once they are placed in an environment where a standard academic curriculum prevails (Ayres *et al.*, 2011). In the US, the legal requirement is that all students with disabilities must have access to the general curriculum, and must work towards making progress within it. Similarly, in Britain and Australia advocates of full inclusion argue that all students with disabilities, including those with severe impairments, should follow the mainstream curriculum in terms of topics to be studied (ACARA. 2013a, 2013b; European Agency for Development of Special Needs Education, 2013). The often naïve advice given to schools is that the ways in which learning activities are planned and implemented should simply be adjusted and geared to the students' developmental stage and ability. This is actually an extremely complex task for teachers, and why inclusion is still a work in progress.

There is growing concern in some quarters that full inclusion is unrealistic for the most disabled students, and may even result in some learners receiving an education that is not appropriate to meet their needs (Imray & Hinchcliffe, 2012). Some experts have queried whether the potential benefits of greater normalization in the mainstream can outweigh all the problems involved in supporting these children in a curriculum that is not necessarily very relevant to them (Kauffman *et al.*, 2005). Similarly, some years ago Dymond and Orelove (2001, p. 111) warned that: 'Functional skills, which were once widely accepted as the basis for curriculum development, have received limited attention as the field has moved to a more inclusive service delivery model.' The same observation can be made today.

For some students with intellectual disability, a special education setting still offers the best environment to meet their needs. The purpose of having special schools and special classes was – and still is – to create an environment in which curriculum content, resources and methods of instruction can be geared appropriately to the students' needs and abilities. A priority in designing such a curriculum is to use content and teaching approaches that ultimately improve the quality of life for intellectually disabled students as they grow toward adulthood.

Learning characteristics of students with intellectual disability

It is generally accepted that children with intellectual disability pass through the same stages in cognitive development as other children, but at a much slower rate. In most aspects of conceptual development, school-age children with mild to moderate intellectual disability tend to be functioning at what Piaget (1963) referred to as the 'concrete operational level' – they understand and remember best the things that they can directly experience. Students with severe to profound disability may be at an even earlier cognitive stage, tied closely to sensory awareness. Teaching for them must always be *reality-based* and must involve 'learning by doing'.

Attention

Individuals with intellectual disability appear often to have problems attending to the relevant aspects of a learning situation. For example, when a teacher is showing the student how to form the numeral 5 with a pencil, or how to use scissors to cut paper, the student is attracted perhaps to the ring on the teacher's finger rather than the task itself. This tendency to focus on irrelevant detail, or to be distracted easily from a learning task, is potentially a major problem for a child with intellectual disability when integrated into mainstream programmes without close supervision. The teacher will need to think of many ways of helping a child with intellectual disability focus on a learning task. Without adequate attention control, any student will fail to learn or remember what the teacher is trying to teach. Attention and memory can both be increased when a learning task is interesting, relevant, involves action on the part of the student and is paired with positive and corrective feedback.

Memory

Many students with intellectual disability also have difficulty storing information in long-term memory (Jarrold & Brock, 2012). This problem is linked, in part, with failure to attend closely to the learning task, as discussed above; but it is also due to the students' lack of effective cognitive strategies for facilitating memorization. To overcome or minimize this memory problem, students with intellectual disability require much greater amounts of repetition and practice to ensure that important information and skills are eventually stored. Many opportunities must be provided for abundant guided and independent practice, revision and overlearning in every area of the curriculum. It takes longer for these students to reach the desired state of automaticity in even the most basic skills.

Generalization

For any learner, the final and most difficult stage of acquiring new learning is that of *generalization*. A stage must be reached when a student can automatically apply new learning in situations not directly linked with the context in which it was first taught. It is typical of most students with intellectual disability that they do not generalize what they learn (Turnbull *et al.*, 2012). They may acquire a particular skill or strategy in one context but fail to transfer it to a different situation. It is recommended that teachers consider ways of facilitating generalization when planning lessons for students with special needs; for example, by re-teaching the same skills or strategies in different contexts, gradually increasing the range of contexts, challenging students to decide whether a skill or strategy could be used in a new situation, and reinforcing any evidence of students' spontaneous generalization of previous learning.

Language delay

One of the main characteristics of children with moderate and severe intellectual disability is the very slow rate at which many of them acquire speech and language. Even a child with mild intellectual disability is likely to be a little behind the normal milestones for language development and may exhibit a more limited vocabulary. A few individuals with severe and multiple disabilities never develop speech, so for them alternative methods of communication may need to be developed, such as sign language and picture or symbol communication systems (Inclusive Technology, 2014).

Language ability is important for cognitive and social development for the following reasons:

- language enables an individual to make his or her needs, opinions and ideas known to others;
- language is important for cognitive development; without language one lacks much of the raw material with which to think and reason;
- concepts are more effectively stored in memory if they have a mental representation in words as well as in sensations and perceptions;
- language is the main medium through which school learning is mediated;
- positive social interactions with other persons are heavily dependent upon effective language and communication skills;
- inner language (self-talk) is important for regulating one's behaviour and responses.

Early intervention programmes in the preschool years place heavy emphasis on developing children's communication skills. These interventions should also be family focused as much as possible. It has been shown that parents can be trained to engage more proactively in stimulating the development of children with language delay (Colmar, 2014).

The development of communication skills is given very high priority in special school curricula, and will be no less important for intellectually disabled students included in mainstream settings. Two obvious benefits of placing a child with intellectual disability in a mainstream class are immersion in a naturally enriched language environment, and the increased need for the student to communicate with others.

Language is best acquired naturally, through using it to express needs, obtain information and interact socially. Where possible, naturally occurring opportunities within the school day are used to teach and reinforce new vocabulary and language patterns. This *milieu approach* is found to be more productive in terms of generalization and transfer of learning to everyday use than are the more clinical approaches to teaching language in isolation (Christensen-Sandfort & Whinney, 2013). It must be noted, however, that teachers do not find it easy to integrate specific language development objectives for an individual student into their content-based classroom lessons (Baecher *et al.*, 2014).

Many students with intellectual disability require the services of a speech and language therapist; but even with this help, improvement can be very slow. This is because the individual receiving help may not appreciate the need for it, and may therefore have no motivation to practise and use what is taught. There is also the usual problem of lack of generalization – what is taught in a clinical setting does not necessarily transfer to the person's everyday speech.

Social development

For many individuals with intellectual disability the development of social competence and skills presents many ongoing difficulties (Nijs & Maes, 2014). The presence or absence of social skills in these students tends to be related to the extent to which they have had an opportunity to socialize in the home and other environments. Within the family, the social interactions between the child and others are likely to be mainly positive, but the same assumption cannot be made for contacts within the community and at school. Although community attitudes towards people with disabilities have become more positive and accepting, there is still likelihood that some children with intellectual disability will experience difficulty gaining acceptance and making friends –

particularly if they have some irritating or challenging behaviours. Some students with intellectual disability are rejected and marginalized by their peers more often on the basis of their irritating behaviour than because they are disabled. For example, the presence of inappropriate responses such as aggression and temper tantrums makes it difficult for some of these children to be socially accepted. Intervention is needed to eliminate these negative behaviours and replace them with pro-social behaviours (see Chapter 7).

If the student with a disability is to make friends and be accepted in the peer group, social skills training may be needed (Peterson & Hittie, 2010). Strategies for developing social skills are described in Chapter 8; but helping students with intellectual disability form lasting friendships with other children in the mainstream is actually quite difficult (Salmon, 2013). Often mainstream students who start out with good intentions to socialize with a disabled peer quickly lose interest and fade away (Smith & Tyler, 2010). In post-school years, socialization remains difficult for many individuals with intellectual disability and often they require regular and ongoing support from a social worker (Nijs & Maes, 2014).

While stressing the need to increase social interaction with others, students with intellectual disability (male and female) also need to be taught *protective behaviours* to reduce the possibility that they become victims of financial or other forms of exploitation. The lack of social judgement of some teenagers and young adults with intellectual disability causes them to be rather naïve and trusting. There is also a risk of sexual abuse because they may not really comprehend right from wrong in matters of physical contact (Alderson, 2014). For their own protection they need to be taught the danger of going anywhere with a stranger, accepting rides in a car, or taking gifts for favours. They need to know that some forms of touching are wrong, and they also need to know that they can tell some trusted adult if they feel they are at risk from some other person. These matters must be dealt with openly in schools and also reinforced by parents. Age-appropriate sex education is an important priority for these children (DHS, 2014).

Self-regulation and self-determination

In recent years, much emphasis has been placed on using cognitive methods to increase self-regulation and self-monitoring in students with intellectual disability (see Chapter 6). While this approach is proving useful for students with mild disabilities, it is very difficult indeed to employ cognitive training with low-functioning students for reasons that will be discussed later in connection with autism.

Self-determination is an area currently attracting greater attention in the education of individuals with intellectual disability (Dowsett *et al.*, 2014; Wehmeyer & Abery, 2013). It is recognized now that too much of the life of a person with moderate or severe disability is typically determined by others; so in recent years educators and caregivers have been encouraged to find many more ways of ensuring that persons with disabilities have opportunities to exercise choice and make decisions. To facilitate this process, goals for increasing independence and self-management must be included in the IEP and curriculum for all students with intellectual disability. Parents, paraprofessionals and volunteers may need to be reminded to allow the children with disabilities in their care to *do more for themselves*.

Teaching approaches for students with intellectual disability

Taking into account the stage of cognitive development of most students with mild to moderate intellectual disability, the priority in teaching is to make the curriculum *reality-based* and *relevant*. For example, reading skills should be developed and practised using real books, real information on the computer screen, recipes, brochures and comic books, as well as through the medium of graded readers, games and flashcards.

For children at the concrete operational stage of cognition, the principle of learning by doing certainly applies (Jimenez & Kemmery, 2013). If they are to learn important number skills for example, they should learn them not only from computer games, instructional materials and practice sheets, but also from real situations such as shopping trips, stocktaking, measuring, estimating, counting, grouping, recording data and comparing quantities. However, a balanced mathematics programme for students with mild intellectual disability should not be restricted only to hands-on activities and functional number skills – efforts must also be made to include opportunities to encourage basic *mathematical thinking* at a slightly more abstract level (e.g. $5 + x = 9$, what is x?) (Rivera & Baker, 2013).

It has already been mentioned that these children need to experience things at first hand and have others mediate (interpret) these experiences. Where first-hand experience of daily situations is not immediately available, it has been demonstrated that using videos and providing a supplementary commentary at an appropriate language level can be beneficial for improving students' understanding. Video therefore offers an innovative solution for bringing more of the school curriculum to life for these students (Graff *et al.*, 2011).

In addition to reality-based learning, children with intellectual disability also need high-quality *explicit instruction*, with the curriculum content broken down into simple steps to ensure high success rates (Peterson & Hittie, 2010). Explicit instruction involves direct teaching of new knowledge to be acquired, and clear modelling of new skills and strategies. It also requires abundant opportunity for students to practise and apply newly taught knowledge and skills while receiving feedback from the teacher. Frequent prompting and cueing by the teacher or instructor during the learning stage also plays an important role in helping the students acquire new skills (Sabielny & Cannella-Malone, 2014). Lessons that employ explicit instruction aim to obtain many successful responses from students during the time available (see Chapter 15). Lessons are made enjoyable and there is heavy emphasis on practice and reinforcement.

Explicit instruction is among the most extensively researched teaching methods, and has consistently proved more effective than independent (unguided) learning for many purposes (Hattie & Yates, 2014). It has been found that instruction using the above principles is extremely effective for students with disabilities, particularly for teaching basic skills involved in literacy and numeracy (Miller, 2009; Turnbull *et al.*, 2012), and for teaching *all* students in the initial stages of new learning.

Other basic strategies to consider when working with students with intellectual disability include the following:

* provide plentiful cues and prompts to enable learners to manage each step in a task;
* make all possible use of cooperative group work; and teach children the necessary group-working skills;

- frequently assess the learning that has taken place against the objectives in the curriculum;
- use additional helpers to assist with the teaching (classroom aides, volunteers, peers);
- involve parents in the educational programme whenever possible;
- most importantly, do not sell students short by expecting too little from them.

Preparation for work

Transition from school to work requires extremely careful planning for intellectually disabled students in the adolescent age range (Carter *et al.*, 2014; McDonnell, 2010). In the US, federal law now mandates age-appropriate preparation for transition. Essential components of the curriculum for all senior students capable of gaining employment must include training in work skills and routines, reliability and punctuality, and regular opportunities to engage in work-experience (Bennett, 2013).

In the past, senior special schools have usually risen effectively to the challenge of developing students' readiness for employment, by providing a strong emphasis on work experience. It is proving to be much more difficult to provide such authentic learning opportunities for senior intellectually disabled students in inclusive mainstream schools. This problem is yet to be resolved.

Specific approaches for students with severe intellectual disability

Several unique approaches have been developed to meet the special needs of students with complex learning difficulties and disabilities (CLDD). Many of these children have no speech and some have limited movement. Four of the approaches are described below that also have some application with students with severe autism.

Intensive interaction

A method known as *intensive interaction* has been developed for use with children who have severe and complex disabilities and who lack verbal communication (Caldwell, 2013; Hewitt, 2012). The interactive approach tries to ensure that much of the teaching and interaction that takes place is based directly on a student's self-initiated actions and reactions, rather than on a pre-planned curriculum imposed by an adult.

In many ways, the method is similar to the natural approach used instinctively by parents when responding to a baby's actions. Something the child does spontaneously leads the adult to react, rather than the other way around. For example, the parent may respond by smiling, reaching out, touching, stroking and speaking and, by doing so, reinforces the child and the behaviour. There is a vital natural ingredient of warm social interaction and communication involved. Often playing simple games or using sensory equipment will create a context for this to happen.

The approach is now well known in the UK, and interest is growing in Australia. For more information on intensive interaction visit the website at: www.intensiveinter-action.co.uk.

Preference-based teaching

This is an approach that has fairly similar theoretical underpinnings to intensive inter-action, and the two can be used in a coordinated manner. It is based on the belief that students enjoy engaging in learning activities much more if the modes of teaching and the materials used are compatible with personal preferences – for example, using sand play rather than water play, or watching television rather than listening to a story. Attention is more effectively gained and maintained, and there are fewer behaviour problems (Reid & Green, 2006). This is a very important consideration when working with young children with severe disabilities and challenging behaviour.

Snoezelen

For many years it has been believed that severely disabled children can be helped most by methods that incorporate sensory stimulation. Great interest was aroused in an approach developed in Holland that is both therapeutic and educational. It uses struc-tured multi-sensory environments containing lights, textures, aromas, sounds and move-ment (Russell & Cohn, 2012). The Snoezelen approach provides both sensory stimulation and relaxation for severely or profoundly disabled individuals (including adults), and has been adopted in a number of special schools in Europe and Australasia. Snoezelen is reported to have particular benefits for individuals who have emotional and behavioural problems combined with intellectual disability, and also for helping autistic children. In some cases Snoezelen has proved useful in reducing self-injurious behaviour (SIB) and self-stimulating behaviour (SSB).

While Snoezelen rooms are unlikely to be developed in mainstream schools, teachers in preschools and special schools do need to note the potential value of intense sensory stimulation for young children with intellectual disability.

Information on Snoezelen can be located at: www.snoezeleninfo.com/main.asp.

Applied behaviour analysis (ABA)

Applied behaviour analysis is a broad term that encompasses several different approaches that can be used within special education (e.g. behaviour modification; discrete trial training; pivotal response training) (Stahmer, 2014). The underlying premise draws on principles of operant conditioning, and believes that new skills and behaviours can be taught, shaped and reinforced by positive rewards or by negative consequences from the environment. Similarly, undesirable behaviours can be reduced or eliminated.

As a teaching technique ABA involves setting clear behavioural objectives for a student, and devising a schedule for rewarding him or her at every incremental step when moving successfully toward that objective (Alberto & Troutman, 2012). The approach has been found effective in teaching new behaviours to children with autism, and also to other students with behaviour disorders. The topic is discussed below, and in much more detail in Chapter 7.

Students with autism spectrum disorder (ASD)

The disability previously referred to simply as 'autism' is now termed *autism spectrum dis-order* (ASD). This reflects evidence that rather than being a single syndrome the disability manifests itself along a continuum, with varying degrees of severity and slightly different behaviour patterns. In general, individuals with ASD tend to have major communication problems, difficulty acquiring new skills and an inability to develop normal social relationships.

Children with autism may or may not also have intellectual disability, but they all share common problems with communication, self-management and social awareness (Scheidecker et al., 2013). While children with mild autistic tendencies can usually be accommodated in the mainstream, those with severe autism are functioning at a level that is too low even to cope with the demands of an adapted mainstream curriculum. In addition, some may be overly dependent on set routines, and are highly sensitive to any change in their environment (APA, 2013). In the most severe cases, the individual may not use speech, may be virtually unresponsive to social contact, and may display ritualistic habits (*stereotypic behaviours*) such as constant body rocking or self-stimulation (Scheidecker et al., 2013). These students often require intensive intervention, as described later.

Among the group of high-functioning individuals with autism are those previously referred to as having Asperger syndrome. The fifth edition of the *Diagnostic and Statistical Manual of Mental Disorders* no longer classifies Asperger syndrome as a distinct category (APA, 2013). These individuals are now regarded as simply located somewhere on the autism spectrum. They have some of the behavioural and social difficulties associated with other degrees of autism, but tend to have language and cognitive skills in the average or even above average range. A few may even exhibit certain talent or knowledge in areas such as music, art, mental calculation and recall of factual information with amazing accuracy.

Most high-functioning individuals receive their education in mainstream schools, where their unusual behaviour patterns can often cause them to be regarded as strange (quirky) by peers and teachers, and they may have difficulty making friends. While lack of friends may not bother some ASD students, others appear to experience deep loneliness (Mazurek, 2014). Some high-functioning autistic students may benefit from personal counselling and social training that focuses on helping them understand the feelings of others, social interaction, dealing with their own problems and how to avoid trouble with other students and with teachers.

Autistic children have been identified in all parts of the world, and the disorder does not appear to be in any way culturally determined. It is a low-incidence disability with approximately 4–10 cases per 10,000 in the population. The lower figure represents the more severe cases; the upper figure includes those children with only mild autistic tendencies. The ratio of males to females is 4 or 5 to 1. There has been a reported increase in the number of identified cases of ASD over the past two decades (Carlon et al., 2011) but this may be due to improved assessment procedures rather than any actual increase in prevalence.

In most cases the underlying cause of autism spectrum disorder is uncertain, and current opinion is that there may be several contributory factors. Studies have shown that in some cases there has been a mutation in the individual's genetic information (DNA), and it is anticipated that mapping the genome of autistic persons may ultimately help with accurate and early detection of the condition (Jiang et al., 2013).

Early detection remains one of the top priorities for providing appropriate intervention for ASD (Schefkind et al., 2014). To be diagnosed as autistic by a clinician, a child must show symptoms of abnormal social and interpersonal development during early childhood, and must meet criteria listed in the fifth edition of the *Diagnostic and Statistical Manual of Mental Disorders* (APA, 2013). *DSM-5* has reduced the number of subtypes of autism and included more symptoms required to meet the criteria, in an endeavour to make diagnosis less subjective and more accurate. A new category termed *social communication disorder* has also been introduced. This applies to individuals who have significant deficits in the social use of language (initiating conversations, responding appropriately, reading non-verbal cues), but do not have restricted interests or repetitive behaviours seen in autism spectrum disorders.

Interventions for autism

Many different approaches have been used to make a child with autism more responsive to teaching, increase communication and to reduce negative behaviours. These interventions have included pharmacological (drug) treatments, diet control, psychotherapy, music therapy, play therapy, Snoezelen, facilitated communication, behaviour modification, cognitive self-management training, and many others. Some approaches are regarded as highly controversial and of doubtful value (Carlon *et al.*, 2011; Levy & Hyman, 2005). Often these programmes are recommended on websites that provide information for parents of autistic children, but usually without including crucial information on their proven efficacy. As Badge (2013, p. 33) has pointed out: 'The claims made and presented to parents on these websites are likely to lead parents to having unrealistic expectations.' It is essential that any intervention should undergo thorough evaluation.

It is generally considered that behaviour modification (applied behaviour analysis) has produced the best results to date (Ashcroft *et al.*, 2010; Virues-Ortaga *et al.*, 2013). However, it should be noted that some authorities have commented on the extremely 'intrusive nature' of interventions such as ABA; for example when used to correct challenging behaviour (Mayton *et al.*, 2014). Against this complaint must be weighed the fact that less intrusive cognitive approaches (designed to develop better self-management) are problematic with low-functioning children, because their application requires a degree of self-awareness and metacognition not usually found in autistic children.

Short-term gains from some of these intervention programmes are reported, but there is considerable variability in response, with some children making much more progress than others (Howlin *et al.*, 2009). Longer-term and lasting benefits seem difficult to achieve, and some children with the most severe forms of autism often appear to make minimal gains despite many hours of careful stimulation and teaching. However, the benefits reported for many children with autism are positive enough to make the investment of time and effort worthwhile.

Teaching, training and management: general principles

Teaching, training and managing children with moderate to severe autism is almost always complex, ongoing and multidisciplinary. It has been said that effective intervention is characterized by structure, intensity of treatment, low adult-to-child ratio and individualized programming (Ashcroft *et al.*, 2010; Manti *et al.*, 2013). Teaching may need to begin at a very simple level – for example, many very young children with autism need first to be taught how to play with toys, and later how to play alongside other children (Hampshire & Hourcade, 2014; Jung & Sainato, 2013). Playing cooperatively with others will be a much later goal.

For non-verbal autistic children, intensive use of alternative communication methods and visual cues (hand signing, pointing, gesture, pictures and symbol cards) are usually necessary in most teaching situations. One approach to help a student improve in self-regulation is the use of visual schedules (picture charts) with a symbol depicting what he or she must do at particular times during a lesson, or during the school day (Carlon *et al.*, 2011). Studies have suggested that for some lower-functioning students the use of tactile symbols (that can be touched by the student) are particularly useful (Aasen & Naerland, 2014). For higher-functioning students an electronic hand-held planner can be useful for storing the daily schedule.

Teaching sessions for children with autism need to be implemented according to a predictable schedule. The classroom environment and routines must always be consistent. Objectives are best achieved by using both direct instructional methods and by maximizing the naturally occurring opportunities in the child's daily life. New information, skills or behaviours need to be taught in small increments through systematic and direct methods. Each child's programme must be based on a very detailed appraisal of his or her current developmental level and existing skills and responses. It is essential to assess the strengths of each individual child and to set goals that will help build on these strengths.

There is general agreement that the focus of any intervention programme should attempt to:

- stimulate cognitive development;
- facilitate language acquisition;
- promote social interactions;
- use visual cues as supplements to all verbal instructions and requests.

All teachers, parents and caregivers must know the precise goals of the programme and must collaborate closely on the methods to be used with the child. It is essential that parents also be trained in the teaching strategies to be used in any intervention programme because the child spends more time at home than at school. The most effective interventions involve the child's family as well as teachers and therapists. Home-based intervention programmes (or home programmes combined with clinic-based intervention) produce better results than purely clinic-based programmes.

Specific programmes and methods

TEACCH

One approach that has become popular in recent years is TEACCH (meaning *Treatment and Education of Autistic and Communication-handicapped Children*) (Mesibov *et al.*, 2005). This approach stresses the need for a high degree of structure in the day for children with ASD, and uses a combination of cognitive and behavioural-change strategies coupled with direct teaching of specific skills. Importance is placed on training parents to work with their own children and to make effective use of support services. A meta-analysis of studies involving TEACCH has suggested that it is effective in increasing social behaviour (Virues-Ortaga *et al.*, 2013).

An important feature of the approach is that it tries to capitalize on autistic children's preference for a visual mode of communication rather than the auditory-verbal mode. Several studies have supported the value of using visual cues, prompts and schedules to hold the child's attention and to represent information in a form that is easily interpreted. Such systems can also operate at home.

Young Autism Program (Lovaas)

One very intensive programme for autistic children is that devised by Lovaas (Lovaas & Smith, 2003). It is often also referred to as Early Intensive Behavioural Therapy (EIBT). The programme begins with the child at age two years and involves language development, social behaviours and the stimulation of play activity. Emphasis is also given to the elimination of excessive ritualistic behaviour, temper tantrums and aggression. The second year of treatment focuses on higher levels of language stimulation, and on cooperative play and interaction with peers. Instruction involves *discrete-trial training*, with skills broken down into their most basic components, and rewarding every positive performance with praise and reinforcement.

The late Ivar Lovaas claimed high success rates for the programme, including increase in IQ. He claimed that almost half of the treated group of children reached normal functioning levels. However, the fact that this programme takes up to 40 hours per week, using one-to-one teaching over two years, makes it very labour-intensive and expensive. While the general principles are undoubtedly sound, it is difficult if not impossible to replicate the approach in the average special preschool.

Pivotal response training (PRT)

This approach, developed by Robert and Lynn Koegel and associates (2006), is based on the principle that intervention in autism should focus heavily on strengthening particular behaviours that have general beneficial effects on self-management and learning. Examples of pivotal behaviours are attention, motivation, response to multiple cues, self-management and the initiation of social interaction. By targeting these areas it is hoped that training will produce broad improvements across areas of sociability, communication, behaviour and academic skills. Pivotal response training employs basic applied behaviour analysis techniques, and has been used effectively in improving language skills, play and social behaviours (Stockall & Dennis, 2014).

An example of a specific pivotal behaviour is *selective attention*. If a child with ASD has major difficulty coping with multiple stimuli in the environment, training would seek to increase selective attention and reduce distractibility. Many benefits then occur, such as greatly improved ability to focus on a learning task and to process information more effectively.

SCERTS model

Detailed information on SCERTS can be found in the two-volume manual by Prizant *et al.* (2006). The acronym SCERTS is derived from Social Communication (SC), Emotional Regulation (ER) and Transactional Support (TS); these are the areas of development prioritized within this approach. The designers of this trans-disciplinary and family-centred model stress that SCERTS is not intended to be exclusionary of other treatments or methods. It attempts to capitalize on naturally occurring opportunities for development that occur throughout a child's daily activities and across social partners, such as siblings, parents, caregivers and other children. The overriding goal of SCERTS is to help a child with autism become a more competent participant in social activities by enhancing his or her capacity for attention, reciprocity, expression of emotion and understanding of others' emotions. In particular, SCERTS aims to help children become better communicators and to enhance their abilities for pretend play.

Infant Start

A programme known as *Infant Start*, developed by staff at the Davis Health Center, University of California, has shown positive effects when implemented by parents of very young children showing signs of potential autism (Rogers & Ozonoff, 2014). In many cases the children who complete the programme return to a near normal developmental trajectory by age three and the symptoms of autism are ameliorated. Details can be found online at: www.ucdmc.ucdavis.edu/publish/news/newsroom/9182.

Social stories and social thinking

Interventions for children with ASD frequently focus on improving their social thinking and social skills. These interventions aim to teach autistic individuals why they and others react socially in the ways that they do, how their own behaviours affect the way others perceive and respond to them, and how this affects their own emotions and relationships with others in different social contexts (Rhodes, 2014).

One approach that appears helpful in developing autistic children's awareness of normal codes of behaviour is the use of *social stories* or *social scripts* (Grennan & Kilham, 2011). These are simple age-appropriate narratives, supplemented by simple illustrations, and personalized to suit the child's behavioural needs. The theme and context of the story help the autistic child perceive, interpret and respond more appropriately to typical social situations; for example, sharing a toy, taking turns or standing in line. Another promising approach is *Children's Friendship Training*, a 12-week parent-assisted social intervention that targets the knowledge and skills for forming relationships (Mandelberg *et al.*, 2014).

Online resources

- Information on intellectual disability can be located on the Mental Help Net website at: www.mentalhelp.net/poc/view_doc.php?type=doc&id=10365.
- Suggestions for teaching students with intellectual disability are available on the Bright Hub Education website at: www.brighthubeducation.com/special-ed-neurological-disorders/79002-tips-for-teaching-students-with-an-intellectual-disability/.
- Detailed information on autism can be found on the Intellectual Disability and Health Website at: www.intellectualdisability.info/diagnosis/autistic-spectrum-disorders.
- The TEACCH approach for autism spectrum disorders is explained at: www.autism-speaks.org/what-autism/treatment/training-and-education-autistic-and-related-communication-handicapped-children.

- The Lovaas Method (and Discrete-trial Training) are clearly described on the Pacific Autism Learning Services website at: http://palsautism.com/faqs.htm.
- Details of the SCERTS approach for autistic children are available at: www.infantva.org/documents/copa-tidew-frank-dec-08-scerts.pdf.
- The Social Thinking website has many useful resources for teachers who need to increase the social awareness and skills of higher-functioning autistic children. Available at: www.socialthinking.com/?view=featured.
- *Snoezelen* multisensory environments are discussed at: www.isna.de/en/snoezelen-engl.html.

Further reading

Alderson, J. (2011). *Challenging the myths of autism*. Scarborough, ON: HarperCollins.

Downing, J.E. & MacFarland, S. (2010). Education and individuals with severe disabilities, promising practices. In J.H. Stone & M. Blouin (Eds), *International encyclopedia of rehabilitation*. Available online: http://cirrie.buffalo.edu/encyclopedia/en/article/114/.

Knapp, J. & Turnbull, C. (2014). *A complete ABA curriculum for individuals on the autism spectrum with a developmental age of 3–5 years: A step-by-step treatment manual*. London: Jessica Kingsley.

Mesibov, G. & Howley, M. (2015). *Accessing the curriculum for pupils with autism spectrum disorders* (2nd edn). London: Routledge.

Sicile-Kira, C. (2014). *Autism spectrum disorder: The complete guide* (Revised edition). New York: Perigee Trade.

Sturmey, P. & Didden, R. (2014). *Evidence-based practice and intellectual disabilities*. Hoboken, NJ: Wiley.

Chapter 3

Students with physical disabilities or health issues

Physical disability is a relatively low-incidence category of special educational need, but these students comprise a relatively diverse group. Unlike disabilities described in the previous chapter, the difficulties considered here do not necessarily arise from impaired intellectual functioning. Many students with physical disability will be of average or better than average intelligence, and can cope well with the mainstream curriculum if assistive technology and adapted equipment are provided (Best *et al.*, 2010; Ullman, 2014; Windman, 2013). For all students with physical disabilities their greatest need is help in accessing the learning environment and engaging in normal classroom experiences.

Having stressed the normality of intelligence in many students with physical disabilities, it is also important to state here that a few individuals with a condition such as *cerebral palsy* may also have significant intellectual impairment. Any disability involving neurological dysfunction or damage can affect intellect, communication and motor skills. These problems are discussed later in the chapter.

The impact of physical disability on learning and development

It is essential for teachers to recognize that a physical disability does not automatically impair a student's ability to learn. Assumptions should never be made about an individual's capacity to learn on the basis of a physical condition. The education of these students must focus on providing them with opportunities to access the same range of social and learning experiences as those available to students without disability. This may require adaptations to be made to the classroom environment, to the ways in which these students move (or are moved) around the classroom, and to the instructional resources they use (Best *et al.*, 2010).

It has been noted that some students with physical disabilities tend to lack confidence in their own self-efficacy, and they present as rather passive learners requiring more than the usual amount of extrinsic motivation (Konings *et al.*, 2005). Teachers, tutors and classroom assistants should take this characteristic into account when providing support. The students often need to be encouraged to make extra effort, to see tasks through to completion and to work steadily towards greater independence. Even those physically disabled students with good learning skills may need a great deal of encouragement in order to achieve their potential. They may also need to draw upon outside services that offer treatment, therapy and counselling in order to function successfully and to maintain a good quality of life.

When teaching new skills to students with physical disabilities it is often necessary for teachers to undertake both *task analysis* (reducing a learning activity to simple steps) and *situation analysis* relating to the learning environment (access, available supports, equipment). It is important to consider any modifications that may be needed in the learning environment to enhance the students' opportunities to participate – for example, seating arrangements, movement routes and resources. For students with very limited flexibility and restricted movement in their limbs, it is often necessary to use adapted classroom furniture and equipment; for example, some physically disabled students require a standing frame or a slanting desk. Some may need to use communication devices, as described later.

It is beyond the scope of this book to provide details of each and every physical disability or health problem. Attention here will be devoted only to the most commonly occurring conditions, namely cerebral palsy (CP), spina bifida (SB), epilepsy, hydrocephalus and traumatic brain injury (TBI), and to common health issues.

Cerebral palsy

Cerebral palsy (CP) is a disorder of posture, muscle tone and movement resulting from damage to the motor areas of the brain occurring before, during or soon after birth (Howard *et al.*, 2010). It may affect one side of the body, or both. CP is one of the more frequently occurring physical disabilities, with a prevalence rate of approximately two cases per 1000 live births. There has been no significant decline in the prevalence rate of this disorder over recent years, even though there have been major advances in prenatal care.

CP exists in several forms (*spasticity*, *athetosis*, *ataxia* and *mixed forms*) and at different levels of severity from mild to severe. Type and severity of the condition are related to the particular area or areas of the brain that have been damaged and the extent of that damage. CP is not curable, but its negative impact on the individual's physical coordination, mobility, learning capacity and communication skills can be reduced through appropriate intensive therapy, training and education. It is anticipated that future brain imaging studies (fMRI) may help to throw more light on the ways in which damage to specific areas of the brain affect the functioning in individuals with CP (Weierink *et al.*, 2013).

Assistive technology (AT) plays a major role in the effective education of students with physical disabilities by enhancing movement, participation and communication, and facilitating access to the curriculum. AT ranges from 'very low tech' equipment such as adjustable slant-top desks, pencil grips, modified scissor grips, specially designed seating, pads and wedges to help position a child for optimum functioning, walking and standing frames, and head-pointers, through to 'high-tech' adaptations such as electric wheelchairs operated by head movements or by air pressure from breath control, modified computer keyboards, touch screens and switching devices. The range of available assistive technology is described by Best *et al.* (2010).

Students with CP often have additional disabilities. At least 10–16 per cent of cases have impaired hearing or vision. Major difficulties with eye-muscle control can lead to fatigue in close-focus tasks such as looking at pictures, typing or reading print. *Epilepsy* is present in up to 30 per cent of cases of CP and a significant number of the children are on regular medication to control seizures. This medication can often have the side effect of reducing the individual's level of alertness and span of attention, thus adding to potential problems in learning.

Some children with severe CP may not develop speech, although their receptive language and understanding may be quite normal. In their attempts to vocalize, they may produce unintelligible sounds and their laughter may be loud and harsh. In addition, they may exhibit other symptoms such as inability to control the tongue, jaw and face muscles, resulting in facial contortions or drooling. These physical problems are beyond the individual's control but can create potential barriers for easy social integration.

It is reported that approximately 60 per cent of individuals with moderate to severe CP also have some degree of intellectual disability, with 25 per cent exhibiting significant cognitive impairment and additional complications (Turnbull *et al.*, 2012). It must be noted, however, that some persons with quite severe CP are highly intelligent, and there is a danger that the potential of some non-verbal CP students is not recognized because of their inability to communicate. One of the main priorities for these individuals is to be provided with an alternative method of communication (Heller & Bigge, 2010).

There have been many suggested treatments and therapies for CP, but few of these have been subjected to really rigorous evaluation. Even *conductive education* – a comprehensive approach originating from Professor Andras Peto in Hungary, and once hailed as a major breakthrough (Pawelski, 2007) – produces very mixed results. It is most likely to be effective with students who have normal intelligence and lack only good motor control. A website giving full detail of conductive education is listed at the end of the chapter under Online Resources.

Instructional needs of students with cerebral palsy

Academic instruction for children with CP will depend mainly upon their cognitive ability and their range of functional movement. Students with mild cerebral palsy and normal intelligence may simply be slower at completing assignments and will need more time and encouragement. Allowance may need to be made for large and poorly coordinated handwriting. For some, adapted devices such as pencil grips and page-turners may be required, and working papers may need to be taped firmly to the desktop. A few students may need to use a word processor with modified keyboard for their assignments. Computers with adaptations such as touch panels rather than a keyboard or a mouse are useful for presenting academic work and as a medium for communication with others.

In addition to problems with movement and speech, many children with CP tend to:

- tire easily and have difficulty attending to tasks for more than brief periods of time;
- take a very long time to perform basic physical actions (e.g. pointing at or picking up an object; eating);
- rely on the teacher or an aide to lift and move them;
- require physical placement in a particular position for work, with padded 'wedges' or cushions to enable them to apply their limited range of movements to best advantage, or be placed and supported in a 'standing frame' with desk-top attached;
- need to be fed and toileted by an aide.

Epilepsy

Epilepsy can be a condition existing in otherwise normal individuals, but is frequently an additional problem that may accompany physical disabilities that have a neurological origin. It is caused by abnormal electrical discharges within specific areas of the cortex. Severity can vary from very mild loss of awareness (mental 'absences' lasting a few seconds) through to severe seizures in which the individual falls to the ground, convulses and may lose consciousness (*tonic-clonic seizure*).

Some instances of epilepsy evident in the primary school years may disappear spontaneously by adolescence or adulthood. But for some individuals the condition requires a lifetime regimen of medication and management. Medication with anti-epileptic drugs is usually successful in controlling seizures in 80 per cent of cases. Teachers need to know details of the child's condition, and how to manage him or her in the case of seizures. All seizure events should be logged and reported to parents.

Spina bifida

Spina bifida (SB) is a congenital disorder, possibly of genetic origin, presenting with different degrees of severity. It affects approximately one child in every 1000 live births. The condition results from a failure of certain bones in the spine to seal over before birth to protect the spinal cord. The milder forms of SB have no significant influence on learning and mobility. It is estimated that approximately 80 per cent of individuals with spina bifida have intelligence within the normal range (Howard *et al.*, 2010). However, learning difficulties are common in the remaining 20 per cent, with major problems in sustained attention (Dennis, 2012). In some cases, visual perception, memory and number skills are also weak. Greater difficulties in learning occur with increasing severity of the disability. In some cases students with moderate to severe spina bifida may have learning difficulties partly due to a more restricted range of experiences during their preschool years. This can contribute to difficulty in understanding some aspects of the curriculum that rely on good general knowledge.

The most serious form of spina bifida, with the greatest impact on the individual's development, is *myelomeningocele*. In this condition, a small part of the spinal cord is exposed at birth and protrudes from a gap in the spine. The cord is usually damaged, and bodily functions below this point may be seriously disrupted, including use of lower limbs. The individual may need to use a wheelchair or leg braces. The management of incontinence presents the greatest personal and social problem for these students.

Approximately 60–70 per cent of children with myelomeningocele may also have some degree of *hydrocephalus* (Howard *et al.*, 2010). The normal circulation and drainage of cerebrospinal fluid within the skull is impaired, resulting in increased intracranial pressure. This relatively rare condition can also exist in children who do not have spina bifida. Treatment for hydrocephalus involves the surgical implanting of a catheter into a ventricle in the brain to drain the excess fluid to the abdominal cavity. A valve is implanted below the skin behind the child's ear to prevent any back flow of cerebrospinal fluid. Teachers need to be aware that shunts and valves can become blocked, or the site can become infected. If the child with treated hydrocephalus complains of headache or earache, or if he or she appears feverish and irritable, medical advice should be obtained immediately.

Children with spina bifida and hydrocephalus tend to be hospitalized at regular intervals during their school lives for such events as replacing shunts and valves, urinary infections or controlling respiratory problems. This frequent hospitalization can significantly interrupt the child's schooling, with subjects such as mathematics being most affected by lost instructional time. Many students in this situation require intensive remedial assistance with their schoolwork.

Traumatic brain injury

The term *traumatic brain injury* (TBI) is used to describe any acquired brain damage resulting from events such as vehicle accidents, serious falls, blows to the head, unsuccessful suicide attempts, sports injury, the 'shaken infant syndrome' and recovery after drowning. An increasing number of school-age individuals acquire brain injury from falls, car accidents and partial drowning. Howard *et al.* (2010) suggest that head injuries now account for some 40 per cent of fatalities in preschool children.

The detrimental effects of TBI can include:

- memory problems;
- attention difficulties;
- slow information processing;
- inability to solve problems and plan ahead;
- speech and language functions disrupted temporarily or permanently;
- impairment of motor coordination;
- onset of epilepsy;
- vision problems;
- severe headaches;
- unpredictable and irrational mood swings or behaviour (aggressive, restless, apathetic, depressed).

Students with TBI often improve dramatically in the first year following injury, but, after that, progress is much slower. Turnbull *et al.* (2012) indicate that for some individuals with TBI there is a slight to moderate decline in functional intelligence, with skills such as reading comprehension and mathematical problem solving presenting as areas of particular difficulty. Frequent problems with word and information retrieval (*anomia*) can slow down the individual's speech and cause great frustration. Many children with TBI express great irritation in knowing an answer to a question in class but being unable to retrieve the necessary words at the right time. Given the complexity of the problems that can occur with TBI, it is common to find that the individuals affected usually require ongoing personal counselling, as well as an adapted learning programme (Helms & Libertz, 2014). Books by Best *et al.* (2010) and Turnbull *et al.* (2012) contain useful sections on teaching and management issues related to TBI in school-age children. The main challenges for the teacher are:

- finding ways of maximizing the individual's attention to a learning task by removing distractions, providing cues, limiting the amount of information presented and giving frequent feedback;
- keeping instructions clear and simple, and not overloading the student with information or tasks;

- breaking down lesson content into manageable units of work that are achievable within the individual's attention span;
- helping to compensate for memory loss by presenting visual cues and graphic organizers to aid recall of information by encouraging visual imagery, rehearsing information more than would be necessary with other learners, teaching self-help strategies such as keeping reminder notes in your pocket, and regularly checking the daily schedule on a hand-held electronic planner;
- helping the individual plan ahead by setting goals and then working towards them;
- understanding and accepting the student's poor ability to concentrate and to complete the work that is set.

Augmentative and alternative communication

It has been mentioned that many students with severe and multiple disabilities, whether congenital or acquired, may lack an oral–verbal method of communication. This can lead others to judge them, wrongly, as functioning at a low cognitive level. The priority for severely disabled persons without speech is to develop an alternative method of communicating (Dodd & Gorey, 2014). The ultimate aim of any augmentative or alternative communication system is to allow the child to converse about the same range of things that other children of that age would discuss.

Alternative communication modes include:

- sign language, finger-spelling, cued-speech and gesture;
- picture and symbol systems that a person can access by pointing or by eye glance on a communication board, screen or book;
- computer-aided communication.

The simplest form of alternative communication is a communication board comprising a small set of pictures or symbols that are personally relevant to the child's life and context. For example, the board may have pictures (widely spaced) of a television set, a glass, a knife and fork, a toilet, a toy, and X for 'no' and a green tick for 'yes'. The child can communicate his or her wishes or basic needs by pointing to or looking at the appropriate picture. Other pictures and symbols are added as the child's range of experiences increases.

General points for mainstream teachers

Many teachers may lack experience in working with physically disabled students. The following list provides some of the information they need to know.

- For students in wheelchairs or walking with leg braces and sticks, it may be necessary to rearrange the classroom desks and chairs to give easier access and a wider corridor for movement.
- Some students with physical disabilities will need to use modified equipment and assistive devices. It is the teacher's responsibility to ensure that the student does make use of these items.
- Secondary school students with physical disabilities may have great difficulty writing and taking notes. Their fine motor movements may be slow and their

coordination very poor and inaccurate. The teacher could establish a peer support network and allow the student to photocopy the notes of other students. Sometimes the teacher may permit a student to use a scribe or submit an assignment as an audiotape rather than an essay.

- Some students with physical disabilities may have a high absence rate due to attending therapy or treatment appointments during school hours; or frequent health problems. Frequent absence means that the teacher may need to provide the student with specific 'catch up' work to do at home, and may need to enlist the help of the support teacher or aide to provide some short-term remedial assistance for the student.
- Some students with physical disabilities (especially cerebral palsy) may also have epilepsy. To control the epilepsy the student may be on medication that also tends to lower their level of responsiveness in class. If seizures appear to increase in severity or frequency, check that the student is actually taking the medication. Report all cases of seizure to parents.
- While applying all commonsense safety procedures, teachers should try not to overprotect students with physical disabilities. Whenever possible, these students should be encouraged to take part in the same activities enjoyed by other students. Teachers of PE and sport need to get practical advice on ways in which physical activities can be adapted to include students with disabilities. Physically disabled students should never be left on the sidelines as mere spectators.

Childhood obesity

While childhood obesity is not classified as a physical disability per se its effects can be somewhat disabling. Certain groups of students with disabilities are particularly prone to weight problems, including those with a disability that restricts their mobility, and those with an intellectual disability or autism who spend a great deal of sheltered and passive time at home. The growing number of overweight children is an issue of concern in schools (and in society generally) (McMullan & Keeney, 2014). This problem is mainly associated with a contemporary lifestyle of sedentary occupations, such as sitting at a computer for hours at a time, easy access to fattening foods, and the presence of advertising that actively promotes such foods. The weight problem is exacerbated for some children by lack of exercise. They even seem to engage less in 'running about' and interacting in vigorous games in the school yard.

Children who are significantly overweight risk a number of health problems as they get older, and their social life and self-esteem are also negatively affected. It is reported that obese children are more likely than others to suffer from asthma (Thompson, 2013) and Type 2 diabetes. It is essential that schools do all they can to increase children's awareness of the need for a healthy lifestyle. Where possible the school curriculum should increase the amount of time devoted to physical education and fitness (Larson *et al.*, 2013); and children with physical and intellectual disabilities should be included fully in all such activities.

Asthma and allergies

Asthma has become a very common condition affecting school-age children. It is due to inflammation of the bronchial airways, resulting in severe breathing problems. Air pollution in cities is one contributing factor. Parents must always notify the teacher if their child has asthma, and discuss the response that needs to be made if the child has an attack while at school. Asthma is one of the leading causes of absence from school; so it is often necessary to provide remedial teaching and 'catch up' homework for these children when they return to school.

Allergies are causing problems for an ever increasing number of students, and teachers need to be alert to any child who may have an extreme reaction to food, pollutants, chemicals, medicines, insect bites, or other agents (Colbert, 2013). The most extreme reaction is referred to as *anaphylactic shock*, which can be life threatening. Schools need to have a list of all students with allergies, together with emergency telephone contact numbers, and a response plan known to all teachers.

Online resources

- The website of the National Institute of Neurological Disorders and Stroke (NINDS) provides information on a number of physical disabilities.
  Cerebral palsy is located at: www.ninds.nih.gov/disorders/cerebral_palsy/cerebral_palsy.htm.
  Traumatic brain injury at: www.ninds.nih.gov/disorders/tbi/tbi.htm.
  Epilepsy at: www.ninds.nih.gov/disorders/epilepsy/epilepsy.htm.
  Spina bifida at: www.ninds.nih.gov/disorders/spina_bifida/spina_bifida.htm.
- *Conductive education* is described fully on the Cerebral Palsy Organization website at: http://cerebralpalsy.org/about-cerebral-palsy/therapies/conductive-education/.
- Tips for teaching students with physical disabilities can be located at: http://specialed.about.com/od/physicaldisabilities/a/physical.htm.

Further reading

Bellon, M. (Ed.). (2014). *Sensory, physical and multiple disorders*. French's Forest, NSW: Pearson Australia.

Best, S.J., Heller, K.W. & Bigge, J.L. (2010). *Teaching individuals with physical or multiple disabilities* (6th edn). Upper Saddle River, NJ: Pearson-Merrill-Prentice Hall.

Effgen, S.K. (2013). *Meeting the physical therapy needs of children*. Philadelphia: F.A. Davis.

Heller, K., Forney, P., Alberton, P., Best, S. & Schwartzman, M. (2009). *Understanding physical, health and multiple disabilities* (2nd edn). Upper Saddle River, NJ: Pearson Education-Merrill.

Hudson, J.P. (2014). *A practical guide to congenital developmental disorders and learning difficulties*. London: Routledge.

Pike, M. (Ed.). (2013). *Disorders of the spinal cord in children*. London: MacKeith Press.

Chapter 4

Students with sensory impairments

Students with sensory impairments comprise a varied group within the population of children with special needs. Often they require teaching approaches and resources that differ somewhat from those normally available in mainstream schools. However, many students with sensory impairments are now included in regular classes and taught by mainstream teachers. The evidence is that very few mainstream teachers have adequate expertise in teaching these students with sensory impairments (Brown *et al.*, 2013).

Vision impairment

In some countries the term *vision impairment* is replacing the older term *visually impaired*. When a child is described as vision impaired, it does not necessarily mean that he or she is blind, it means that the child has a serious defect of vision that cannot be corrected by wearing spectacles. In the population of children with impaired vision, there are those who are totally blind, those who are 'legally' blind and those with low vision (partial sight).

While impaired vision is a low-incidence disability, it is important to note that it also occurs as a secondary handicap in many cases of severe and multiple disabilities. For example, many students with cerebral palsy also have serious problems with vision, as do some individuals with traumatic brain injury (Howard *et al.*, 2010). There is also a very small population of students who are both deaf and blind, and who therefore require extremely skilled teaching (Mockler, 2014).

Impaired vision has many potential causes, including structural defects or damage to the retina, lens or optic nerve, inefficiency in the way the brain interprets and stores visual information, or an inability of the retina to transmit images to the brain. Prematurity and very low birth weight can contribute to vision problems in childhood, with *retinopathy of prematurity* (ROP) being reported as one of the most common causes of impaired vision in very young children. Some vision problems are inherited, including those associated with *albinism*, congenital cataracts and degeneration of the retina, while others may be due to disease or to medical conditions such as diabetes or tumours. Loss of vision in persons who have previously had normal sight involves very significant psycho-social readjustment (Southwell, 2012).

Special educational needs of children with impaired vision

Early years

Vision is important for developing gross and fine motor skills. Blind children and those with very low vision may often be delayed in acquiring basic motor skills such as crawling, walking and feeding. Young children with impaired vision benefit from many physical activities that help them develop body awareness, depth perception, movement and coordination. These children need to be encouraged, within the realms of safety, to explore and interact with their immediate environment.

Absence of sight can also lead to delays in cognitive development and concept formation (Bardin & Lewis, 2008). Early sensory stimulation is therefore vital for young blind children, and needs to be accompanied by constant verbal interpretations by the parent or caregiver. The child should be given different objects to explore through touch, and taught how to examine small objects and large objects in order to build relevant concepts. Parents and teachers need to provide a blind child with verbal input, while seizing opportunities throughout the day to encourage the child's use of intact senses. Children with impaired vision are obviously much less able to acquire knowledge and skills through observation and incidental learning, so the environment and events happening within it must be *described*, to increase the child's awareness of things he or she cannot see. Auditory skills need to be encouraged through appropriate activities that involve careful listening.

Social development

Impaired vision can affect an individual's confidence and self-esteem (Bowen, 2010) and this in turn can reduce willingness to initiate social contacts. Teachers need to be proactive in helping blind and partially sighted students become involved in the social group (Smith & Tyler, 2010). For vision-impaired students able to cope with learning in the mainstream, inclusion can be extremely beneficial for overall social development. However, for some students the socialization process in the classroom and in the playground can often be problematic. This is partly due to lack of opportunity to mix and interact with other children from an early age, and thus observe and acquire social behaviours. It is also due to the fact that blind children can't see the many important non-verbal aspects of social interaction and communication such as nodding in agreement, looking surprised, smiling and respecting personal space when engaging in conversation (MacConville & Rhys-Davies, 2007). Social development is further restricted if members of the peer group feel shy or are lacking in confidence when interacting with a person who is blind or partially sighted. It is sometimes helpful to foster better understanding in the peer group by discussing openly with the class the problems that a person with impaired vision may have in dealing with schoolwork and with the physical environment. Obviously, if such discussion is attempted, it should only be done with the student's agreement, and must be done with due sensitivity.

Accessing the curriculum and the environment

There are several areas in which blind children and those with seriously impaired vision need to be taught additional skills. These areas include mobility, orientation, the use of Braille and assistive technology (Smith & Tyler, 2010).

Mobility

Blind students and those with very low vision need to be taught mobility skills to enable them to move safely and purposefully in their environment. Any person with severely impaired vision needs mobility skills and confidence to negotiate the outside environment, including crossing the road, catching buses or trains, and locating shops. Increased mobility adds significantly to the quality of life for persons with impaired vision. While the classroom teacher and parents can certainly assist with the development of mobility skills, a mobility-training expert usually carries out the detailed planning and implementation of the programme.

Mobility skills include:

*   *self-protection techniques* – for example, in unfamiliar environments, holding the hand and forearm loosely in front of the face for protection while trailing the other hand along the wall or rail; checking for doorways, steps, stairs and obstacles; using auditory information to locate objects (e.g. air-conditioner, an open doorway; traffic noise);
*   *long-cane skills* – moving about the environment with the aid of a long cane swept lightly on the ground ahead to locate hazards and to check surface textures;
*   *using electronic travel aids* – for example, 'sonic spectacles' with a built-in device that emits a sound warning to indicate proximity to objects;
*   *using public transport* – an important part of training involves teaching the individual how to use and negotiate buses and trains.

Orientation

Orientation is the term used to indicate that a person with impaired vision is familiar with a particular environment and at any time knows his or her own position in relation to objects such as furniture, barriers, doors or steps. Teachers should realize that, for the safety and convenience of students with vision impairment, the physical classroom environment should remain constant and predictable (Salisbury, 2008). If furniture has to be moved or some new static object is introduced into the room, the blind student needs to be informed of that fact and given the opportunity to locate it in relation to other objects. In classrooms it is necessary to avoid hanging posters and other items at head height, and to make sure that equipment such as boxes and books are not left on the floor. Doors should not be left half open with a hard edge projecting into the room.

Mobility and orientation together are two of the primary goals in helping the blind student move towards increased independence. Without these skills the quality of life of the blind person is seriously restricted.

Braille

Braille is of tremendous value as an alternative communication medium for those students who are blind or whose remaining vision does not enable them to perceive enlarged print. Braille is a complex code, so its use with students who are below average in intelligence is not always successful. Obviously if an individual's cognitive level is such that he or she would experience difficulties in learning to read and write with conventional print, Braille is not going to be an easier code to master. However, if a child's intelligence is adequate, the younger he or she begins to develop some Braille skills the better, as this will prepare the child to benefit from later schooling and university study.

A simplified system similar in principle to Braille is called Moon. It is reported to be easier to learn, particularly for children who have additional disabilities (Salisbury, 2008). Moon uses only 26 raised shapes, based on lines and curves, to represent the standard alphabet, plus ten other symbols.

In recent years there has been debate around the issue of whether communication technology (screen-to-speech and speech-to-text applications for computers) has made touch systems such as Braille and Moon obsolete. Persons in the blind community have expressed varied opinions, but most believe that Braille is still important because it provides an independent means of accessing, recording, storing and revisiting information. This is deemed more effective for study than purely transient audio input. However, in mainstream schools there can often be a delay in providing a blind student with relevant curriculum materials in Braille. For this reason, secondary students who are blind are reported to prefer talking books and audio recordings for convenience and ease of access to new information (Adetoro, 2012).

Assistive technology

In the same way that students with physical disabilities can be helped to access the curriculum and participate more effectively in daily life through the use of assistive technology, children with impaired vision can also be assisted. Many devices have been designed to enable the partially sighted student to cope with the medium of print. *Low-vision aids* are magnification devices or instruments that help the individual with some residual sight to work with maximum visual efficiency. The devices include a variety of hand-held or desktop magnifiers, and closed-circuit television or microfiche readers (both used to enlarge an image).

For blind students, calculators and clocks with audio output, dictionaries with speech output, compressed speech recordings and thermoform duplicators are used to reproduce Braille pages or embossed diagrams and maps. Some students with impaired vision benefit from modified furniture such as desks with bookstands or angled tops to bring materials closer to the child's eyes without the need to lean over, or with lamp attachments for increased illumination of the page.

Teachers in mainstream classes should note that although assistive devices are of very great benefit to partially sighted students, many of these students will try to avoid using them in class because they feel that using them draws unwanted attention to their disability (MacConville & Rhys-Davies, 2007). This emotional sensitivity to assistive technology as a marker of disability can begin in the primary school years, but occurs most frequently among vision-impaired students in mainstream secondary schools.

Teaching students with impaired vision

Teachers in the mainstream with no prior experience of vision-impaired children may tend to hold fairly low expectations of what these children can do and accomplish. It is essential, however, to provide many new challenges for these students and encourage them to do as much as possible. Having a problem with vision should not exclude the children from access to normal classroom experiences, although significant modifications to materials and methods may need to be made (Amato *et al.*, 2013; Supalo *et al.*, 2008). The following general advice may help mainstream teachers with vision-impaired students in their classes.

- Almost all students with impaired vision in mainstream classes will have low vision rather than total or legal blindness. It is essential to encourage them to use their residual vision effectively, because exercising remaining vision is helpful, not harmful.
- Seat the student in the most advantageous position to be able to see the whiteboard or screen.
- Ensure that your own material on whiteboard, PowerPoint or computer screen is neat and clear, using larger script than usual. Keep the whiteboard surface clean to ensure clarity of text.
- Enlarge the font in all text, notes and handouts to one of the following point sizes: 24, 36, 48.
- Use a photocopier when necessary to make enlarged versions of notes, diagrams and other handouts for the student.
- Avoid overloading worksheets with too much information.
- Allow partially sighted students to use a thick-tip black pen that will produce clear, bold writing.
- When necessary, prepare exercise paper with darker ruled lines.
- Allow much more time for students with impaired vision to complete their work.
- Read written instructions aloud to students with impaired vision, to reduce the amount of time required to begin a task and to ensure that the work is understood.
- Use very clear verbal descriptions and explanations, because explanation must compensate for what the student cannot easily see.
- Use an abacus and other equipment to establish early number skills through manipulation and touch.
- Train other students and the classroom aide to support the student with impaired vision when necessary – for example, by taking notes during the lesson, clarifying points or repeating teacher's explanations.
- Call on blind students frequently by name during lessons to engage them fully in the group-learning processes. Verbally acknowledge and value their contributions.
- Call upon other students clearly by name so that the blind student knows who is responding.
- Make sure that any specialized equipment is always at hand and in good order. If the student with impaired vision uses magnification or illumination aids or other devices, make sure that you know when and how the equipment needs to be used, and ensure that the student does not avoid using the equipment.
- Some forms of vision impairment respond well to brighter illumination, but in some other conditions bright light is undesirable. Obtain advice on illumination from support service personnel who are aware of the student's characteristics.
- If the student has extremely limited vision, make sure that any changes to the physical arrangement of the room are explained and experienced by the student to avoid accidents. The student needs to develop fresh orientation each time an environment is changed.
- Try to ensure that the student establishes a network of friends within the class. Social interaction is often not easily achieved without assistance.
- Obtain all the advice you can from the visiting support teacher and other advisory personnel. In the UK, there are now quality standards clearly specified for visiting support services (TeacherNet, 2010).

Transition to work or further study

Helping vision-impaired students prepare for employment or further study requires a team approach – teachers, parents, peer group, mentors, counsellors – and of course the student (Ravenscroft, 2012; Willings, 2013).

The following strategies are regarded as important when preparing vision-impaired students for transition.

- Careers teachers and counsellors should familiarize themselves with all barriers that may exist for vision-impaired students' successful post-secondary transitions.
- For students contemplating tertiary study, help the student explore what support options will be available for them in that setting.
- Discuss with the student his or her strengths, interests and aspirations, and provide appropriate career counselling and informed advice.
- Encourage and facilitate a student's increasing independence, self-confidence, resilience and assertiveness.
- In the final school year, gradually align any accommodations currently provided in the school with those the student may realistically encounter in workplace, college or university. This may mean phasing out certain school supports at an appropriate time.
- Assist the student directly by arranging job placements and trial internships.
- Give adequate time to teaching these students 'interview skills', so that they can present themselves well during interviews for employment or university.

Hearing impairment

Hearing impairment is a general term used to describe all degrees and types of hearing loss and deafness. Impaired hearing does not mean that an individual cannot detect any sounds; he or she may simply hear some frequencies of sound much more clearly than others. Individuals are usually referred to as *deaf* if they are unable to detect speech sounds and if their own speech is disordered. In some countries, those who can hear some sounds and can make reasonable use of their residual hearing are either termed *hard of hearing* or *partially hearing*.

Types and degrees of hearing loss

Many students with impaired hearing have no other disability; but hearing impairment can often be present as a secondary problem in children with intellectual disability, cerebral palsy or language disorders. Most hearing loss can be classified as either *conductive* or *sensori-neural*. The key features of each type are summarized below.

Conductive hearing loss

Conductive hearing loss occurs when sounds do not reach the middle ear or inner ear (cochlear) because of some physical malformation, blockage or damage. Common causes are excessive build-up of wax in the ear, abnormality of the ear canal, a ruptured eardrum, dislocation or damage to the tiny bones of the middle ear, or infection in the middle ear (*otitis media*). Hearing loss due to middle-ear infection is usually temporary and will improve when the infection is treated successfully. If infections are allowed to continue untreated, damage may be done to the middle ear resulting in permanent hearing loss. The use of a hearing aid may significantly help an individual with conductive hearing loss.

Sensori-neural loss

Sensori-neural hearing loss is related to the inner ear and the auditory nerve. The most serious hearing losses are often of this type. As well as being unable to hear many sounds, even those that are heard may be distorted. The problem of distortion means that the wearing of a hearing aid may not always help, because amplifying a distorted sound does not make it any clearer. Some individuals with sensori-neural loss are particularly sensitive to loud noises, perceiving them to be painfully loud.

Assessing hearing loss

Hearing is measured in units called decibels (dB). Zero dB is the point from which people with normal hearing can begin to detect the faintest sounds. Normal conversation is usually carried out at an overall sound level of between 40 and 50 dB. Loss of hearing is expressed in terms of the amplification required before the individual can hear each sound. The greater the degree of impairment, the less likely it is that the child will develop normal speech and language, and the more likely it is that they will need special education services. Individuals with a hearing loss above 95 dB are usually categorized as 'deaf' or 'profoundly deaf'.

Other categories are:

- *Slight loss*: 15–25 dB★.Vowel sounds still heard clearly. Some consonants may be missed.
- *Mild loss*: 25–40 dB★. Can hear only loud speech; usually requires hearing aid; may need speech therapy; some difficulty with normal conversation.
- *Moderate loss*: 40–65 dB★. Misses almost all speech at normal conversational level; requires hearing aid; serious impact on language development; speech therapy and special education often required.
- *Severe loss*: 65–95 dB★. Unable to hear normal speech; major problems with language development; hearing aid required (but may not help in some cases); language training and other special services required.
- *Profound loss*: above 95 dB★. Cannot hear speech or other environmental sounds; severe problems in language acquisition; normal conversation impossible; alternative forms of communication usually required (e.g. sign language; cued speech); special class placement often indicated.
  [*Note*: ★ The specific dB range varies slightly from country to country]

The difficulties experienced by children with slight to moderate hearing loss often remain undetected for several years, placing the child at risk of failure in school (DCSF, 2009). This is particularly the case if the hearing problem is intermittent and related, for example, to head colds or middle-ear infections. Early detection of hearing loss must lead to appropriate early intervention.

Impact of hearing loss on learning and development

An inability to hear clearly places a young child at risk of delay in many areas, including the acquisition of spoken language, literacy skills and social development. For example, the speech of children with significantly impaired hearing often has very poor rhythm and phrasing, together with a flat and monotonous tone of voice. Many factors, including time of onset, severity, type of hearing loss and different instructional approaches, all interact to produce large variations in spoken language performance. Early detection of hearing loss is vital, so that intervention can begin in the preschool years (Szymanski et al., 2013). A priority goal in the education of all children with impaired hearing is to advance their language skills as much as possible. Any improvement in language will allow each child to make better use of his or her intellectual potential, understand much more of the curriculum and develop socially.

Helping a deaf child acquire intelligible speech can be a long and difficult process and early intervention and active parental involvement are essential elements in language stimulation. One well-respected programme for this purpose is the Ling Method (or Auditory Verbal Approach) (Ling & Ling, 1978). In some cases, speech training and auditory training are also advocated for hearing-impaired students. Speech therapists or language teachers may, for example, use speech and articulation coaching based mainly on behavioural principles of modelling, imitation, reinforcement and shaping. In recent years, however, speech therapists and teachers have placed much more importance on trying to stimulate language development through the use of naturally occurring activities in the classroom (milieu approach). Such teaching is thought to result in better transfer and generalization of vocabulary and language patterns to the child's everyday life (Christensen-Sandfort & Whinney, 2013).

The inability to hear language from an early age not only creates a major problem in developing speech but can also have a negative impact on intellectual development. It is often said that deaf students' limited vocabulary slows down development of cognitive skills necessary for learning in school. In recent years there has been some criticism of this viewpoint and it is now suggested that although deaf children may lack depth in *spoken* language, they still encode and store information and experience in other ways. They often have some other more visual representations of language such as signing or gesture that enable them to express their ideas.

Many hearing-impaired children are now included in mainstream classes. It is argued that they experience maximum social interaction and communication by mixing with other students who use natural spoken language. They are exposed to more accurate language models than might be the case in a special class containing only hearing-impaired students. It is also hoped that students with normal hearing will develop improved understanding and tolerance for individuals who are slightly different from others in the peer group. Where deaf children are included in regular classes, some schools ensure that the hearing students are also taught basic sign language in order to promote communication.

Including students with significantly impaired hearing in mainstream classes relies fairly heavily on the availability of expert advice from visiting teachers and from regional hearing support services. In some countries where many schools are in country regions or in remote areas (e.g. Australia), providing this service can be problematic (Checker et al., 2009). Advances in communication technology in recent years have opened up new opportunities for using 'tele-intervention' to provide regular service to hearing-impaired students, their teachers and their parents (Houston & Stredler-Brown, 2012). This is of great benefit to students with impaired hearing living in remote areas. Direct work with students can occur through audio-video links, and techniques can be demonstrated to teachers and parents.

Basic academic skills

It is frequently reported that the academic attainment level of children with impaired hearing lags well behind that of their hearing peers. Often this problem is due not only to difficulties in processing oral information from teachers but also to lack of adequate proficiency in basic literacy and numeracy skills. Careful attention must be given to the explicit teaching of reading and spelling skills to students with impaired hearing. It is typical of these students that as they progress through primary school they fall three to four years behind the peer group in terms of reading ability (Robertson, 2009). For example, Trezek et al. (2010) indicate that by age 19, students with significant hearing loss typically read at the level of a nine-year-old child. This reading lag has a detrimental impact on their performance in all subjects across the curriculum.

Many of their difficulties in reading and spelling are thought to stem from their problem in accurately perceiving speech sounds. Limited phonemic awareness results in serious difficulty in learning decoding and encoding skills. At one time, it was believed that deaf and hard-of-hearing students need to learn to read by visual memory methods alone because they lack the underlying capacity to master decoding. It was thought, for example, that teaching printed words alongside their manual sign language equivalents would enable students to build up a meaningful sight vocabulary of words. However, such an approach is limited in the long term because it does not teach a system that would help a reader to unlock unfamiliar words. The visual approach used alone is no longer popular among educators, and instructional methods now aim to help these students develop phonological awareness and acquire an understanding of orthographic units (letters and letter groups) and their relation to speech (Cupples et al., 2014). The significant improvement in the quality of hearing aids in recent years has been beneficial in this respect by helping students detect speech sounds more accurately (Robertson, 2009). While the beginning stages of reading instruction can focus on building a basic sight vocabulary by visual methods, later the teaching of word-analysis (decoding) skills must also be stressed for students with hearing loss. Phonics-based instruction is still viable for these students if it is supplemented by visual materials and, in some cases, cued speech (Harris et al., 2013; ICLI, 2014). Without the phonic concept, students' ability to read and spell unfamiliar words will remain seriously deficient. It is also essential when providing reading instruction for hearing-impaired children that due attention be given to developing comprehension strategies. A restricted vocabulary and limited awareness of complex sentence structures can cause major problems in fluency and comprehension (Trezek et al., 2010).

The written expression of deaf children is often reported to be problematic, with syntax and vocabulary being the major weaknesses (Strassman & Schirmer, 2013). Difficulties often include inaccurate sentence structure, incorrect verb tenses, difficulties representing plurals correctly and inconsistencies in using correct pronouns. The written work of older deaf students has many of the characteristics of the writing of younger children, and may also contain 'deafisms' involving incorrect word order (e.g. 'She got black hair long', instead of 'She has long black hair').

Spelling instruction needs to be direct and systematic rather than incidental. For deaf children, it is likely that more than the usual amount of attention will need to be given to developing visual memory to enable them to spell and check words by eye as well as ear. The 'look-say-cover-write-check' strategy is particularly helpful and needs to be taught thoroughly (see Chapter 12).

Modes of communication

While listening and speaking remain the preferred methods of communication for students with mild and moderate degrees of impairment, for those who are severely to profoundly deaf alternative manual methods may be needed. These methods include gesture, sign language, cued speech and finger-spelling.

Sign language

There are different forms of sign language all sharing obvious characteristics in common but also having some unique features (e.g. Signed English, Auslan, American Sign Language). Deaf children from deaf families will almost certainly have been exposed to, and become competent in, manual communication even before entering formal education. There is no strong evidence that early exposure to sign language has a detrimental effect on later oral communication skills, such as speech and lip reading (Meadow, 2005).

Sign language remains a controversial issue in the field of deaf education. Often the use of sign language is the only thing that attracts the attention of others to the fact that a person is deaf. Many teachers, and some parents who are not deaf, feel that to encourage manual forms of communication will cause the child to be accepted only in the deaf community rather than in the wider community of hearing persons. They also believe that the use of signing will retard the development of speech, thus isolating the child even further. Experts suggest, however, that sign language should be respected as a language in its own right, with its own vocabulary, grammar and semantics, and it should be valued and encouraged as an effective mode of communication (Beal-Alvarez & Huston, 2014).

Oral–aural approach (oralism)

The belief underpinning *oralism* is that to be accepted and to succeed in a hearing world you need to be able to communicate through oral–verbal methods. The approach virtually places a ban on manual communication and stresses instead the use of residual hearing, supplemented by lip reading and speech training. Teachers should note, however, that hearing-impaired students' ability to lip read is often greatly overestimated (MacConville & Palmer, 2007). Attempting to interpret words from cues on the speaker's lips is an extremely difficult and inaccurate method of understanding the communication of others.

Cued speech

A manual system known as *cued speech* was developed to help resolve the many visual ambiguities inherent in 'reading the lips'. Cued speech uses hand signs alongside the mouth of the speaker to differentiate between similar sounds or words (Colin *et al.*, 2013).

Total communication approach

The relative popularity of signing versus oralism ebbs and flows from decade to decade. In response, *total communication* (TC) or simultaneous communication (SC) deliberately combines signing and gesture with oral–aural methods to help deaf children comprehend and express ideas and opinions (Howard *et al.*, 2010). A combination of oral and manual training at an early age appears to foster optimum communicative ability (Turnbull *et al.*, 2012).

Assistive technology

Hearing aids

Hearing aids are designed to amplify sound, and are of various types including the typical 'behind the ear' or 'in the ear' aid and radio frequency (FM) aids (Crowe, 2012). An audiologist assesses the specific needs of the child and a hearing aid is prescribed to suit the individual's sound-loss profile. The aid is adjusted as far as possible to give amplification of the specific frequency of sounds needed by the child. No hearing aid fully compensates for hearing loss, even when carefully tailored to the user's characteristics.

The great limitation of the conventional hearing aid is that it amplifies all sound, including background noise in the environment. The advantage of the radio frequency (FM) aid is that it allows the teacher's voice to be received with minimum interference from environmental noise. The teacher wears a small microphone and the child's hearing aid receives the sounds in the same way that a radio receives a broadcast transmission. The child can be anywhere in the classroom, and does not need to be near to or facing the teacher, as with the conventional aid.

Many hearing-impaired students do not like to be seen wearing a hearing aid, especially in mainstream situations and particularly in secondary schools. They will take every opportunity to hide it away and not use it. Some of these students report that they feel more socially at ease, and thus able to fit in more easily with their peers, if they do not wear the aid (MacConville & Palmer, 2007). Teachers have a responsibility to make sure the hearing aid is used and is maintained in good order.

Cochlear implants

A cochlear implant is a device used to produce the sensation of sound by electrically stimulating the auditory nerve. The device has four parts: processor, transmitting coil, receiver and electrode array (Crowe, 2012). The implant is able to bypass the functions of the hair cells in the inner ear that are often damaged or defective in cases of sensorineural loss.

Many developed countries now carry out the surgery required to implant this form of assistive device at a very young age. Cochlear implants are normally recommended only for children who are profoundly deaf and cannot benefit at all from other forms of hearing aid. While the child can begin to perceive the electrical stimulation soon after surgery, it normally takes at least a year for gains in the child's language skills to become evident. The child's effective adaptation to the cochlear implant needs much support and encouragement from the parents. Many children with cochlear implants still rely on sign language or cues to understand fully what is said. Smith and Tyler (2010, p. 347) have remarked, 'Teachers need to understand that students with cochlear implants may have speech that is difficult to understand, and they will be receiving intensive speech and language therapy.'

There is increasing evidence that integrating various forms of technology and software into teaching of students with impaired hearing can bring positive results. For example, CD-ROM-based packages, such as the auditory and language training program *Fast ForWord* (Scientific Learning Corporation) are showing some promise in helping children with mild hearing loss or with an auditory processing disorder to improve phonemic awareness and listening attention (Howard *et al.*, 2010). In the domain of reading, Mueller and Hurtig (2010) describe a successful strategy for enhancing reading activities for deaf students by combining technology with sign language input.

Teaching students with impaired hearing

The following basic strategies for teaching hearing-impaired students may also be helpful to students with other learning difficulties in the classroom. It is recommended that teachers:

- make greater use of visual methods of presenting information whenever possible;
- use simple language when explaining new concepts; very clear enunciation by the teacher is important (Lam & Tjaden, 2013);
- teach all new vocabulary thoroughly; write new words on the whiteboard, ensuring that students with hearing impairment see the word and say the word;
- revise new vocabulary regularly; and revise new language patterns (e.g. 'Twice the size of...', 'Mix the ingredients...', 'Invert and multiply...');
- repeat instructions clearly while facing the class;
- do not give instructions while there is noise in the classroom;
- write instructions as short statements on the whiteboard whenever possible;
- attract the student's attention when you are about to ask a question or give out information;
- check frequently that the student is on task and has understood what he or she is required to do;
- provide the student with printed notes when possible, to ensure that key content from the lesson is available for later study;
- make sure a deaf student can see the other students who are speaking or answering questions when group discussion is taking place;
- repeat the answer that another student has given if you think the hearing-impaired student may not have heard it;
- involve the student in the lesson as much as possible;
- ensure that the student has a partner for activities and assignments;
- encourage other students to assist the hearing-impaired student to complete any work that is set – *but* without doing the work for the student;
- do not talk while facing the whiteboard – a deaf student needs to see your mouth and facial expression;
- do not walk to the back of the room while talking and giving out important information;

- reduce background noise when listening activities are conducted;
- do not seat the student with impaired hearing near to sources of noise (e.g. fan, open window, generator); the student should be seated where he or she can see you easily, can see the whiteboard and can observe the other students;
- make sure that you know how to check the student's hearing aid, and check it on a daily basis;
- modifications are often required for assessment and testing in accordance with the nature and degree of a student's hearing impairment (Cawthorn & Leppo, 2013);
- seek advice regularly from the regional advisory service and from the visiting support teacher, and use such advice in your programme.

Online resources

- Information on blindness and vision impairment is available on the National Dissemination Center for Children with Disabilities website at: www.nichcy.org/Disabilities/Specific/Pages/VisualImpairment.aspx.
- Curry, S.A. & Hatlen, P.H. (2012). *Meeting the unique needs of visually impaired pupils through appropriate placement.* Online article at: www.eccadvocacy.org/section.aspx?TopicID=451&DocumentID=5282.
- Willings, C. (2014). *Resource books on visual impairments.* Annotated list available at: www.teachingvisuallyimpaired.com/resource-books-on-visual-impairments.html.
- Transition from school to work (or to study) for blind and low-vision students is discussed at: www.teachingvisuallyimpaired.com/transitions.html.
- Practical strategies for teaching children with sensory impairments available at the Texas School for the Blind and Visually Impaired website: www.tsbvi.edu/Education/strategies.htm.
- Information on teaching deaf and hearing-impaired students available at the National Dissemination Center for Children with Disabilities website at: http://nichcy.org/disability/specific/hearingloss.
- Doorn, R. (2010). *Teaching hearing impaired children.* Article available on TeachMag website at: http://teachmag.com/archives/130.
- The issue of including hearing-impaired students in the mainstream is addressed in a paper at: www.brighthubeducation.com/special-ed-inclusion-strategies/42913-hearing-impairment-teaching-strategies-for-an-inclusive-classroom/.

Further reading

Cavitt, W. & Gwise, T. (2013). *A blind child's pathway to learning: Developing cognition without sight.* Bloomington, IN: Author House.

Easterbrooks, S.R. & Beal-Alvarez, J. (2013). *Literacy instruction for students who are deaf and hard-of-hearing.* New York: Oxford University Press.

Niparko, J.K. (Ed.). (2009). *Cochlear implants: Principles and practices* (2nd edn). Philadelphia, PA: Lippincott, Williams and Wilkins.

Nitttouer, S. (2010). *Early development of children with hearing loss.* San Diego, CA: Plural Publishing.

Salisbury, E. (Ed.). (2008). *Teaching pupils with visual impairment.* London: Routledge.

Spencer, P.E. & Marschark, M. (2010). *Evidence-based practice in educating deaf and hard-of-hearing students.* New York: Oxford University Press.

Chapter 5

Gifted and talented students

In previous chapters, attention has been devoted to the characteristics and needs of students with various forms of learning difficulty or disability. This chapter explores the special needs of a group of students who are often assumed to have no problems in learning – namely those of high intellectual ability and those who possess specific talents. It is now accepted that these students require special attention if their full potential is to be realized. Sulak (2014) has commented that such potential, especially in academic areas, may only develop if students are provided with appropriate experiences and advanced instruction. Some important ways of meeting their needs are discussed in this chapter.

Prevalence

It is generally agreed that based on measured intelligence approximately 3–5 per cent of the school population can be regarded as potentially intellectually gifted. In Britain these students are referred to now as '*highly able students*' or students with '*high learning potential*' (Smithers & Robinson, 2012). Within this population there are varying degrees of giftedness, ranging from 'moderate' to 'profound'. Less than one child in every 100,000 would be classed as 'profoundly gifted'.

Many intellectually gifted students – but by no means all – are high achievers in most academic subjects in the school curriculum. Many – but by no means all – may also display exceptional ability and creativity in areas such as art and design, technology, music, drama, dance, sports, gymnastics, interpersonal skills and leadership (Groth-Marnat, 2009). In addition to these intellectually and academically gifted students, there are also many others in our schools, not necessarily of above average intelligence, with exceptional talent in specific areas. These talented students also require special attention to enable their talents to develop to the full. Taken together, intellectually gifted and other talented students comprise some 10–12 per cent of the school population.

Identifying gifted learners

In the US there is no national mandate that all states must identify their gifted and talented students or make special provision for them. It is left to individual states to determine their own policy – and many have done so. Most other countries have a similar laissez-faire approach. In an ideal world there would be a comprehensive approach to identifying gifted students in our schools. This would combine informal observation by parents and teachers, evaluation of students' work samples and test results, formal assessments of intelligence, aptitude and talent, and discussions among relevant experts. In reality, identification currently occurs mainly through recognizing students' excellent classroom work and test results, and their higher-than-average commitment and interest in learning. Unfortunately, this informal approach tends to result in many students with good potential, but only average classroom performance, falling through the net. Studies have shown that teachers are not good at identifying gifted students who are *underachieving* in school – so improving teachers' expertise in identification therefore remains a high priority.

In the UK, concern has been expressed that capable students are not being identified systematically, and are not being sufficiently extended by the teaching they receive. In an effort to combat this weakness, future school inspections will focus particularly on how well the school is meeting the needs of highly able students (OfSTED, 2013a, 2013b). In addition, Geake (2009) recommends that there should be a much stronger focus on principles and practices of gifted education in all pre-service and in-service teacher education courses.

In the US, the influential National Association for Gifted Children (NAGC) and the Council for Exceptional Children (CEC) have attempted to address this problem by recommending standards for the training of all teachers in gifted education. NAGC comments that:

> Classroom teachers are the primary agent for identifying and serving gifted and talented students in our nation's schools. Ensuring that highly able learners are recognized and subsequently served through systematic programming is of the highest priority. It is critical that all teachers are able to recognize a high-ability student who may need more depth and complexity in instruction or be referred for further assessment and services.
>
> (NAGC-CEC, 2013, n.p.)

In order to strengthen provision for gifted students, Bates and Munday (2005) have argued strongly that every school should have a recognized and enacted policy that delineates how these students will be identified and how special provision will be made for them. Schools should also determine how teaching and learning within regular classrooms will be differentiated to meet their needs. As one positive move in this direction, all schools in the UK are now expected to appoint a member of staff with appropriate expertise to the role of Leading Teacher. This person will be responsible for promoting and monitoring gifted and talented education, in much the same way that a Special Educational Needs Coordinator (SENCo) oversees special education support.

Defining giftedness, talent and creativity

Over the years, experts have debated the nature of giftedness, and whether it stems from innate potential or simply arises as a result of high motivation and hard work – the view held in many Asian countries (Porter, 2012). The consensus is that giftedness does have a genetic component that represents a *potential* for advanced development; but such development then only occurs if many other factors combine in positive ways. Cross and Coleman (2014, p. 94) have suggested that giftedness develops from

> ...a complex series of interactions that include the coordination of many traits of the individual student, such as motivation and perseverance, with context variables

such as teacher expertise and opportunities for practice, along with the general ability levels of the individual in terms of academic domains, and levels of creativity.

Some definitions of giftedness suggest that *creativity* and originality are essential components in all forms of giftedness. Renzulli (2005), for example, proposed that giftedness arises from a positive interaction among three human traits – above average ability, a high degree of task commitment (motivation, persistence and effort) and creativity. Others have suggested that creativity, while clearly essential in some fields, is not a necessary ingredient in *all* forms of outstanding ability or talent. Often intellectually and academically gifted students are not necessarily highly creative in the artistic or performance areas, although they may be extremely creative in problem solving and in generating new ideas.

While the exact relationship between giftedness and creativity remains a topic for debate, it has become popular to argue that every student has some creative ability, and that this attribute must be recognized, valued and encouraged in schools. There is concern expressed sometimes that current education reforms, particularly those concerned with raising academic standards, have caused the typical school curriculum to become too narrow, focusing almost exclusively on mastery of subject matter and measurable outcomes. It is feared that this may result over time in fewer opportunities for students to engage in a range of non-academic activities that foster creativity.

For many years the terms *gifted* and *talented* had been used interchangeably in the literature, as if the two are synonymous. However, the official line taken in Britain is that the two terms are not synonymous. The term *gifted* is used to describe learners who have the ability to excel *academically* in one or more school subjects. *Talented*, on the other hand, describes learners who have the ability to excel in *practical* ways, such as in sport, leadership, artistic ability, or in an applied skill. In practice it has proved difficult for schools to differentiate between gifted students and talented students, and for this reason the concept has come in for some criticism (Smithers & Robinson, 2012).

The Canadian psychologist Françoys Gagné (2009) also views giftedness and talent as separate concepts, but arrives at this conclusion from a different perspective. Gagné's 'Differentiated Model of Giftedness and Talent' (DMGT) regards 'gifts' as outstanding *innate aptitudes* with which certain individuals are born. These aptitudes relate to competencies within the intellectual, creative, social, socio-affective, physical and sensory domains; and it is within these same domains that specific talents may be developed. However, an individual's latent talent will only develop as a result of sustained personal effort and long commitment (Gladwell, 2008; Hattie & Yates, 2014). From Gagné's (2009) perspective it is easy to understand that some gifted students can be in a state of arrested development unless educational opportunities are optimum, environmental factors are positive, and intrapersonal factors are conducive to talent development. Socio-economic disadvantage is one important negative environmental factor; and poor quality of teaching is another.

The official view adopted in the US differs somewhat from that taken in Britain. The US federal definition tends to blur the distinction between giftedness and talent. It states therein that gifted students are

> children or youth who give evidence of high achievement capability in areas such as intellectual, creative, artistic, or leadership capacity, or in specific academic fields,

and who need services and activities not ordinarily provided by the school in order to develop those capabilities fully.

(Porter, 2012, p. 1)

The current discourse in the US focuses on 'talent development' as being a principal goal in education for *all* students; and the view is that outstanding potential ability exists in any domain. It is the responsibility of US schools to identify students with high capabilities and to provide appropriate education. However, in practice this has usually meant using only intelligence testing as the means of identifying students to be placed in gifted education programmes. There is little evidence to date to suggest that schools have become more effective in a broader sense in identifying students' creative, artistic or leadership potential or in providing appropriate teaching (Smithers & Robinson, 2012).

Underachievement

Gifted underachievers may not be recognized as such by their teachers because they produce classroom work and test results that are satisfactory, but not outstanding. Their high potential remains unrecognized, so nothing is done to vary their programme or provide additional support and motivation. Unfortunately, underachievement is often associated with early dropping out from school – which in turns affects the life prospects for the individual (Landis & Reschly, 2013).

There are many reasons why certain high-ability students may underachieve in school. Among the most common reasons are:

- *Boredom* – perhaps the curriculum is not sufficiently challenging to hold the student's interest and attention. The average pace at which topics are covered in the programme may be much too slow for students who are able to learn at a fast rate. There may be too much time devoted to revisiting material they have already mastered. Even in early childhood education settings there is evidence in several countries that the daily curriculum contains too little substance and intellectual challenge for young children of high ability, thus getting them off to a poor start (OECD, 2006).
- *Personal or emotional problems* – the student may be experiencing difficulties at home or within the peer group. These problems can severely undermine students' motivation and can impair their ability to concentrate and devote effort to study. Other problems may stem from the very fact that the student is gifted. Some students of high ability are overly obsessed with producing results that are always perfect, and are constantly fearful of failure. Some highly gifted individuals are thus prone to experience stress, anxiety and depression and often require personal counselling and support (Wood, 2010).
- *Peer pressure* – a few students of high ability may conceal their talents from their classmates in order not to stand out as 'different'. For example, they may be reluctant to hand in work of a high standard, or to speak out in class and ask or answer questions, even though they have much to contribute. Both boys and girls may deliberately underachieve so as not to be thought different and rejected by peers for being 'too smart'. This is especially true during adolescence (Coleman & Cross, 2014).

- *Poorly developed work and study habits* – some gifted students are not naturally inclined to work hard, to set themselves goals, to make a commitment and to devote the necessary effort. Simply because an individual has high potential does not in any way ensure that he or she is motivated to develop that potential through hard work. In addition, a few gifted students have never been taught effective study habits, so they do not always tackle assignments efficiently or successfully. Montgomery (2009, p. 225) comments that, 'The latest research on curriculum and learning needs has shown that the gifted need to be helped to develop study and research skills, reasoning capabilities and creative problem-solving.'
- *Learning disability* – a few students who are very talented and/or of high intelligence may also have a specific disability (SpLD) in areas such as reading, spelling, writing or mathematics, or may have attention deficit hyperactivity disorder (Assouline *et al.*, 2010). These students are often referred to as 'twice exceptional'. Dyslexic students, for example, may be intellectually gifted but have major problems with writing assignments and reading fluently with good comprehension. Often a gifted student with these difficulties is thought to be a low achiever by the teacher, and may even be placed in a low-ability group. It must also be remembered that some students with severe physical or sensory disabilities may be gifted and talented, but their disability impedes their ability to reveal their potential.
- *English as a second language* – students whose first language is not English can have difficulty in performing to the best of their ability in schools where English is the medium of instruction (Allen & Cowdrey, 2014). The problem relates not only to difficulties with understanding spoken and written language but also to a reluctance (sometimes related also to cultural differences) to ask and answer teachers' questions in class or to request additional help and explanations.
- *Socio-economic disadvantage* – some potentially gifted students may underachieve for a variety of reasons related to social disadvantage. For example, poverty leading to lack of resources in the home, dysfunctional family, low expectations and lack of support for learning are all factors associated with underachievement in school (Reed *et al.*, 2009). Improving outcomes in attainment, aspirations, motivation and self-esteem must be one of the key aims for gifted education for the most disadvantaged students.

Meeting the needs of gifted and talented students

There are two main ways to maximize progress for gifted students and to minimize underachievement – one is early identification, and the other is implementation of effective strategies to meet gifted students' intellectual and affective needs. Identification has been discussed already. Effective strategies for meeting the needs of gifted learners include organizational options and teaching methods. Organizational options may include, for example, allowing young gifted children to begin their schooling before the normal age of entry, creating part-time or full-time special groups (or 'cluster groups') containing only high-ability students, enrolling gifted students in separate specialist schools or 'academies' that cater for students with exceptional gifts and talents, 'grade skipping' (moving a student up to a higher age group for all or some subjects), early transfer to secondary school or to university, organizing a range of activities, training opportunities, clubs and competitions after school hours, enrolling students in special part-time programmes for gifted and talented learners, and establishing mentoring systems. Some of these options will be described in more detail later.

The current policy of inclusive education has called into question options that place high-ability students into specialist schools or classes for the gifted. These are frowned upon because they separate gifted students from their age peers. Instead, it is argued that gifted students should remain in the mainstream and receive a suitably differentiated programme, matched to their abilities and talents. An ideally differentiated programme for a gifted student would set appropriate goals, provide relevant learning activities (e.g. inquiry-based projects; problem solving; critical thinking) geared to ability level, allow for a faster pace of learning, spend less time on curriculum basics and revision, capitalize on the student's special interests and strengths, and monitor the student's progress closely (Kettler, 2014; VanTassel-Baska, 2014). The gifted student's programme would simply be one of several alternative programmes operating together in a mixed-ability classroom under the system known as 'tiered instruction'. Tiered instruction usually provides appropriate activities for different groups of students at three or more levels of difficulty. The potential benefits claimed for the differentiated approach are that students of high ability remain as members of a mixed-ability class and are able to interact socially and intellectually with other students of differing abilities. The high-achieving students may also act indirectly as role models for other students in the mainstream class in terms of study habits, work output and motivation. The potential disadvantage of differentiation (and it is a serious disadvantage) is that many teachers find it almost impossible to sustain many different levels and types of activities operating at the same time within the same classroom (Hertberg-Davis, 2009). The larger the class size, the more difficult the task becomes. Research has shown that very little differentiation of instruction typically occurs for gifted students in the average classroom; instead, these students tend to be given 'more of the same' or 'busywork' if they finish assignments quickly. Delisle (2006, p. 52) goes so far as to comment that, 'This error of inclusion and its ragtag "solutions" of differentiation and cooperative learning have done enormous harm to the appropriate education of gifted children.'

In contrast to those who advocate inclusion in the mainstream for students of high ability, most educators, community groups and researchers working in the field of gifted education believe that grouping by ability, for at least part of the time, is necessary if gifted students are to reach their full potential (Gross, 2004; National Association for Gifted Children, 2003; Smithers & Robinson, 2012). It is argued that teachers can be much more effective in providing challenging and rewarding curricula for students of high ability, and the pace of instruction can be much faster, if these students are grouped together for teaching and learning purposes (Gargiulo, 2009). Ability grouping can also be beneficial because it allows students of high ability to work closely and productively with others of similar ability. It has also been found in at least one study that students in gifted classes exhibit more interest in school and report better student-teacher relationships than similar students retained in regular classes (Vogl & Preckel, 2014).

Regardless of where students of high ability are taught (segregated setting, or in the mainstream) there are three main approaches to meeting their instructional needs – acceleration, extension and enrichment. These approaches are not mutually exclusive and can be used in combination.

Acceleration

Acceleration refers to any method adopted to cater for the gifted student's faster pace of learning and to avoid students having to repeat material they already know. Colangelo and Assouline (2009) describe acceleration as a powerful and effective strategy. Studies have shown unequivocally that acceleration can contribute greatly to gifted students' motivation and academic achievement; and in most cases has no negative effect on their social adjustment (Rimm & Lovance, 2004). Acceleration can, of course, be a feature within a gifted student's differentiated programme in the regular classroom, or it can be achieved through some of the practices described below.

- *Grade skipping* – the gifted student works with an older group or class for certain lessons; or the student may be permanently promoted to a higher age group. Early admission to secondary school or university represents another extreme example of this model. This form of acceleration, while useful for some exceptionally advanced students, does not necessarily suit all gifted children. Promotion to higher grade is also a difficult system to sustain over several years of schooling, particularly if a student changes schools. It should also be noted that acceleration will not help a gifted student at all if the programme into which the student is promoted is of poor quality.
- *Curriculum compacting* – the teacher omits certain topics, exercises or tasks in a course of study and modifies assignments so that a student can skip work already known to achieve the learning objectives in a shorter period of time (Peterson & Hittie, 2010).Teachers need to have a deep understanding and command of curriculum content to be able to adapt and condense courses or to devise alternative assignments effectively in this way. It is not an easy option.
- *Independent learning contracts* – an individualized work plan is designed for the student of high ability, allowing him or her to work fairly independently or with a mentor for specific periods each week (Clark, 2012). Such programmes usually involve the provision of more advanced learning resources (texts, computer software, DVDs, Internet connection) and more challenging learning objectives.

Extension

The strategy known as extension enables high achievers to go much more deeply into an area of study. This can be achieved in part by compacting the curriculum to save time, and then using that time to work on more challenging assignments. E-learning in all its forms has opened up many new possibilities for doing this in recent years (see Chapter 15). Such extension activities often rely heavily on students' independent learning skills and self-management. Students need first to receive direct teaching in the application of particular researching and data-processing skills to enable them to go beyond the objectives set for most members of the class. The extension approach also tends to involve students in more first-hand investigation and problem solving, with an emphasis on development of critical and creative thinking (Kettler, 2014).

Enrichment

Enrichment is the term used to describe any approach that seeks to broaden the field of study to include more applications and concepts (but not necessarily more difficult concepts) and to encourage creative or exploratory activities related to the central theme. It can be thought of as an expansion of the standard curriculum for those who are ready and able to go beyond the basic objectives. Enrichment is often achieved through the use of classroom learning centres, computer-assisted learning, project work, resource-based learning and individual or cooperative study contracts (Houghton, 2014). Enrichment is also the main function of the extra-curricular activities, clubs, competitions and summer schools that many schools organize. These activities often serve the additional purpose of encouraging specific talent development in areas other than the academic.

Both extension and enrichment can also be facilitated through *mentoring systems*. Mentoring makes use of adults or older students with special expertise in a particular area as tutors or guides for gifted students with an interest in, and aptitude for, that field. The area of study may be academic or may be related, for example, to the arts, recreation, sports or technology. Often mentoring sessions take place as extra-curricular activities.

The reality is that many teachers working with mixed-ability classes do not find it a simple matter to incorporate opportunities for acceleration, extension and enrichment into their everyday mainstream programmes. These approaches demand above average creativity, organizational and managerial skills on the part of the teacher. In the case of acceleration through the grades, the approach also requires the full backing and ongoing support of the whole school.

Most attempts to meet the needs of gifted students in mainstream schools have consisted of ad hoc activities intended to enrich students' learning experiences; but often these activities are not well integrated and purposeful and may result in very few lasting benefits. Some enrichment attempts lack any academic rigor and substance. These points are made here not to suggest that adopting a differentiated approach for students with gifts and talents is not worthwhile but to indicate that strategies for acceleration, extension and enrichment require very careful planning, conscientious implementation, close monitoring and the support of the whole school community.

General principles of teaching gifted learners

In order for the teaching of intellectually gifted students to be effective, teachers need to use many open-ended, challenging and extended tasks, requiring them to engage in high-level thinking, analysing, evaluating, synthesizing and creating new ideas. The amount of investigative work, problem solving, and creative or expressive opportunities should be increased in any topic studied; and the depth and complexity of the subject matter increased. It is also important to promote independence in learning and to encourage curiosity, persistence and confidence to talk through and share ideas. Gifted students also need to engage in self-evaluation and goal setting.

No matter whether gifted and talented students are taught within the mainstream or in cluster groups, Gilman (2008) suggests that there is a need to include the following components:

* individualized planning;
* access to advanced materials;
* faster pace of instruction;
* opportunities to reason and think critically;
* encouragement of free expression of ideas, and allowing disagreements;
* direct teaching of essential study skills and research strategies.

Specific implementation models

Over the years, many different programmes, models and curricula have been devised to serve the needs of gifted and talented students. A few of these models are described here, with others listed in the Online Resources at the end of the chapter.

Enrichment Triad Model and Schoolwide Enrichment

The Enrichment Triad Model (ETM) (Renzulli, 1976) and the *Schoolwide Enrichment Model* (SEM) (Renzulli & Reis, 1997) are examples of well-designed approaches to foster and support gifted students and other learners. The Enrichment Triad Model presents students with a variety of activities that enable them to explore a given topic from different perspectives and at different levels of challenge. It moves students of high ability beyond the regular curriculum and opens up new areas of interest. All students first engage in a range of introductory activities (Type I enrichment) to become conversant with the topic and to identify interesting issues worthy of further investigation. All students are then taught necessary investigative and data-processing skills required to explore and report some of these issues in greater depth and breadth (e.g. online searches, interviewing, note-taking, summarizing, diagramming, tabulation) (Type II enrichment). Finally, students can focus on specific issues or personal interests related to the central theme, and study these in much greater depth through independent or collaborative research (Type III enrichment). While Type III activities are available to all students in the class, they can also be tailored to stretch and challenge fully the students of high ability.

Most recently, the Renzulli Learning System (RLS) has used the Enrichment Triad Model to motivate and increase achievement in a broad range of students. RLS involves the use of search engine technology to match carefully selected web-based curriculum resources with specific student strengths and interests. The designer states that RLS provides learners with the skills and resources necessary to acquire advanced-level content and thinking skills, and creates authentic opportunities for students to apply their skills (Duke University Talent Identification Program, 2014).

The goal of the *Schoolwide Enrichment Model* (SEM) (Renzulli & Reis, 1997) is to strengthen a school's overall provision for gifted students and others by infusing enriched learning experiences and higher learning standards into the general curriculum. This is regarded as preferable to setting up separate programmes for students of high ability. SEM has three main goals: (i) to develop talents in all children; (ii) to provide a broad range of advanced-level enrichment experiences for all students; and (iii) to provide suitably challenging extension opportunities for students, based on their strengths and interests. The teaching approaches and activities in the model have come from research evidence on effective pedagogy in the gifted education field, and of course also embody key elements of the Enrichment Triad Model.

Various versions of ETM and SEM have been adapted in different countries and contexts. One example in the UK is OWLETS (*Original Ways of Learning through Enrichment Technology and Socialization*: Houghton, 2014), involving children in the first years of schooling. OWLETS aimed to address the common lack of provision for exceptionally able young children by engaging them more fully in their learning, and by supporting their social development. Some students who had undertaken OWLETS in their early years were interviewed later when they were older. They all suggested that they had benefited from opportunities to socialise and work collaboratively with similarly gifted peers.

Parallel Curriculum Model

The Parallel Curriculum Model (PCM) evolved from earlier work on curriculum adaptation by educators such as Carol Tomlinson in the US. PCM is based on the premise that every learner is somewhere on a path towards gaining expertise in a particular subject. The parallel curriculum sets out to develop further the existing abilities of all students and to extend the specific talents of students who perform at advanced levels.

PCM offers four curriculum parallels that incorporate the element of ascending intellectual demand. The four parallels comprise: (i) a *Core Curriculum* of key knowledge, concepts and skills related to the subject; (ii) *Connections*, helping students connect new content with prior knowledge in this and other subject areas, and apply skills across disciplines; (iii) *Practice*, to help students function effectively in a particular discipline area; and (iv) *Identity*, helping students identify with the subject more deeply by connecting it with their own lives, interests and aspirations. These four curricular components can be used singly or in combination to help teachers plan and implement units of work around a central theme. Teachers must first determine each student's current performance level and from this information develop intellectual challenges that will move him or her along a continuum towards expertise (Tomlinson *et al.*, 2008).

Autonomous Learner Model

The Autonomous Learner Model (ALM) has the stated aim of giving students the content, process and product knowledge that enables them to take responsibility for implementing and evaluating their own learning (Betts, 1985). The model focuses on gifted and talented students in Grades 1 to 12. ALM has flexibility in that it can be used with students in the regular classroom, in small group settings, or as an individual course. Among the basic principles of the model are emphases on self-esteem, student interests and broad-based content topics. ALM consists of five major dimensions:

- *Orientation* – understanding giftedness, group building activities, self/personal development.
- *Individual development* – inter/intra-personal understanding, learning skills, use of technology, university/career awareness, organizational and productivity skills.
- *Enrichment* – courses, explorations, investigations, cultural activities, community service, excursions, camps.
- *Seminars* – small group presentations of futuristic, problematic, controversial, general interest or advanced knowledge topics.
- *In-depth study* – individual projects, group projects, mentorships, presentations, assessment of self and others.

To some extent, independent study of this type matches the preference of some high-ability students to work alone; but it must be noted that not all gifted students exhibit this preference (French & Shore, 2009).

The CLEAR Curriculum Model

This model integrates three approaches that have proved to be effective in gifted education, namely: differentiation, increasing depth and complexity of the curriculum, and Schoolwide Enrichment (Azano, 2013; Foster *et al.*, 2011). The acronym CLEAR is derived from **C**ontinuous assessment, **L**earning goals, **E**xperiences, **A**uthentic products and **R**ich curriculum. The curriculum content and learning activities are designed so that all students are appropriately challenged and fully engaged to ensure higher achievement. A comprehensive overview of this model (with specific examples) can be found at the link specified in the Online Resources listed below.

Online resources

- *GT Voice* is an independent UK-based network for individuals and organizations supporting the education of able, gifted and talented children and young people. www.gtvoice.org.uk/.
- In the US the National Association for Gifted Children provides much useful information. www.nagc.org/.
- Also based in the US, National Research Center for the Gifted and Talented is a good source and has several research programmes in operation. www.gifted.uconn.edu/.
- The Department for Education and Skills in the UK prepared a guide titled *Effective provision for gifted and talented children in primary education*. Available online at: http://webarchive.nationalarchives.gov.uk/20130401151715/www.education.gov.uk/publications/eOrderingDownload/GTPrimary.pdf.
- The Ministry of Education in New Zealand has published a document titled *Gifted and talented students: Meeting their needs in New Zealand schools* (2012), Wellington: Learning Media. Available online at: http://gifted.tki.org.nz/For-schools-and-teachers.
- In Australia there are signs that the various states are strengthening their policies on gifted education. A good example is that now operating in Victoria through the Department of Education and Early Childhood Development (2014), *Aiming High: A strategy for gifted and talented children and young people 2014–2019*. Online at: www.education.vic.gov.au/Documents/about/programs/learningdev/giftedtalentedstrat.pdf.

Models and approaches:

- A description of the *Renzulli Learning System* can be located at: https://tip.duke.edu/node/850.
- Information on the *CLEAR Curriculum Model* can be located at: http://nrcgtuva.org/presentations/CEC2011.pdf.
- A clear description of the *Enrichment Triad Model* can be found at: http://enrichmenttriadmodel.weebly.com/what-is-triad.html.
- The *Schoolwide Enrichment Model* is explained fully on the University of Connecticut Center for Gifted Education and Talent Development website at: www.gifted.uconn.edu/sem/semexec.html.
- The *Parallel Curriculum Model* is explained at: http://presentlygifted.weebly.com/parallel-curriculum-model.html.
- The *Autonomous Learner Model* is described at: http://nmgifted.org/ALM/ALM_model.html.

Further reading

Callahan, C.M. & Hertberg-Davis, H.L. (Eds). (2012). *Foundations of gifted education*. New York: Routledge.

Davis, G., Rimm, S. & Siegle, D. (2011). *Education of the gifted and talented* (6th edn). Boston, MA: Merrill.

Kaplan, S.N. (2009). Layering differentiated curriculum for the gifted and talented. In F. Karnes & S. Bean (Eds), *Methods and materials for teaching the gifted* (pp. 107–136). Waco, TX: Prufrock.

Montgomery, D. (Ed.). (2009). *Able, gifted and talented underachievers*. Chichester: Wiley-Blackwell.

Montgomery, D. (2015). *Teaching gifted children with special needs*. London: Routledge.

Pfeiffer, S.I. (2012). *Serving the gifted: Evidence-based clinical and psychoeducational practice*. London: Routledge.

Renzulli, J.S., Gentry, M. & Reis, S.M. (2014). *Enrichment clusters* (2nd edn). Waco, TX: Prufrock.

Weinfeld, R. Jeweler, S., Barnes-Robinson, L. & Roffman, B. (2013). *Smart kids with learning difficulties* (2nd edn). Waco, TX: Prufrock.

Chapter 6

Self-management and self-regulation

One of the common observations concerning many students with learning problems is that they have become passive learners. They show little confidence in their own ability to bring about improvement through their own efforts or initiative. In contrast to this, studies over many years have yielded data indicating that self-regulated students tend to do well in school, and are more confident, diligent and resourceful. This is particularly important now that schools are using more e-learning strategies that call for self-management and self-direction (Wang, Shannon & Ross, 2013). One of the goals of education must therefore be to help all students achieve this level of self-efficacy by teaching them how to regulate and monitor their own performance in the classroom.

Self-regulation and self-management are essential competencies that children need to develop if they are to become autonomous learners. In the case of students with intellectual disability, emotional disturbance or learning disability, the skills and strategies involved in self-management and self-regulation may need to be explicitly taught (Hoff & Ervin, 2013; Regan & Martin, 2014). When these children acquire adequate self-management, it is much easier for them to be accommodated effectively in inclusive classrooms.

Definition of terms

The categories self-regulation, self-direction and self-management are often used interchangeably in educational discourse, but in the field of psychology each has its own precise meaning.

*   *Self-regulation* is the term commonly used in relation to an individual's ability to monitor his or her own approach to learning tasks and to modify strategies as necessary (Mason *et al.*, 2009). Self-regulation in learning involves *metacognition* – the ability to 'think about one's own thinking' and to monitor and control cognitive processes such as attention, strategy application, rehearsal, recall, comprehension and self-correction. Self-regulation also includes the ability to manage one's emotions, to control anger or frustration, and to cope with stress (Ennis & Jolivette, 2014; Levin & Nolan, 2013). Self-regulation in the context of classroom learning is discussed more fully later in the chapter.
*   *Self-direction* shares much in common with what some psychologists refer to as *self-determination*. Self-direction refers to the ability to show initiative, set personal goals and initiate appropriate actions and strategies to achieve those goals (Abar & Loken, 2010). Interest has been shown in recent years in the concept of 'self-directed

learning', as an essential source of personal motivation in schools, universities and in adult life (Boyer *et al.*, 2014).

* *Self-management* is one aspect of self-regulation and refers to an individual's ability to function independently in any given environment without the need for constant supervision, prompting or direction from others. In the classroom, for example, it relates to such behaviours as knowing how to organize one's materials, knowing what to do when work is completed, recognizing when to seek help from the teacher or a peer, understanding how to check one's own work for careless errors, how to maintain attention to task, how to observe the well-established routines such as ordering lunch, having sports equipment or books ready for a specific lesson, knowing when a change of lesson or room is to occur, and so on. All these skills are easily acquired by students without learning problems or disabilities, but can be difficult for some students with special needs. The possession of adequate self-management and self-direction is one factor that can facilitate inclusion in mainstream classrooms.

* *Executive functioning* (also known as *cognitive control*) is the term applied to an individual's ability to manage essential processes involved in daily life by planning, prioritizing, managing time, being well organized, maintaining attention, persisting long enough to complete a task, inhibiting inappropriate reactions and regulating one's emotions. Metacognition and working memory are closely involved. Executive functioning is often reported to be weak in students with learning disabilities.

Self-management in children

The specific self-management skills and executive processes required by a child in school will tend to differ slightly from classroom to classroom according to a particular teacher's management style, routines and expectations, and according to the nature of the curriculum. For example, in some classrooms a premium is placed upon passive listening, note-taking and sustained on-task behaviour, while in other classrooms initiative, group-working skills and cooperation with others are essential prerequisites for success. The self-management skills required in an informal classroom setting tend to be very different from those needed in a more formal or highly structured setting. Knowing how to respond to the demands and constraints of different lessons or settings is an important aspect of a student's growth towards independence (Mercer *et al.*, 2011).

The type of classroom learning environment created by the teacher, and the teacher's instructional approach, can both markedly influence the development of self-management and independence in children. Some teachers and tutors seem to operate with students in ways that foster their *dependence* rather than encourage their independence. For example, they may offer too much help and guidance for children with special needs in an attempt to prevent possible difficulties and failures. They may virtually spoon-feed the children using individualized support programmes that offer very few challenges and call for no initiative on the child's part. Too much of this support restricts the opportunities for a child to become autonomous.

The possession of self-management skills by a child with a disability or a learning difficulty seems to be one of the most important factors contributing to the successful inclusion in a regular classroom (Salend, 2011). Some students, for example those with intellectual disability or with social, emotional or psychological disorders, frequently exhibit very poor self-management (Wehmeyer & Field, 2007). Even students with milder forms of disability or learning difficulty often display ineffective self-management and need positive help to become more autonomous learners. It is essential, therefore, that all students with special needs, whether placed in special settings or in the regular classroom, be helped to develop adequate levels of independence in their work habits, self-control and readiness for learning. One of the major goals of intervention with such students is to increase their independence by improving their self-management.

Teaching self-management

When students are able to manage routines in the classroom and look after their own needs during a lesson, the teacher is able to devote much more time to teaching rather than managing the group. Evidence is accumulating to support the view that specific training in self-management and self-regulation can be effective in promoting students' independence (Adani et al., 2012; Hoff & Ervin, 2013). Intervention studies involving self-management and strategy training have suggested that there are very strong positive effects (e.g. Mooney et al., 2005).

To teach self-management, first teachers must recognize that such teaching is important and necessary. Second, teachers need to consider precisely which skills or behaviours are required in order to function independently in their particular class-rooms – for example, staying on task without close supervision, self-monitoring, using resource materials and technology appropriately, or seeking help from a peer. Third, students' current strengths and weaknesses in these skills must be assessed. Finally, any skills that are lacking must be explicitly taught using direct methods and corrective feedback.

Teaching self-management skills as part of an inclusive programme should have a high priority, particularly with young children and those with developmental delay. For students with special needs, a five-step procedure can be used to teach self-management.

- *Explanation* – discuss with the student why a specific self-managing behaviour is important. Help the student recognize when other students are exhibiting the target behaviour.
- *Demonstration* – the teacher or a peer models the behaviour.
- *Role play* – the student practises the behaviour, with descriptive feedback.
- *Cueing* – prompt the student when necessary to carry out the behaviour in the classroom.
- *Maintenance* – praise examples of the student displaying the behaviour without prompting.

It is important to teach the particular skills or behaviours to the point where the student no longer needs to be reminded or prompted. When teachers are constantly reminding the students of what to do, they are maintaining the students' dependence. Teachers may need to remind children with special needs rather more frequently than other students, and may have to reward them more frequently for their correct responses, but the long-term aim is to help these children function independently. It is always necessary to check at regular intervals to ensure that the student has maintained the behaviours over time.

Locus of control

Self-management links quite closely with the personality construct known as *locus of control*. To understand locus of control one needs to recognize that individuals attribute what happens to them in a particular situation either to internal factors (e.g. their own ability, efforts, decisions or actions) or to external factors (e.g. luck, chance, things outside their control). Children with an internal locus of control recognize that they can influence events by their own actions and believe that they do to some extent control their own destiny. At classroom level, an example of internality might be when students recognize that if they concentrate on the task and work carefully, they get much better results. Appreciating the fact that outcomes are under one's personal control is a key component of one's feelings of 'self-efficacy' and a strong defence against passivity (Pajares & Urdan, 2006; Pandya & Jogsan, 2013).

Internalization of locus of control usually increases steadily with age if a child experiences normal success and reinforcement from his or her efforts in school and in daily life outside school. However, it has been found that many children with learning problems and with negative school experiences remain markedly external in their locus of control in relation to school learning, believing that their efforts have little impact on their progress and that they lack ability (Bender, 2007). Young children enter school with highly positive views of their own capabilities, but this confidence rapidly erodes if they experience too many early failures and frustrations.

The child who remains largely external in locus of control is likely to be the child who fails to assume normal self-management in class and is prepared to be managed or controlled by others such as the teacher, parent, teacher's aide or more confident peers. There exists a vicious circle wherein the child feels inadequate, is not prepared to take a risk, seems to require support, gets it, and develops even more dependence upon others. The teacher's task is one of breaking into this circle and causing the child to recognize the extent to which he or she has control over events and can influence outcomes. It is natural for a teacher, tutor or aide to wish to help and support a child with special needs, but it should not be done to the extent that all challenge and possibility of failure are eliminated. Failure must be possible and children must be helped to see the causal relationship between their own efforts and the outcomes. Children will become more internal in their locus of control, and much more involved in learning tasks, when they recognize that effort and persistence can overcome failure.

It is important that teachers and parents publicly acknowledge and praise children's positive efforts, rather than emphasizing lack of effort or difficulties. Teachers' use of praise has been well researched. Praise seems particularly important for low-ability, anxious, dependent students, provided that it is genuine and deserved, and that the praiseworthy aspects of the performance are specified. A child should know precisely why he or she is being praised if appropriate connections are to be made in the child's mind between effort and outcome. Trivial or redundant praise is very quickly detected by children and serves no useful purpose. *Descriptive* praise, however, can be extremely helpful; for example: 'Good work, David! You used your own words instead of simply copying from the reference book.'

In general, teachers' use of descriptive praise has a strong positive influence on children's beliefs about their own ability and the importance of effort. When praise is perceived by children to be genuine and credible, it appears to enhance their motivation and feelings of control.

Attribution retraining

A markedly external locus of control usually has a negative impact upon a student's willingness to persist in the face of a difficult task. It is easier for the child to give up and develop avoidance strategies rather than persist if the expectation of failure is high. In the intervention approach known as *attribution retraining* (McInerney & McInerney, 2013), students are taught to appraise carefully the results of their own efforts when a task is completed. They are encouraged to verbalize their conclusions aloud: 'I did that well because I took my time and read the question twice', 'I listened carefully and I asked myself questions'. The main purpose in getting students to verbalize such attribution statements is to change their perception of the cause of their successes or failures in schoolwork. Verbalizing helps children focus their attention on the real relationship between their efforts and the observed outcomes. In most cases, attribution retraining seems to have maximum value when it is combined with the direct teaching of effective cognitive strategies necessary for accomplishing particular tasks. It is also recommended that teachers consider incorporating aspects of attribution training (thinking about reasons for one's success) into the school curriculum for all students (Chodkiewicz & Boyle, 2014).

Strategy-based instruction

Cognitive strategies are mental plans that help students complete learning tasks, solve problems and self-regulate (University of Kansas, 2014). A typical strategy includes both cognitive aspects (thinking and planning) and behavioural aspects (acting, responding, self-monitoring) that guide the individual's engagement with the task. *Strategy-based instruction* (SBI) involves teaching students to apply effective step-by-step thoughts and procedures to guide their self-monitoring when approaching and completing a particular task or problem (Waters & Schneider, 2010). There is ample evidence that strategy-based instruction in task-specific self-regulation can be very effective in improving learners' autonomy (McInerney & McInerney, 2013; Nguyen & Gu, 2013). An Effect Size of .69 has been reported for strategy training (Hattie, 2012). Any Effect Size above .40 is regarded as a very positive effect.

Teachers should always provide a clear model of how to tackle new learning tasks efficiently, to maximize the chances of early success. A teacher who says: 'Watch and listen. This is how I do it – and this is what I say to myself as I do it', is providing the learner with a secure starting point. The teacher who simply says, 'Here is the exercise. Get on with it', is often providing an invitation to failure and frustration. All too often teachers exacerbate students' learning problems by failing to demonstrate the most effective ways of approaching each new task. Appropriate skills and strategies are not taught explicitly and may therefore remain obscure to many students.

It was noted in Chapter 1 that many students with general or specific learning difficulties appear to lack appropriate skills and strategies for tackling schoolwork. They do not seem to understand that these tasks can be carried out effectively if approached with a suitable plan of action in mind. For example, attempting to solve a routine word problem in mathematics usually requires careful reading of the problem, identification of what one is required to find out, recognition of the relevant data to use, selection of the appropriate process, completion of the calculation and a final checking of the reasonableness of the answer. This approach to solving the mathematical problem involves application of a cognitive strategy and utilization of procedural knowledge (knowing how to carry out the steps in a specific calculation). There is clear evidence that teaching students with learning difficulties in mathematics how to apply this type of self-management strategy can enhance their achievement (Adani *et al.*, 2012).

The typical teaching procedure used in strategy-based instruction usually follows this sequence:

- *Modelling* – the teacher performs the task or carries out the new process while thinking aloud. This involves self-questioning, giving self-directions, making overt decisions and evaluating the results.
- *Overt external guidance* – the students copy the teacher's model and complete a similar task, with the teacher still providing verbal directions and exercising some control.
- *Overt self-guidance* – the students repeat the performance while using self-talk.
- *Covert self-instruction* – the students perform several similar tasks while guiding their responses and decisions using inner speech.

Typical self-questions, statements and directions a student might use when attempting to solve a problem in mathematics would include: *What do I have to do? Where do I start? I will have to think carefully about this. I must look at only one problem at a time. Don't rush. OK, I need to multiply these two numbers and then subtract the answer from 100. That's good. I know that answer is correct. I'll need to come back and check this part. Does this make sense? I think I made a mistake here, but I can come back and work it again. I can correct it.* These self-monitoring statements cover problem definition, focusing attention, planning, checking, self-reinforcement, self-appraisal, error detection and self-correction. They are applicable across a fairly wide range of academic tasks. Sometimes the steps involved in tackling a specific task are printed on a cue card displayed on the students' desks while the lesson is in progress. The students may also need to be taught a method for remembering the steps for implementation (e.g. a mnemonic). Examples of mnemonics are provided later in the chapters on literacy and numeracy.

Maintenance and generalization

Students with learning problems tend to take very much longer than other students to accept and adopt new learning strategies, so the teaching process needs to be sustained until independent use is finally established. Maintenance and generalization of taught strategies have always been problematic, particularly for students with learning difficulties. Students may learn successfully how to apply a given strategy to a specific task but not recognize how the same approach could be used more widely in other contexts. To help students overcome this problem, teachers might:

- provide strategy training that makes use of a variety of different authentic tasks from across the curriculum;
- discuss different situations in which a particular strategy could be applied;
- involve students as much as possible in creating or adapting strategies to the demands of particular tasks.

Effective use of strategies within the school curriculum can be fostered by direct teaching, abundant practice, discussions about the value of strategies, and how and when to apply them. Cooperative learning activities, peer tutoring, sharing views on how problems can be solved or tasks accomplished, can help to foster, generalize and maintain strategy use.

It is important to ensure that the specific strategies taught to students are actually needed in the daily curriculum to facilitate their immediate application. Students will find most relevance in strategies they can use to complete classroom assignments and homework more successfully. Strategies should be taught that focus particularly on tasks the students usually find too difficult.

Metacognition

Effective strategy training incorporates elements of self-regulation training together with cognitive and metacognitive instruction (Waters & Schneider, 2010). It is essential that students not only complete tasks independently but also monitor, reflect upon and control their own performance. Metacognitive instruction focuses on tactics that require a learner to monitor the appropriateness of his or her thoughts and responses, and to weigh up whether or not a particular strategy needs to be applied in full, in part or not at all in a given situation. This self-regulation of thought and action includes mental activities such as pre-planning, monitoring, regulating, evaluating, self-correcting or modifying a response.

It is considered that metacognition helps a learner recognize that he or she is either doing well or is having difficulty understanding the task. A learner who is monitoring his or her own ongoing performance will detect the need to pause and check, perhaps begin again before moving on, weigh up possible alternatives or seek outside help. It is essential that teachers encourage students to think about their own thinking and the quality of their own performance in a variety of learning situations.

Metacognition involves inner verbal self-instruction and self-questioning (self-talk) in order to focus, reflect, control or review. The scaffolding that teachers provide should therefore include modelling this self-talk to help students develop their own inner language. Effective use of self-talk is vital for better self-regulation in both learning and classroom behaviour (see *cognitive behaviour modification* below).

Reading comprehension, written expression and mathematics problem solving are examples of academic areas that can be improved by cognitive and metacognitive strategy training (Brissiaud & Sander, 2010). Students can be taught how to approach printed information and mathematical problems strategically, and then given abundant opportunities to practise the application of the strategies on a wide variety of texts, tasks and problems. It is said that research has shown strategy instruction to be a very effective method to enable older students with disabilities and learning difficulties to meet the demands of secondary and post-secondary education. Strategy training gives them confidence to find, study and express information independently (University of Kansas, 2014). The Center for Research on Learning at the University of Kansas has explored most facets of strategy training and has produced helpful information for teachers. The online resources listed at the end of this chapter include reference to the Kansas Strategic Instruction Model (SIM). Several examples of cognitive strategies are provided in later chapters.

Cognitive behaviour modification

Cognitive behaviour modification (CBM) is closely related to metacognitive strategy training, but also embodies behavioural principles. The term *cognitive behaviour intervention* (CBI) is also used. It involves procedures to help students gain better independent control over their own behaviour by using inner self-talk to guide their thoughts and actions. CBM is different from other forms of behaviour management in that the students themselves, rather than teachers or powerful others are the agents for change. The approach is more commonly referred to as *cognitive behavioural therapy* (CBT) when used in clinical settings to modify maladaptive behaviour and dysfunctional emotions (e.g. phobias, anxiety disorders, stress and anger control) (Garvik *et al.*, 2014).

Typically, students with a behaviour problem in class are taught to memorize and use a mental 'script' that enables them to monitor their behaviour in a particular situation and then make appropriate decisions. An example might be a student who has great difficulty in staying on task and who often gets out of her seat to wander around during the lesson. A small timing device with a beeper might be placed on her desk and she would be taught to monitor her own on-task behaviour every time the beeper sounds. If she is on task, she praises herself: 'Good! I am working. I am finishing the task. I must keep working. I have remained in my seat.' At the end of each lesson the teacher may reward the student in some way if she has remained seated and on task. Training in self-control techniques of this type is considered to be particularly useful for improving the self-management of students with mild intellectual disability, autism and attention deficit hyperactivity disorder (ADHD). The application of cognitive behaviour modification in cases of behaviour disorder is discussed in the next chapter.

Online resources

- The Center for Research on Learning at University of Kansas provides helpful information on learning strategies at: www.ku-crl.org/sim/strategies.shtml.
- The Strategic Instruction Model (SIM) at the University of Kansas is described at: www.ku-crl.org/sim/brochures/SIMoverview.pdf.
- A clear description of metacognition can be found at North Central Regional Education Laboratory at: www.ncrel.org/sdrs/areas/issues/students/learning/lr1metn.htm.
- Locus of control is explained fully at: www.wilderdom.com/psychology/loc/LocusOfControlWhatIs.html.
- Attribution retraining is described at: www.collegetransition.org/promisingpractices.research.attributional.html.
- Cognitive behaviour modification is discussed from a classroom perspective at: http://blue197757.tripod.com/untitled-page-5.html.

Further reading

Chapin, B. & Penner, M. (2012). *Helping young people learn self-regulation.* Chapin, SC: Youth Light Inc.

Dawson, P. & Guare, R. (2010). *Executive skills in children and adolescents* (2nd edn). New York: Guilford Press.

Dawson, P. & Guare, R. (2012). *Coaching students with executive skills deficits.* New York: Guilford Press.

Reid, R. & Lienemann, T. (2013). *Strategy training for students with learning disabilities* (2nd edn). New York: Guilford Press.

Wolsey, T.D. & Fisher, D. (2010). *Learning to predict and predicting to learn: Cognitive strategies and instructional routines.* Boston, MA: Pearson-Allyn and Bacon.

Chapter 7

Managing classroom behaviour

Effective teaching and well-managed classroom behaviour are two mutually supportive influences on students' learning. Teachers in primary and secondary schools place great importance on managing students' behaviour and helping students gain control over their own conduct. Many teachers report that one of their main concerns in the classroom is the child who disrupts lessons, cannot work cooperatively with others, seeks too much attention from teacher or peers (Landers *et al.*, 2013). Teachers feel that although they know what the child needs in terms of basic instruction and support, it proves impossible to deliver appropriate teaching because the child is unreceptive. Turnbull *et al.* (2012) suggest that some 9 per cent of school-age students present with intense behaviour problems, while another 15 per cent are at risk for developing such problems unless taught effective ways of self-control. Poduska and Kurki (2014, p. 83) have remarked: 'Moving evidence-based practices for classroom behavior management into real-world settings is a high priority for education and public health.' This chapter presents an overview of some of the approaches for preventing or reducing behaviour problems in school through effective use of proactive strategies.

The effects of misbehaviour

There are numerous negative outcomes from behaviour problems in school, both for the students and their teachers. Students who are creating the problems usually miss out on many important learning opportunities by spending a huge amount of time off task, and they tend to have a very poor and unhappy quality of life in school. Their social development may be affected because they tend to alienate members of their peer group. The general classroom climate is often affected negatively, because the teacher is unable to relax and use methods which do not require tight control.

Teachers of children with behaviour problems need the personal and professional support of their school principal and other teachers. In particular they need understanding from colleagues that the student's behaviour is not due to their own inability to exercise effective classroom management. Unless a school adopts a collaborative approach to the management of difficult and disruptive behaviour, certain problems tend to arise. These problems include:

- individual teachers feeling that they are isolated and unsupported by their colleagues;
- teachers feeling increasingly stressed by the daily conflict with some students;
- the problem becoming worse over time.

In the case of a child with serious behaviour problems, it is essential to involve the child's parents fully in the implementation of any behaviour change programme. The parents and school staff should together agree on the goals and strategies for such intervention, and be consistent in applying the same management strategies in school and at home.

Preventing behaviour problems

Shepherd (2010, p. 134) has written, 'Behaviour management provides students with a safe and secure environment in which learning can take place, teaches students the necessity of having rules and consequences, and helps students develop self-discipline and self-control.' The underlying principle of behaviour management practices in schools today is 'being positive rather than punative' (Wheeler & Richey, 2013, p. 108). Teachers are encouraged now, under a positive and preventive approach, to catch students being good and to praise them for appropriate behaviour, rather than waiting to reacting to bad behaviour. There is a strengthened focus now on improving students' positive engagement with classroom learning activities, rather than on punishing bad behaviour (Sullivan *et al.*, 2014).

It is generally agreed that the first step in preventing problem behaviour at the classroom level is to have a well-organized, predictable and supportive learning environment, an interesting curriculum, effective teaching methods and well-established routines (Wheeler & Richey, 2013). It is particularly important to employ teaching methods, activities and resources that *engage* students fully in the learning process, and that help to make students feel successful.

Behaviour management policy

The next step, at whole-school level, is to have a clear policy on behaviour management issues. In the UK, Section 89 (1) of the *Education and Inspections Act 2006* indicates that all maintained schools must set out measures in their behaviour policy which aim to: regulate students' conduct; promote good behaviour, self-discipline and respect; prevent bullying; and ensure that pupils complete assigned work (Gov.UK, 2006). A typical policy will describe ways in which individual teachers and all school staff should approach general matters of discipline and classroom control. The policy may also make specific reference to the management of students with significant emotional or behavioural disorders, and to students with disabilities. A clear school policy is the basis for consistent implementation and practice by all staff.

A school-level policy document must be much more than a set of rules and consequences. A good policy will make clear to students, teachers, parents and administrators that schools should be safe, friendly and supportive environments in which to work. In many ways, a school policy on student behaviour should be seen as dealing more with matters of welfare, safety and social harmony rather than procedures for punishment and enforcing discipline. The heart of any behaviour management policy should be the stated aim of teaching all students responsible and effective ways of managing their own behaviour and making appropriate choices. A good policy in action will help students recognize the personal and group benefits that self-control and responsible behaviour can bring.

A three-tier model of intervention

Increasingly, behaviour management is seen to require a *three-tier approach*, similar to that now used in remediation of learning difficulties – as described in Chapter 1. Tier 1 involves making school expectations and rules clear to all students, and explicitly teaching them self-management skills for appropriate behaviour. Tier 2 provides additional guidance for some students who, at times, begin to display poor behaviour. Tier 3 involves intensive behaviour change intervention at the level of an individual student with a severe and ongoing behaviour disorder (Dunlop, 2013; Jenkins *et al.*, 2013). Strategies for working with students at any of the three tiers are described below.

Positive behaviour support

The typical approach to behaviour problems in schools has always tended to be reactive and aversive rather than preventive. A more effective Tier 1 model attempts instead to be proactive and thus reduce the likelihood that serious problems will arise (Shepherd, 2010). For example, schools in the US are now encouraged to adopt a *Positive Behaviour Intervention and Support* model (PBIS) that requires a school-wide approach to creating a safe school environment where teachers can teach and students can learn (Boden *et al.*, 2013). PBIS offers a combination of practices, including social skills instruction, proactive supervision, reinforcement of self-controlled behaviour, provision of positive adult role models and building school-family-community links (Dunlop, 2013). The approach also requires schools to implement curricula that genuinely engage students, and in which they can succeed. In schools where the approach is adopted there is evidence of fewer instances of challenging behaviour, and attainment standards have improved.

PBIS intervention strategies include:

- modifying or eliminating classroom conditions that increase the probability of challenging behaviour arising (for example, reducing group size, arranging seating differently, changing teaching method, eliminating interruptions and distractions);
- teaching students self-control strategies;
- using positive reinforcement, rather than reprimands;
- providing active and supportive supervision;
- discussing behaviour codes and personal rights and responsibilities with students;
- explicitly teaching students the behaviours they need to display.

In the US a version of this approach is referred to as *Schoolwide Positive Behaviour Support* (SWPBS) (Turnbull *et al.*, 2012). The approach in operation involves all teachers clearly and consistently defining classroom expectations, teaching students how to meet these expectations, defining consequences for inappropriate behaviour and implementing the consequences where required (Feuerborn & Chinn, 2012).

The British Institute of Learning Disabilities has produced much useful material on positive behaviour support with reference to students and adults with intellectual disability. The link can be found under Online Resources. PBIS has been suggested as a helpful approach for students with autism spectrum disorders, due to its clear structure and predictable routines (Alter & Vlasak, 2014).

A team approach

There has to be recognition at whole-school level that behaviour problems are best dealt with from a shared perspective, and tackled with a team approach. When cases of disruptive or challenging behaviour are reported, it is important to consult with other teachers to discover whether the student also has a problem when in their classes. All teachers who have contact with the student will need to collaborate to use a consistent approach when dealing with the behaviour. Occasionally of course it is necessary to seek outside expert advice when a child's behaviour does not respond to standard forms of effective management; but in many cases behaviour can be modified successfully within the school setting.

To facilitate positive behaviour support at the whole-school level, it is recommended that *behaviour support teams* comprising teachers should be established in the school. These teams have the role of implementing behaviour policy, encouraging positive approaches to classroom management, helping to solve specific problems related to behaviour and learning, and assisting with staff development.

Behaviour support teams also operate at regional level, serving a number of different schools. For example, in the UK, multi-agency *Behaviour and Education Support Teams* (BESTs) have been established in many areas to work closely with schools and families to address the needs of children and young people with emotional, behavioural and school attendance problems. Schools drawing on the services of BESTs include those with high proportions of students with, or at risk of developing, behavioural problems and poor attendance. Similar support teams now operate in most states in Australia and the US.

Schools in the UK placed a strong focus on improving students' behaviour and reducing truancy rates. On the latter issue the schools have been reasonably successful (Gov. UK., 2013b). The initiative called *Social and Emotional Aspects of Learning (SEAL)* stresses the importance of creating a safe and supportive school environment. *SEAL* also provides valuable curriculum resources and deals with many relevant topics such as bullying and conflict resolution (Woolf, 2013).

The *SEAL* programme introduced in Britain should not be confused with the SEALS model in the US. The American model is titled *Supporting Early Adolescent Learning and Social Success* (SEALS). It targets the training for teachers to meet the needs of young adolescents during the transition to middle school (Farmer, 2011). The aim is to increase their understanding of the psycho-social dynamics operating during early adolescence, and to enhance efficacy in working with at-risk students. In particular, SEALS encourages positive classroom climate and teaches strategies to increase students' sense of connectedness (belonging) to their school community, while reducing feelings of emotional risk.

Classroom behaviour

While it is true that some students exhibit negative behaviour in school that is a reflection of stresses or difficulties outside school, it is also evident that disruptive behaviour can result from factors within the learning environment. For example, an unsuitable curriculum or inappropriate teaching methods quickly lead to poor behaviour because students who are bored or frustrated may well become troublesome. In addition, research has shown that class size, grouping and seating arrangements are factors influencing behaviour.

Teachers who are most effective in management tend to be vigilant in the classroom, and are more proactive in preventing behaviour problems. They also set appropriate and achievable tasks for students to attempt, they avoid 'dead spots' in lessons, they keep track of student progress, and they check work regularly to provide timely and constructive feedback.

A sound starting point for establishing a good classroom climate is the democratic process of creating classroom rules, building on sound principles set out in the school policy. Classroom rules are essential for the smooth running of any lesson and should be negotiated jointly by students and the teacher early in the school year. Students should appreciate why rules are necessary, and must agree on appropriate consequences if a rule is broken. Rules should be clear, consistent, expressed in positive terms (what the students *will do*, rather than *must not do*) and few in number. The rules should be based on respect for personal rights and responsibilities, and on respect for the rights of others. While the actual rules are important, the process by which they are developed is just as important. Students should feel ownership through contributing to their formulation. Rules might include matters related to noise level during lessons, movement within the classroom, seeking assistance, making opinions heard, respect for the ideas of others, safety, personal property and sharing of equipment.

All teachers should have their own *discipline plan* in mind, to enable them to know in advance what to do if classroom behaviour is disruptive (Rogers, 2014). The plan gives a teacher confidence when the pressure is on. Corrective actions a teacher might decide to use include:

* tactical ignoring of the student and the behaviour (for low-level disruptions);
* simple directions ('Ann, get back to work please');
* positive reinforcement ('Good, Ann');
* question and feedback ('What are you doing, Mark? OK, I will come and help you');
* rule reminders ('David, you know our rule about noise. Please work quietly');
* simple choices ('Excuse me, Joanne. You can either work quietly with Susan, or I will have to move you to a different seat – OK?');
* isolation from peers (student is taken aside to discuss the problem, then placed in a quiet area to do the work);
* removal from class (time out under supervision in a different room).

Teachers may also use strategies such as deflection and diffusion to take the heat out of a potential confrontation. Teacher: 'Sally, I can see you're upset. Cool off now and we will talk about it later; but I want you to start work please.' The judicious use of humour can also help to defuse a situation without putting the student down. One approach that never works is to lecture students endlessly about their perceived misdemeanours.

Sometimes it is appropriate to ask senior students to write a self-reflection about an incident of inappropriate behaviour in which they have been involved. They must say what they did, what they should have done and what they are going to do to remedy the situation. This reflection might then become the basis of a discussion with the teacher or school counsellor, and could be used as a starting point from which to formulate a plan of action for behaviour change.

Identifying the problem

According to Levin and Nolan (2013) a discipline problem exists whenever an incident interrupts the teaching process, interferes with the rights of others to learn and results in lost instructional time. Children who are constantly seeking attention, interrupting the flow of a lesson and distracting other children are very troubling to teachers. Naturally, teachers feel professionally threatened by children who constantly challenge their discipline. The feeling of threat can cause the situation to get out of hand, and a teacher can get trapped into confrontations with a child rather than looking for possible solutions that will provide responsible choices and save face for the child and the teacher.

All too often teachers react overtly to undesirable behaviour, thus reinforcing it. Many behaviour problems in the classroom, particularly disruptive and attention seeking behaviours, are rewarded by the adult's constant reaction to them. For example, the teacher who spends a lot of time reprimanding children is in fact giving them a lot of individual attention at a time when they are behaving in a deviant manner. This amounts to a misapplication of social reinforcement, and the teacher unintentionally encourages what he or she is trying to prevent.

If a teacher has a student who often displays inappropriate behaviour in the classroom, it is useful to reflect upon possible reasons for this behaviour. The following questions may be helpful when teachers attempt to analyse a case of disruptive behaviour:

* How frequently is the behaviour occurring?
* In which lesson or activity is the negative behaviour less frequent (e.g. more highly structured sessions, or the freer activities)?
* At what time of day does the behaviour tend to occur (a.m. or p.m.)?
* How is the class organized at the time (whole class, groups, individual assignments)?
* What am I (the teacher) doing at the time?
* What is my immediate response to the behaviour?
* What is the child's initial reaction to my response?
* How do other children respond to the situation?
* What strategies have I used in the past to deal successfully with a similar problem?

Modifying behaviour

It should be understood that changing a student's behaviour is often difficult. Sometimes the behaviour we regard as inappropriate has proved to be quite effective for the child in attaining certain personal goals. It has been practised frequently and has become very well established. In order for a positive behaviour change to occur, the child must first *desire* to change. The responsibility of the teacher is then to help the child understand exactly *how* to bring about and maintain the change.

Lane *et al.* (2013) suggest that there are four key elements to a behaviour change programme in school:

* any new behaviour to be established should be recognized as valuable by the student;
* methods to be used to eliminate an undesirable behaviour and teach a new behaviour should be evidence-based (i.e. of proven efficacy);

- close monitoring of progress towards the goal is essential;
- administrative processes and structures existing within the school should be such that behaviour change methods can be implemented consistently by all personnel involved and across all contexts.

One approach that is commonly used to bring about change is referred to as *behaviour modification*. It is based on principles of applied behaviour analysis (ABA) (Alberto & Troutman, 2012). In this approach three assumptions are made:

- all behaviour is learned;
- behaviour can be changed by altering its consequences;
- factors in the environment (in this case the classroom) can be engineered to reward and maintain specific behaviours.

When using ABA, problematic behaviour is observed and analysed to identify factors that are causing and maintaining the behaviour. A programme is then devised to reshape this behaviour into something more acceptable through a consistent system of rewards (reinforcement), ignoring or punishment. In cases of very persistent negative behaviour, such as aggression or severe disruption, positive reinforcement procedures alone may not be sufficient to bring about change. In such cases it may be necessary to introduce negative consequences and reductive procedures, such as loss of privileges, loss of points, or time out. Attention must also be given to improving the student's own self-monitoring in order to increase his or her self-control over the problem behaviour.

Behaviour modification approaches are sometimes criticized on the basis that control is exercised by powerful others rather than the individual. It is suggested that manipulation of the individual's behaviour is somehow out of keeping with humanistic views on the value of interpersonal relationships, the social nature of learning and the need for personal autonomy. However, the very precise planning and management of a behaviour modification programme requires careful observation of how the child, the teacher and other children are interacting with one another and influencing each other's behaviour. Far from being impersonal, the techniques used to bring about and maintain change are usually highly interpersonal.

The behavioural approach is now regarded as an evidence-based method, its efficacy having been reported in an impressive number of research studies over a long period of time. In particular, ABA techniques are of great practical value for those working with students who have severe disabilities, autism, emotional disorders and challenging behaviour.

Cognitive approaches for self-control

The main goal of any type of behaviour-change intervention should be the eventual handing-over of control to the individual concerned so that he or she is responsible for managing the behaviour. One way of achieving this is to employ the cognitive behaviour modification (CBM) approach described in Chapter 6. Cognitive behavioural approaches are often viewed (wrongly) as the province of the clinical psychologist or counsellor, but in fact they should be part of a classroom teacher's repertoire of skills (Cooper *et al.*, 2013).

Application of CBM requires the teacher or trainer to provide coaching in the use of *self-talk* to help the student monitor his or her own reactions to challenging situations. The self-talk enables the student to process aspects of the situation rationally and enables him or her to manage responses more effectively. A key ingredient in the approach is teaching the student to use self-statements that serve to inhibit impulsive and inappropriate thoughts or responses, allowing time for substitution of more acceptable responses – for example, to be assertive but not aggressive; to approach another student in a friendly rather than confrontational manner.

The intervention must help the student analyse inappropriate behaviour and understand that lashing out at others or arguing with staff, for example, is not helping them in any way. Next the student is helped to establish both a *desire to change* and the *goals* to be aimed for over the following week (i.e. to stop doing the negative behaviour and to start doing the more positive behaviour). Over a number of sessions the student is helped to change negative thoughts and beliefs to more appropriate positive perspectives.

Strategies for reducing disruptive behaviour

Teachers can lose almost half of their teaching time in some classrooms due to students' disruptive behaviour. This behaviour upsets the orderly conduct of teaching and prevents a teacher from achieving the objectives for a particular lesson. Frequent disruptive behaviour may also impair the quality of personal and social interaction within the group by destroying a positive classroom climate (Rogers, 2014). Sometimes simple changes such as modifying seating arrangements, restructuring working groups, reducing noise level and monitoring more closely the work in progress will significantly reduce the occurrence of disruptive behaviour. The following strategies are also recommended.

Tactical ignoring

If a child begins some form of disruptive behaviour (e.g. shouting to gain attention), the teacher ignores that child's response, and instead turns away and gives attention to another student who is responding appropriately. When the first student is acting appropriately, the teacher will ensure that he or she is immediately noticed and called upon.

Clearly it is not sufficient merely to ignore disruptive behaviour. It is essential that planned ignoring be combined with a deliberate effort to praise descriptively and reinforce the child for appropriate behaviours at other times in the lesson – 'catch the child being good'.

Signal interference

Many teachers use the strategy of signal interference to indicate to a student that his or her behaviour is becoming inappropriate (Levin & Nolan, 2013). The use of non–verbal indicators such as staring hard at the student, frowning or shaking the head are often sufficient to bring that student back on task without disrupting the attention of others in the class.

Proximity interference

Proximity interference refers to the common strategy of moving much closer to the student (almost invading the personal space) and giving your undivided attention. This usually has the effect of redirecting the student's efforts back on the lesson, again without affecting the attention of the other students. Teachers seem to have fewer problems if they move around the classroom frequently, monitoring the students closely as they work.

Reinforcement and rewards

In order to modify behaviour according to ABA principles, particularly in young or immature children, it may be helpful to introduce a reward system. If social reinforcers such as praise, smiles and overt approval are not effective, it will be necessary to apply more tangible rewards, selected according to students' personal preferences. Children differ, and what one child may find rewarding another may not.

For students with special needs, some teachers use tokens to reinforce behaviour or work in class. Tokens are simply a means of providing an immediate concrete reward. Tokens are usually effective because of their immediacy and students can see them accumulating on the desk as visible evidence of achievement. Tokens can be traded later for back-up reinforcers such as time on a preferred activity, being dismissed early or receiving a positive report to take home to parents. While not themselves sensitive to individual preferences for particular types of reinforcement, tokens can be exchanged for what is personally reinforcing.

Most textbooks on educational psychology provide some general rules for using reinforcement. It is worth repeating them here.

* Reinforcement must be given immediately after the desired behaviour is shown, and at first must be given at very frequent intervals.
* Once the desired behaviours are established, reinforcement should be given only at carefully spaced intervals.
* The teacher must gradually shift to unpredictable reinforcement so that the newly acquired behaviour can be sustained for longer and longer periods of time without reward.

Time out

Time out refers to the removal of a student completely from the social group situation to a different part of the room, or even to a separate but safe setting for short periods of isolation. While time out may appear to be directly punishing, it is really an extreme form of ignoring. The procedure ensures that the child is not being socially reinforced for inappropriate behaviour.

Time out also allows for 'cooling off' of emotions. A set place should be nominated for this (e.g. a corner of the school library where worksheets may be stored for use by the student). He or she should be under supervision for all the time spent out of the classroom. The work set should be achievable, given his or her ability level – but avoid making the session so 'enjoyable' that time out becomes a preferred option; for example don't set assignments on the computer with Internet access.

The student will not return to that particular lesson until he or she is in a fit emotional state to be reasoned with, and some form of behaviour contract can be entered into between teacher and student. Following a period of time out it is usually beneficial to have the child participate in a debriefing session in which he or she is encouraged to discuss the incident, reflect upon the behaviour, identify behaviour that might have been more effective and set a goal for improvement.

If the time out technique is being used, it is important that every instance of the child's disruptive behaviour be followed by social isolation. The appropriate behaviour will not be established if sometimes the inappropriate behaviour is tolerated, sometimes punished, and at other times the child is removed from the group. It is essential to be consistent.

In 2014 the Department for Education in the UK stated that:

> Schools can adopt a policy which allows disruptive pupils to be placed in isolation away from other pupils for a limited period. If a school uses isolation rooms as a disciplinary penalty this should be made clear in their behaviour policy.
>
> (DfE, 2014b)

The issue of excluding a student from school for a short or longer term for extreme reason is addressed under Section 51A, *Exclusion of pupils from schools*, in the Education Act 2011. The legal requirements pertaining to this can be found online at: www.legislation.gov.uk/ukpga/2011/21/section/4.

Behaviour contracts

A behaviour contract is a written agreement signed by all parties involved in a behaviour-change programme. After rational discussion and negotiation, the student agrees to behave in certain ways and carry out certain obligations. In return the staff and parents agree to do certain things. For example, a student may agree to arrive on time for lessons and not disrupt the class. In return the teacher will sign the student's contract sheet indicating that he or she has met the requirement in that particular lesson, and add positive comments. The contract sheet accompanies the student to each lesson throughout the day. At the end of each day and the end of each week, progress is monitored and any necessary changes are made to the agreement. If possible, the school negotiates parental involvement in the implementation of the contract, and the parents agree to provide some specific privileges if the goals are met for two consecutive weeks, or loss of privileges if it is broken. When behaviour contracts are to be set up, it is essential that all teachers and school support staff are kept fully informed of the details.

Good Behaviour Game

The Good Behaviour Game has existed in various forms for many years, but has recently seen an increase in its application in the US (Poduska & Kurki, 2014). It is an approach that rewards students for displaying appropriate on-task behaviours during lessons. The class is usually divided into two teams at specific times and points are given (interdependent group-contingency technique) to a team for all appropriate behaviour displayed by its members. The team with the most points at the end of the session (or end of the week) wins a group reward. Obviously the strategy needs to be used frequently enough to have the desired impact.

Social stories

Another cognitive approach to behaviour change is the use of 'social stories'. The use of stories with autistic children was discussed in Chapter 2. Social stories can also be used with young or intellectually disabled students to help them discriminate between appropriate and inappropriate patterns of behaviour.

Haggerty *et al.* (2005) explain that social stories, with pictures of the children engaging in desirable and undesirable behaviour, can be used to help the children observe and reflect upon their own behaviour and the reaction it gets from others. For example, a first picture might show the children lining up in front of a cake stall at the school Open Day. One child is pushing another out of the line in order to take his place. The children on each side are looking very unhappy. In the next picture two of the other children are beginning to push the naughty child away from the line and a fight starts. In the third picture the lady in charge of the cake stall is telling the children that she will stop selling the cakes unless children line up in a neat queue. The final picture shows a neat queue of children with happy faces, each paying in turn for a cake. The story can be prepared, read and discussed with several children in a small group, but social stories are most frequently used to target the negative behaviour of one particular child. In such cases the story is personalized with the child's own name and the activity conducted individually. The story approach can also be used to help children who are shy or lacking in social skills.

Punishment

Punishment represents yet another way of eliminating undesirable behaviours – but the use of punishment in schools is a contentious issue. The principal objection to punishment, or *aversive control*, is that while it may temporarily suppress certain behaviours, it may also evoke a variety of undesirable outcomes (fear, a feeling of alienation, resentment, an association between punishment and schooling, a breakdown in the relationship between teacher and student). Punishment may also suppress a child's general responsiveness in a classroom situation as well as eliminating the negative behaviour.

If it is absolutely necessary to punish a child, the punishment should be administered immediately after the unacceptable behaviour is exhibited. Delayed punishment is virtually useless. Punishment also needs always to be combined with positive reinforcement and other tactics to rebuild the child's self-esteem. The goal of intervention should be to help students gain control over their own emotions and behaviour, but this goal will not be achieved if aversive control is the only method implemented.

Aggressive behaviour

Aggression can manifest itself in many forms – aggression against persons, property, verbal aggression, sexual aggression, and even aggression against self (Crotty *et al.*, 2014). Teachers are bothered most by aggressive behaviour in children (Nields, 2014), and increases in work-related stress among teachers are related in part to increases in acting-out and aggressive behaviour among students. Teachers need to acquire some simple strategies for dealing with students' anger.

A cognitive behavioural approach can be effective in helping students understand and control their own anger – although the students must genuinely want to change their own behaviour if the approach is to work. This can be regarded as one important aspect of self-regulation and self-determination (Kelly & Shogren, 2014). There is value in teaching all students (and particularly those with aggressive tendencies) to apply 'conflict resolution' strategies so that they can control threatening situations by negotiation and compromise. In typical cognitive approaches participants may explore the following issues:

* the nature of anger;
* when anger can be justified;
* when anger becomes a problem;
* things that trigger our anger;
* how to take control when we are becoming angry;
* how to use self-instruction and relaxation strategies.

Cullen-Powell *et al.* (2005) reported benefits for students in upper primary and secondary school from a 16-session 'self-discovery programme' (three modules over one school year) to teach relaxation and self-control strategies that students can implement when feeling anxious, stressed or confrontational. It is worth noting that often students with emotional and behavioural problems are not particularly proficient in oral language skills, and sometimes their aggressive behaviour is used to compensate for their inability to win an argument or convey their feelings. Intervention for such students needs to focus on improving communication competencies as well as modifying overt behaviours (Oliver *et al.*, 2014).

It is reported that less aggression is found in schools where a caring and supportive environment has been nurtured and where curricular demands are realistic. Schools where there is constant frustration and discouragement seem to breed disaffection and stimulate more aggressive and anti-social behaviour in students (Levin & Nolan, 2013).

Bullying

It is crucial not to ignore bullying in schools as this is a problem that will not cease of its own accord (Menard & Grotpeter, 2014). The lives of too many children are made miserable when they become the victims of bullying. For the victim, bullying is known to cause absenteeism, psychosomatic illnesses, low self-esteem, impaired social skills, a feeling of isolation, learning problems, depression and, in extreme cases, suicidal tendencies (Landstedt & Persson, 2014). From the number of adults who report the severe impact that bullying had on them, it is clear that the experience frequently has long-lasting effects. For the perpetrator of the bullying at school, there is some evidence that this can become an established behaviour pattern that leads later to violence in adult life.

Some estimates put the prevalence of bullying at about one child in every ten; but self-report studies reveal many more students who later indicate that they were bullied when they were at school but did not report it. Both boys and girls are involved in bullying other children. School climate appears to be an area of influence on prevalence of bullying, with schools that have poor teacher–student relationships and a 'non-inviting' atmosphere exhibiting more cases (Wang, Berry & Swearer, 2013).

Bullying may take several different forms – direct physical attacks, verbal attacks, or indirect attacks such as spreading hurtful rumours verbally or online, or by excluding someone from a social group. Physical bullying is different from generally aggressive behaviour because bullies pick their targets very selectively. There are often characteristics of victims that make them targets for bullies – for example, they may appear to be vulnerable, weaker, shy, nervous, overweight, of different ethnic background, or 'teacher's pet'. There is some evidence that students with intellectual disability are sometimes subjected to teasing and bullying in both mainstream and special school settings. Unpopular children and those with behaviour disorders or poor personal and social skills are more likely than others to be victimized (Henley, 2010).

Bullies are often older or more physically advanced than their victims. Four out of five bullies come from homes where physical or emotional abuse is used frequently, and are therefore victims themselves to some degree. They appear to have less empathy than non-bullies. When bullying is carried out by gangs of students, factors come into play such as the importance of roles and status within the group. Some individuals feel that they are demonstrating their power by repressing the victim. Even those who are not themselves bullies get carried along with the behaviour and do not object to it or report it. Few would ever intervene to help the victim.

Within a school's behaviour management policy there should be agreed procedures for handling incidents of bullying so that all staff approach the problem with similar strategies. Much bullying occurs in the schoolyard, particularly if supervision is poor. Increased out-of-class supervision is one intervention that schools can introduce to reduce bullying. Obviously the behaviour of the bully or the gang members needs to be addressed with direct intervention; but, in addition, the issues of consideration and respect for others and the right of every student to feel safe also need to be discussed.

Cyber bullying

Recent data from several countries suggest an alarming increase in 'cyber bullying' wherein the student becomes the target for derogatory comments, malicious gossip and lies posted on social networking websites, instant messaging, emails and by mobile phone (Nordahl et al., 2013). In the case of older adolescents, the bullying can also take the form of sending embarrassing photographs involving the victim. These examples are often linked to lack of positive peer relationships in school (Scott et al., 2014).

Unfortunately, as with other forms of bullying, children tend not to report such bullying to their parents. The effects of cyber bullying can be a lowering of school grades, poorer self-esteem, anxiety, depression, lost interests, and in extreme cases suicide. In his advice to parents Beane (2008) suggests that signs of cyber bullying to watch for include the child seeming to be constantly upset, anxious or secretive, particularly after spending time on the computer or mobile phone, and spending more time than usual in online chatrooms. Beane's book also provides a number of helpful hints for parents and teachers on how to monitor a child's use of information and communication technology and how to deal with problems of cyber bullying.

Teachers should discuss with their classes at an appropriate time what cyber bullying is and its effect on the person targeted. It is suggested that issues of bullying and aggressive behaviour should become the focus of attention within the school curriculum – perhaps under the general heading 'human relationships'.

Attention deficit hyperactivity disorder

A few children in our schools display chronic problems in maintaining attention to any learning task. They may also exhibit hyperactive and impulsive behaviour. These children are generally classified now as having *attention deficit hyperactivity disorder* (ADHD). A few children with ADHD may also be diagnosed with 'conduct disorders' – defined as a pattern of persistent and repetitive violations of the rights of others, lack of empathy and respect, and a disregard for age-appropriate social norms and rules (APA, 2013). ADHD can accompany certain other disabilities such as cerebral palsy, traumatic brain injury, autism, specific learning disability and emotional disturbance.

Reviews of the extensive literature available now on ADHD seem to suggest that some 5–10 per cent of school-age children may present with symptoms of ADD or ADHD (Wright *et al.*, 2009). In the past ten years there has been an increase in the number of students diagnosed with ADHD and these children now represent approximately one quarter of all referrals for psycho–educational assessment.

DSM-5 lists symptoms of ADHD divided into the two categories of 'inattention' (failure to listen or pay attention to details, difficulty organizing and staying on task) and 'hyperactivity and impulsivity' (excessive fidgeting, movement, an inability to remain seated, excitability and excessive talking) (APA, 2013). To be diagnosed with ADHD, children must have at least six symptoms from the inattention criteria and/or the hyperactivity and impulsivity criteria. Older adolescents and adults (over age 17) must present with at least five clear symptoms. This new fifth edition of *DSM* has placed greater emphasis on identifying symptoms of ADHD across several settings, rather than looking solely at classroom behaviour (Prosser & Reid, 2013). *DSM-5* has also placed increased emphasis on the fact that ADHD is not limited to the childhood years, and may be diagnosed in some adults.

No single cause for ADHD has been identified, although the following have all been put forward as possible explanations: genetic influences, central nervous system dysfunction (perhaps due to slow maturation of the motor cortex of the brain), subtle forms of brain damage too slight to be confirmed by neurological testing, allergy to specific substances (e.g. food additives), adverse reactions to environmental stimuli (e.g. fluorescent lighting), maternal alcohol consumption during pregnancy and inappropriate management of the child at home or school. Most authorities now agree that the ADHD syndrome represents a neuro-behavioural disorder with multiple possible causes.

ADHD children, while not necessarily below average in intelligence, usually exhibit poor achievement in most school subjects. Weak concentration and restlessness associated with ADHD have usually impaired the child's learning during the important early years of schooling. However, students with ADHD do differ as individuals in their resilience to such problems, with some displaying more than others of what is now termed 'academic buoyancy' (Martin, 2014).

Many ADHD students also have problems with peer relationships and in developing social competence. Some of these students seem to lack an understanding of the emotional reactions and feelings of others, resulting in many negative confrontations and other inappropriate social interactions (Kats-Gold & Priel, 2009).

Interventions for ADHD

Because of the possibility that ADHD is caused by different factors in different individuals, it is not surprising to find that quite different forms of treatment are advocated;

and what works for one child may not work for another. Treatments have included diet control, medication, psychotherapy, behaviour modification and cognitive behaviour modification. There have also been other 'alternative' therapies of doubtful value. Any approach to the treatment of ADHD needs to attend to *all* factors that may be causing and maintaining the behaviour. The most effective treatment requires effective teaching strategies to be integrated with a behaviour management plan, parent counselling, home management programme and (often) medication.

The use of medication in the management of ADHD remains a controversial issue, and teachers often express doubts about the appropriateness and ethics of using drugs to control behaviour (Moldavsky *et al.*, 2014). In the US, almost 60 per cent of students with ADHD are taking medication such as Ritalin or Adderal to reduce their hyperactivity and to help them focus attention more effectively on schoolwork. In Britain and Australia, the use of medication as a first resort is a little less common, with the focus being more on behavioural interventions. While medication does appear to have a positive impact on students' activity level, attention and school achievement (Scheffler *et al.*, 2009), it is not without side effects such as loss of appetite, drowsiness, insomnia, headaches and increased nervousness.

There is strong agreement among experts that children with ADHD need structure and predictability in the learning environment. Effective teaching strategies must be used to arouse and hold the child's interest. Children with ADHD need to be engaged as much as possible in interesting work, at an appropriate level, in a stable environment. Enhancing the learning of children with ADHD will also involve:

- providing strong visual input to hold attention;
- using computer-assisted learning (CAL);
- teaching the students better self-management and organizational skills;
- monitoring them closely during lessons and finding many opportunities to praise and reinforce them descriptively when they are on task and productive.

Online resources

- The Association for Positive Behavior Support (APBS) provides guidelines for *Positive Behavior Support: Standards of Practice*. Available online at: www.apbs.org/files/apbs_standards_of_practice_2013_format.pdf.
- The British Institute of Learning Disabilities (BILD) website: www.bild.org.uk/about-bild/aboutbild/.
- Welsh Government (2012): *Practical approaches to behaviour management in the classroom: A handbook for classroom teachers in primary schools*. Available online at: www.nsmtc.co.uk/media/WAG%20Behaviour%20Management.pdf.
- A plan of action for developing a school-wide behaviour management system can be located at: www.behavioradvisor.com/SchoolWideSystem.html.
- Details of the University of Oregon behavioural support programme (Effective Behavior Support: EBS) can be found at: http://cecp.air.org/resources/success/ebs.asp.
- Wakefield, M. & Paley, S. (n.d.) *Positive behaviour support: A guide for schools*. Birmingham: British Institute of Learning Disabilities. Available online at: http://teachersupport.info/get-support/practical-guides/pupil-behaviour?gclid=CPrIw7WWrb8CFU8JvAodfnQAbg.

- Information concerning ADHD can be found on the Attention Deficit Disorder Association website at: www.add.org/?page=ADHD_Fact_Sheet.

Further reading

Alberto, P.A. & Troutman, A.C. (2013). *Applied behavior analysis for teachers* (9th edn). Upper Saddle River, NJ: Pearson-Merrill.

Ashbaker, B.Y. & Morgan, J. (2015). *The paraprofessional's guide to effective behavioural intervention.* London: Routledge.

Barkley, R.A. (2014). *Attention-Deficit Hyperactivity Disorder: A handbook for diagnosis and treatment* (4th edn). New York: Guilford Press.

Chandler, L.K. & Dahlquist, C.M. (2015). *Functional assessment: Strategies to prevent and remediate challenging behavior in school settings* (4th edn). Boston, MA: Pearson.

Chaplain, R. (2015). *Managing behaviour in the primary classroom.* London: Routledge.

DuPaul, G.J. & Stoner, G. (2014). *ADHD in the schools* (3rd edn). New York: Guilford Press.

Levin, J. & Nolan, J.F. (2013). *Principles of classroom management* (7th edn). Upper Saddle River, NJ: Pearson Education.

Paul, S. (2014). *Beyond bullying.* London: Routledge.

Wheeler, J.J. & Richey, D.D. (2013). *Behavior management: Principles and practices of positive behavior supports* (3rd edn). Columbus, OH: Pearson-Prentice Hall.

Chapter 8

Social skills and peer group acceptance

Students' ability to do well in school depends upon not only their intelligence, motivation, diligence, self-regulation, prior experience, quality of teaching and home background, but also on their social adjustment and social competence. Any student, regardless of ability, is at risk in school if they lack social skills and are rejected or victimized by others. It is for this reason that establishing good social relationships with other children has been described as one of the most important goals for education.

Individuals with functional social skills are less likely to engage in problem behaviour, are better at making friends, are able to resolve conflicts peacefully, and have effective ways of dealing with persons in authority. As well as having appropriate positive pro-social skills, a socially competent individual also avoids having negative behavioural characteristics that prevent easy acceptance by others – for example, high levels of irritating behaviour (interrupting, poking or shouting), impulsive and unpredictable reactions, temper tantrums, abusive language or cheating at games. In many cases these undesirable behaviours need to be reduced very significantly by behaviour modification or through cognitive self-management.

Lack of social competence is often reported in children with learning difficulties or disabilities, and those with emotional disorders (Sullivan & Sadeh, 2014). Their problems in achieving acceptance in a social group, and their lack of ease in social situations, can be just as debilitating as academic failure. They can feel socially isolated in school and they tend to disengage from learning. A study conducted in Scotland found that students with special needs expressed a desire for more support to socialize with peers and to take part in social activities (Scottish Government, 2013).

Social development begins before a child even reaches school age; and early influences can shape that development positively or negatively. It is evident that poor peer relationships during the school years can have a lasting detrimental impact on social and personal competence in later years. Shepherd (2010, p. 155) has observed that: 'The importance of social skills cannot be underestimated. Children with deficits in social skills are at risk for unemployment, aggressive interactions in the community, juvenile delinquency, and adult mental health problems.' There is obviously an urgent need to enhance the social acceptance and social competence of children with special needs when they are placed in regular classrooms (Mannix, 2009). This applies to many children with intellectual disability, physical or sensory impairments, learning disabilities and emotional problems. Children with autism and those with ADHD are particularly at risk (Cotugno, 2009). Inclusive education settings create a potential opportunity for these children to engage in more positive social interaction with their peers – but social acceptance of students with special needs does not occur spontaneously (Friend &

Bursuck, 2011; Nowicki, 2012). The results of most studies of inclusion have shown that merely placing a child with a disability in the mainstream will not automatically lead to his or her social integration into the peer group. The situation is most problematic for children who have an emotional or behavioural disorder (Sullivan & Sadeh, 2014), and there is a danger that such children become marginalized, ignored or even openly rejected by classmates.

Opportunities for social interaction

At least three conditions must be present for positive social interaction and development of friendships among children with and without disabilities. These conditions are:

*   *Opportunity* – being within proximity of other children frequently enough for meaningful contacts to be made. Inclusive schooling provides proximity and frequency of contact. It creates the best possible chances for children with disabilities to interact with their peers, and also to observe and imitate the social behaviours of others.
*   *Continuity* – being involved with the same group of children over a reasonable period of time; and also seeing some of the same children in their own neighbourhood out of school hours.
*   *Support* – being helped to make contact with other children in order to work and play with them; and if possible being directly supported in maintaining friendships beyond school. In this matter, it is important for parents to be encouraged to nurture their child's peer friendships outside of school hours.

When students with disabilities are placed in regular settings without adequate preparation or ongoing support, three problems may become evident:

*   children without disabilities do not readily demonstrate acceptance of those with disabilities;
*   children with disabilities, contrary to popular belief, do not automatically observe and copy the positive social models that are around them;
*   some teachers do not intervene to promote children's positive social interaction.

It is necessary for teachers to identify as soon as possible any children in their classes who appear to be without friends at recess and lunch breaks and who seem unable to relate closely with classmates during lessons. Unfortunately, there is evidence to suggest that some teachers may not pay adequate attention to this issue of isolation or lack of social interaction, instead being more preoccupied with the students who behave badly or are off task during lessons (Landers *et al.*, 2013).

Creating a supportive environment

A positive and supportive school environment is, of course, important for the social development of all children, and it provides a foundation that enables children to feel a 'connectedness' to the school community. Creating classroom environments where competition is not a dominant element is the first step in facilitating social development. Cooperation, rather than competition, needs to be encouraged. Students must be involved frequently in group activities that encourage social cooperation, collaboration and mutual support.

To facilitate social interaction for children with special needs in regular classrooms three conditions are necessary:

- the general attitude of the teacher and the peer group towards students with special needs must be positive and accepting;
- the environment should be arranged so that the child with a disability has the maximum opportunity to spend time socially involved in group or pair activities both in the classroom and at recess;
- children with special needs must be taught the specific skills and behaviours that may enhance social interaction with peers.

Facilitating social interaction

The following strategies can be used to increase the chances of positive social interaction for students with disabilities.

- Making more frequent use of non-academic tasks (e.g. games, model-making, painting) because these place the child with special needs in a situation where he or she can more easily fit in and contribute (DeRosier, 2014).
- Using 'peer tutoring' and 'buddy systems'. Several versions of these exist, including Classwide Peer Tutoring (CWPT). Research over two decades has confirmed the effectiveness of peer tutoring for improving learning and social outcomes for students at all age and ability levels (McMaster *et al.*, 2006).
- Making a particular topic – for example, 'friends' or 'working together' – the basis for class discussion. 'If you want someone to play with you at lunchtime how would you make that happen?' 'If you saw two children in the schoolyard who had just started at the school today, how would you make them feel accepted?'
- Encouraging peer-group members to maintain and reinforce social interactions with less-able or less-popular children. Often they are unaware of the ways in which they can help. They, too, may need to be shown how to initiate contact, how to invite the child with a disability to join in an activity, or how to help that classmate with particular school assignments.
- Using the class activity called *Circle Time* as an opportunity for children to discuss aspects of social behaviour, such as helping one another, preventing bullying or teasing, building self-esteem, looking for strengths in other people and showing interest in the ideas of others. Circle Time is often used in kindergarten and early primary years, but the value of having students coming together in a relaxed situation in which they can voice their opinions can extend easily into secondary schools.

For students with a disability who have difficulty finding a friend or coping in class, it can also be helpful to introduce the *Circle of Friends* as a peer-group support strategy (Friend & Bursuck, 2011). The system operates by involving some of a child's classmates as natural supporters to help the child acquire more positive behaviours and self-management. Specific members of the circle are detailed to greet the child each day, to be friendly and helpful at all times, to assist with routines at lunch and break times, to make sure the child is counted in for all activities, and to help the child solve any problems that may arise. However, this support element should not be so dominant that over time it causes the child to become over-dependent and passive. Peers should be aware that the goal is not to do everything for the child and remove all challenges but rather help the child become more competent and assertive. The role of the teacher is to facilitate and encourage this process.

A difficulty that can arise with any attempt to improve social acceptance is that some students actually resent any obvious intervention by a teacher to 'fix them up' with a friend. This is particularly the case with adolescents who are ultra-sensitive to peer group opinion. They prefer to solve their social and other problems themselves (Friend & Bursuck, 2011). The reality is that teachers cannot really 'force' friendships to be established between students with special needs and others; they can only hope to establish the conditions under which this may occur spontaneously.

Importance of group work

The regular use of group work in the classroom is one of the main ways of providing children with opportunities to develop social skills through collaborating with others. Careful planning is required if group work is to achieve the desired educational and social outcomes. The success of collaborative group work depends on the composition of the working groups and the nature of the tasks set for the students (Malekoff, 2014).

When utilizing group work as an organizational strategy, it is important to consider the following basic principles.

- Initially there is merit in having groups of children working cooperatively on the *same task* at the same time. This procedure makes it much easier to prepare resources and to manage time effectively. When each of several groups is undertaking quite different tasks, it can become a major management problem for the teacher.
- Choice of tasks for group work is very important. Tasks have to be selected that *require* collaboration and teamwork. Children are sometimes seated in groups in the classroom but are actually expected to work on individual assignments. Not only does this negate the opportunities for collaboration, it also creates difficulties for individuals in terms of interruptions and distractions. It is essential that all tasks have a very clear structure and purposes that are understood by all.
- It is not enough merely to establish groups and to set them to work. Group members may have to be taught how to work efficiently together. They may need to be shown behaviours that encourage or enable cooperation – listening to the views of others, sharing, praising each other and offering help. If the task involves the learning of specific curriculum content, teach the children how to rehearse and test one another on the material. There is great value in discussing openly with a class the best ways of making group work effective, and identifying the skills necessary to cooperate productively with others.
- The way in which individual tasks are allotted (division of labour) should be carefully planned. Each child needs to understand clearly his area of responsibility – for example, 'John, you can help Craig with his writing, then he can help you with the lettering for your title board.' Contingent praise for interacting with others should be descriptive: 'Good, Sue. You are taking turns and working very well with Sharon.'

- Teachers should monitor closely what is going on during group activities and must intervene when necessary to provide suggestions, encourage the sharing of a task, praise examples of cooperation and teamwork, and model cooperative behaviour themselves. Many groups can be helped to function efficiently if the teacher (or classroom assistant or a parent helper) works as a group member without dominating or controlling the activity.
- The size of the group is important. Often children working in pairs is a good starting point. Select the composition of the group carefully to avoid obvious incompatibility among students' personalities. At times a teacher needs to intervene to help a particular child gain entry to a group activity or to work with a carefully chosen partner.
- When groups contain students with special needs, it is vital that the specific tasks and duties to be undertaken by these students are clearly delineated. It can be useful to establish a system whereby the results of the *group's* efforts are rewarded by the way in which they have worked together positively and supportively. Under this structure, group members have a vested interest in ensuring that all members learn, because the group's success depends on the achievement of all. Helping each other, sharing and tutoring within the group are behaviours that must be modelled and supported.
- Talking should be encouraged during group activities. It is interesting to note that sub-grouping in the class has the effect of increasing transactional talk (talk specifically directed to another person and requiring a reply) by almost three times the level present under whole-class conditions.
- Seating and work arrangements are important. Group members should be in close proximity but still have space to work on materials without getting in each other's way.
- Group work must be used frequently enough for the children to learn the skills and routines. Infrequent group work results in children taking too long to settle down. Group work can become chaotic if the tasks are poorly defined or too complex. Other problems arise if the students are not well versed in group-working skills, or if the room is not set up to facilitate easy access to resources.

Social skills training

Social skills are the specific behaviours an individual uses to maintain effective interpersonal communication and interaction with others. Social skills comprise a set of competencies that allow individuals to cope effectively within the social environment.

While some students with disabilities are very popular with classmates in the mainstream, particularly if they have a pleasant personality, others with similar disabilities or with emotional and behavioural difficulties are particularly at risk of social isolation. One of the main reasons why certain children are marginalized or ignored is that they lack appropriate social skills that might make them more acceptable. They are in a Catch-22 situation, since friendless students have fewer opportunities to practise social skills, and those who do not develop adequate social skills are unable to form friendships. It is argued that early training in social skills can be instrumental in reducing or preventing problem behaviour in later years. Such instruction should be embedded in the natural context of events that occur within the children's social environment.

Research shows that there is very limited transfer or maintenance of social skills when they are taught (coached) in contrived exercises unrelated to real situations. The most meaningful settings in which to enhance the child's skills are usually the classroom and schoolyard.

The teaching of social skills usually involves establishing some or all of the following behaviours. Each skill should be considered relative to the particular child's age and specific needs; it is pointless to teach skills that are not immediately useful in the child's regular environment. The list below is similar to that found in most published programmes for social skills training:

*   making eye contact;
*   greeting others by name;
*   gaining attention in appropriate ways;
*   talking in a tone of voice that is acceptable;
*   knowing when to talk, what to talk about and when to hold back;
*   initiating a conversation;
*   maintaining conversations;
*   answering questions;
*   listening to others and showing interest;
*   sharing with others;
*   saying 'please' and 'thank you';
*   helping someone;
*   being able to collaborate in a group activity;
*   taking one's turn;
*   smiling;
*   accepting praise;
*   giving praise;
*   accepting correction without anger;
*   making apologies when necessary;
*   coping with frustration;
*   managing conflict.

In each individual case, the first step is to decide what the priorities are for this child in terms of specific skills and behaviours to be taught. The skills to be targeted need to be of immediate functional value to the child within the setting in which he or she operates. In this respect, advice from parents can be very useful (Frey et al., 2014). Studies suggest that, to be effective, social skills training needs to: (i) target the precise skills and knowledge an individual lacks; (ii) be intensive and long term in nature; and (iii) promote maintenance, generalization and transfer of new skills into the individual's daily life.

In situations where specific intervention is needed beyond normal everyday attention to children's social skills (e.g. children with autism, or with emotional disorders), training is based on a combination of modelling, coaching, role playing, rehearsing, feedback and counselling. At times, video recordings are also used effectively to provide examples of social behaviours to discuss and imitate, or to provide a child with feedback on his or her own performance or role play (Wang & Spillane, 2009). The use of Social Stories (see Chapter 2 and Chapter 7) has also proved to be effective in encouraging children's awareness of social skills.

In typical interventions to improve social skills the following steps are involved:

- *Definition* – describe to the child the skill to be taught and indicate how its use helps social interactions to occur. Illustrate the skill in action by pointing out examples happening in the peer group. Key points can be reinforced using video, pictures, cartoons or a simulation using puppets. The teacher may say, 'Look at the two girls sharing the puzzle. Tell me what they might be saying to each other.'
- *Model the skill* – break the skill down into simple components and demonstrate these clearly yourself, or have a selected child do this.
- *Imitation and rehearsal* – the child tries out the same skill in a structured situation. For this to occur successfully, the child must be motivated to perform the skill and must attend carefully and retain what has been demonstrated.
- *Feedback* – this should be informative. 'You've not quite got it yet. You need to look at her while you speak to her. Try it again.' 'That's better! You looked and smiled. Well done.' Feedback via a video recording may be appropriate in some situations.
- *Provide opportunity for the skill to be used* – depending upon the skill being taught, use small group work or pair activities to allow the skill to be applied and generalized to the classroom or other natural setting.
- *Intermittent reinforcement* – watch for instances of the child applying the skill without prompting at other times in the day and later in the week. Provide descriptive praise and reward. Aim for maintenance of the skill once it is acquired. To a large extent, social skills, once established, are likely to be maintained by natural consequences – that is, by more satisfying interactions with peers.

Limitations of social training

Training in social skills is not a matter simply of teaching a child something that is missing from his or her repertoire of behaviours but may also involve *replacing* an undesirable behaviour that is already strongly established with a new alternative behaviour. The negative behaviours often taken as indicative of lack of social skill in some children (e.g. aggression, non-compliance, verbal abuse) may actually be very rewarding behaviours for the individuals concerned, and may represent more powerful and effective forces than the new pro-social skills we attempt to teach. This residual influence of pre-existing behaviours is one of the reasons why skills taught during training are often not maintained – they are competing with powerful behaviours that have already proved to work well for the child.

It must also be noted that even when children with disabilities are specifically trained in social skills, some may still not find it any easier to make friends. Students with intellectual disability or with non-verbal learning disabilities often report ongoing loneliness even after successfully participating in a social skills programme (Court & Givon, 2007). Unexpected outcomes may also occur – for example, some students may feel *less* socially competent after training because the training has made them more acutely aware of their own deficiencies. The old rule 'first, do no harm' certainly applies in social interventions.

Finally, it seems clear that poor social acceptance is often an accompaniment to poor achievement in class. Unless achievement within the curriculum can also be increased, social adjustment and acceptance may remain a problem for some children. With this in mind, attention is focused in the following chapters on evidence-based approaches for teaching basic academic skills.

Online resources

- A list of children's books useful for teaching social skills can be located online at: www.pinterest.com/jillkuzma/books-i-love-for-teaching-social-skills/.
- Additional information on social skills training can be found on the *Encyclopedia of Mental Disorders* website at: www.minddisorderscom/Py-Z/Social-skills-training. html.
- Additional information on *Circle of Friends* can be obtained from: www.circleof-riends.org/Program.html.
- Resources for social skill training for students with autism spectrum disorders can be found online at: http://socialskillstraining.org/.
- Several useful resources such as lesson plans and curricula for social development and social skills can be found on the *About.com: Special Education* website at: http://specialed.about.com/od/characterbuilding/Character_Building_Character_ Education.htm.
- The University of Kansas website has suggestions for *'Strategies for effectively interacting with others'*. Available online from the Center for Research on Learning at: www.ku-crl.org/sim/strategies.shtml.
- A useful source of information is the Center on the Social and Emotional Foundations of Early Learning at: http://csefel.vanderbilt.edu/resources/strategies.html.
- An evaluation of the effectiveness of social skills training is provided by DoE (US Department of Education, Institute of Education Sciences). (2013). *Early childhood education interventions for children with disabilities intervention report: Social skills training*, What Works Clearinghouse. Retrieved 12 September 2014 from http://what-works.ed.gov.

Further reading

DeRosier, M.E. (Ed.). (2014). *Social skills assessment through games*. Cary, NC: Interchange Press.

Gerhardt, P.F. & Crimmins, D. (2013). *Social skills and adaptive behavior in learners with autism spectrum disorders*. Baltimore, MD: Brooks.

Kostelnik, M.J., Whiren, A.P., Soderman, A.K., Rupiper, M. & Gregory, K.M. (2014). *Guiding children's social development and learning* (8th edn). Stamford, CT: Cengage.

Malekoff, A. (2014). *Group work with adolescents*. New York: Guilford Press.

Roffey, S. (Ed.). (2012). *Positive relationships: Evidence based practices across the world*. Dordrecht: Springer.

Wilkerson, K.L. (2014). *Promoting social skills in the inclusive classroom*. New York: Guilford Press.

Chapter 9

The effective teaching of reading

The ability to read is among the most important skills that students need to learn, because reading provides the key to acquiring new information in all areas of the curriculum. It is the main means by which children can become independent learners. Failure to learn to read with adequate proficiency places any child at risk of failing in most school subjects. Even in this technological age, reading still represents the main method of obtaining information, and is also used for recreation and enjoyment; and reading can stimulate a child's imagination and emotions. In life beyond school, people with good literacy skills are able to take advantage of the many opportunities that occur, and are likely to have higher self-esteem, better jobs and higher wages than those with poor literacy skills.

Unfortunately, many children with special educational needs have major difficulties learning to read, and without effective intervention they fall increasingly behind their age peers in school achievement (Connor *et al.*, 2014). Ongoing failure undermines any child's confidence and motivation, leading eventually to disengagement from learning and the belief that learning to read is simply too difficult. Early intervention is therefore absolutely essential so that a child is helped to make good progress before detrimental feelings of helplessness set in. This is the underlying principle in the Response to Intervention model (RtI) described in Chapter 1.

Reading difficulties can affect the progress of up to 30 per cent of children in some schools, and the problem is not confined to those with disabilities or with other identified special needs (Lonigan & Shanahan, 2008). Even a few students regarded as gifted sometimes exhibit problems with reading and spelling. Weakness in reading remains the principal reason for the high number of referrals for additional support in schools. It is obvious, therefore, that schools must adopt the most effective initial teaching methods to prevent this problem and ensure that almost every child gets off to a smooth start in reading. All kindergarten and primary school teachers working with beginners need very strong professional preparation that gives them the pedagogical knowledge and skills for effective Tier 1 teaching (Noll & Lenhart, 2014). Unfortunately, it seems that all too often trainee teachers are still not being equipped with the expertise necessary for starting young children on a sure path to literacy.

A sound start

The Response to Intervention (RtI) model is predicated on the assumption that at Tier 1 (beginning stage) *all children* in the first year of schooling will receive high-quality instruction that maximizes their opportunity to learn. The overwhelming consensus emerging from research is that Tier 1 instruction in reading for children aged 5–6 years must be direct, explicit and systematic, and should not rely on incidental learning through informal immersion in books. Teaching should be aimed primarily at developing efficient letter knowledge, decoding skills, word recognition and comprehension (Buckingham, 2014; IES, 2009a). In Britain, it is now generally accepted that explicit instruction in phonic principles needs to be a key component in all early reading programmes (Gov.UK., 2013c; National Foundation for Educational Research, 2013). However, in Australia, where the informal 'whole-language approach' was extremely popular in recent decades, intensive phonics teaching is still fighting an uphill battle at this time (Moore, 2014).

The ability to decode unfamiliar words using knowledge of letter-to-sound relationships (phonics) leads to optimum progress in reading for most children. In the earliest stages of learning to read, children have not yet built up a large vocabulary of words they know instantly by sight, so they must use knowledge of letters and groups of letters to help them identify unfamiliar words. Children cannot really become independent readers unless they master the alphabetic code. In recognition of this fact the Department of Education in the UK introduced a *Phonics Screening Check* for students at the end of Year 1, to identify any who required addition teaching (DfE, 2012). When children with reading difficulties are referred for diagnostic assessment it is still quite common to find that the problem is caused by a lack of phonic knowledge and no confidence in decoding.

While decoding ability and word recognition are clearly essential foundations for reading, children must also be able to process with understanding the information they are reading in a text. For this reason, an early reading programme contains not only explicit teaching and practice in phonic decoding but also instruction in applying comprehension strategies. This approach also incorporates many aural and oral language enrichment activities to encourage careful listening, build oral vocabulary, establish familiarity with language patterns, and introduce books and materials that foster children's interest in reading.

The simple view of reading

Most reading experts now agree that the process of reading comprises two complementary abilities: (i) decoding and (ii) language comprehension. This belief has become widely known as the 'simple view of reading' (Gustafson *et al.*, 2013; Hoover & Gough, 1990). This simple view has gained popularity with cognitive psychologists and educators who favour a skills-based approach to teaching, and with some government education systems.

The simple view of reading is not without its critics. Some educators suggest that it is *too simple*, and that reading is a much more complex language process that draws on many other sub-skills and domains of knowledge. In particular, it is suggested that the simple view overlooks the vital importance of *fluency* in reading – fluency being the ultimate outcome from effortless decoding, rapid word recognition and reading with understanding (Ring *et al.*, 2013). The most recent comprehensive view of reading now incorporates five aspects – phonological awareness, alphabetic principle, vocabulary, fluency and language comprehension (Vesay & Gischlar, 2013).

Regardless of any minor criticisms of the simple view of reading, the focus it places on decoding and language comprehension provides teachers with a strong sense of direction for most teaching purposes in the beginning stages of literacy. The simple view of reading underpins the remaining material in this chapter.

The role of phonemic awareness

Before a child can understand the principle and operation of the alphabetic code, he or she must first understand that spoken words are made up of separate sound units (*phonemes*). For example, the word *tree* actually comprises the sounds /t/ /r/ /ee/ (or /tr/ /ee/) and the word *tin* contains the phonemes /t/ /i/ /n/. The ability to identify these sounds in spoken words is termed *phonemic awareness*. If a child lacks this awareness it is impossible for him or her to understand that a letter or a group of letters in print represents a unit of sound within a word, and that these sound units can be identified and put together (synthesized) to build the word. A child cannot acquire functional phonic skills without first understanding how to break down spoken words into component sounds (a process referred to as *segmenting*) and how to put sound units together to build a word (referred to as *blending*). While some children discover for themselves that spoken words are made up of sounds and that sounds can be manipulated mentally to construct words when reading and spelling, it should never be assumed that all children reach this understanding unaided. Studies have shown that students with reading difficulties or with language disorders are frequently very slow indeed to acquire phonemic awareness and it is the main underlying cause of their problem. Activities to develop phonemic awareness are therefore essential components in all language and reading programmes for beginners.

Intensive training in phonemic awareness is not required by each and every child; some will have discovered for themselves that phonemes are the building blocks of the words they hear. Teachers need to identify individuals who do need explicit teaching and additional practice. It is often useful to inspect children's early attempts at spelling (invented spellings) as these can reveal the extent to which they have developed some phonemic awareness and letter knowledge. The same is true of older students with learning difficulties.

For young children, the skill of segmenting words can be taught explicitly by spending a little time taking words apart into their component sounds and syllables. For example: 'What's in this picture, Jackie? Yes. It's a frog. Listen. Let's say frog very slowly. Let's stretch the word out ... /FR/–/O/–/G/. You try it.' The child could also be asked to count and clap the number of sounds heard in the word. Analysing a few target words each day in this way can be one of many informal activities used within the various teaching approaches described later. Specific programmes can also be used to develop children's segmenting and sequencing skills necessary for reading and spelling. Two good examples are *Sound Check: Books 1 and 2*, and *Sound Swap*, both by Pollard (2004).

Children can be helped to understand how even single-syllable words may be taken apart by using what are termed onset-rime activities. For example, in the word 'stick', /st/ is the *onset* and /ick/ is the *rime*. Being able to break simple words into onset and rime units provides a good foundation for more demanding word analysis and segmentation later.

Teachers and tutors can also create activities that will help children gain more experience in blending sounds to build words. For example, using the simple 'I Spy' game: 'I spy with my little eye a picture of a /CL/ – /O/ – /CK/. What can I see?' Blending skill should also be applied and practised in every context when the student is reading aloud and needs to sound out a particular word.

Teaching letter-to-sound correspondences

Once a child is able to perform oral and aural activities that involve segmenting and blending (and some children can already do this on entry to school), it is opportune to teach directly the common letter-to-sound correspondences – the most basic building blocks of phonic skills. Studies have indicated clearly that teaching phonics early and systematically produces superior results to those obtained by whole-language approach or the whole-word recognition method (Torgerson *et al.*, 2006). Current evidence suggests that the method known as *synthetic phonics* (learning to identify words in print by building (synthesizing) them from their component sounds) produces the best results (Grant, 2014). Synthetic phonics helps children acquire a word-analysis technique that they can continue to develop and apply independently for themselves.

In contrast to the synthetic phonics approach, the method called *analytic phonics* teaches children essential letter-sound relationships by analysing words they can already recognize in print. For example, the sound of letter /t/ is taught from words such as '*tin, top, tap, tip*'. Or, the consonant blend /cl/ might be taught from the words '*class, clap, clip*' and so forth. Analytic phonics is favoured as a method by some teachers because it moves in the direction from whole to part, rather than part to whole. However, research has not shown it to be more effective than synthetic phonics.

Since 2006 all schools in England have been expected to use the synthetic phonics approach when teaching early reading; and as stated above, since 2012 a *Phonics Screening Check* has been introduced to help teachers identify any students who are falling behind in their letter knowledge and decoding skills. In 2014 a large number of six-year-old children were still reported to be below the expected standard in phonic skills in Britain (Petersen, 2014). Unfortunately, too many teachers in the UK (and in Australia) still try to use a combination of reading methods (including 'look-and-say'), which greatly reduces the time available to teach phonic skills thoroughly (Grant, 2014). It is also evident that many primary school teachers are not really aware of *how* to teach phonics explicitly (Fielding-Barnsley, 2010; Tetley & Jones, 2014).

Reading experts differ in their views on exactly how letter-sound correspondences should be introduced. As a general principle, all agree that phonic knowledge and decoding skills should not be taught and practised totally out of context. Letter knowledge is only useful if it helps with the reading and writing of meaningful text. While students do need specific time devoted to mastering phonic units and working with word families, every effort must be made to ensure that this learning is quickly applied to meaningful reading and writing.

Much phonic knowledge can be taught or reinforced from the words young children are already meeting in storybooks their teachers are sharing with them every day. However, simply embedding some occasional and incidental instruction in decoding within a whole-language programme is *totally inadequate* for most children. This unsystematic approach to phonics lacks intensity and does not ensure that young children master decoding ability to the necessary level of automaticity. By way of contrast, evidence suggests that 10–20 minutes a day spent in enjoyable word study in the early years enables young children to master the fundamental relationships among letters and sounds and how to apply this knowledge (Hepplewhite, 2011).

It is reasonable to ask if there is any prescribed order in which to introduce beginners to the common associations between letters (graphemes) and sounds (phonemes). The consensus view is that there is no single best order. In practice the order is often dictated by the nature of the reading materials or programme the children are using. However, when working with children who have reading difficulties, it is useful to consider how the task of learning letter–sound correspondences might be organized into the most logical sequence. One systematic approach begins by selecting highly contrastive sounds such as /m/, /k/, /v/, and avoiding confusable sounds such as /m/ and /n/, or /p/ and /b/. It is also helpful to teach first the most consistent letter–sound associations. The following consonants often provide a useful starting point because they represent only one sound, regardless of the letter or letters coming after them in a word: j, k, l, m, n, p, b, h, r, v, w. Identifying initial consonants can be made the focus within many of the general language activities in the classroom.

Obviously, to enable children to engage in meaningful decoding, vowel sounds and their letters must be taught very early. Vowel sounds are far less consistent than consonants in their letter-to-sound relationships. After first establishing the most common vowel sound associations (/a/ as in apple, /e/ as in egg, /i/ as in ink, /o/ as in orange and /u/ as in up) these can be used in simple word-building activities with consonant-vowel-consonant (CVC) words. More complicated variations involving vowels are best tackled much later in combination with other letters when words containing these units are encountered in word families and in text (e.g. -ar-, -aw-, -ie-, -ee-, -ea-, -ai-, etc.).

With the least able children it is likely that much more time and attention will need to be devoted to mastery of letter-to-sound correspondences. This can be achieved not only by direct teaching and daily practice but also through games and activities. There are also many programmes designed to teach basic phonic knowledge in a very systematic way. For example, THRASS (*Teaching Handwriting, Reading and Spelling Skills*: Davies, 2006) is designed to teach students how specific letters and letter groups represent the 44 phonemes in the English language. The programme has many supplementary teaching materials for practice and reinforcement. Approaches such as THRASS, using direct teaching and synthetic phonics, are highly appropriate for students with learning difficulties who otherwise remain confused about the fact that some of the same sound units in English can be represented by different orthographic units (e.g. /-ight/ and /-ite/) and how the same orthographic pattern can represent different sounds (e.g. /ow/ as in flower or /ow/ as in snow). Another example of a successful synthetic phonics programme is *Jolly Phonics* (Lloyd & Lib, 2000). This sets out to teach 42 basic sound-to-letter correspondences, taught in seven groupings through a multisensory and synthetic phonics approach. *Letterland Phonics* (Letterland International, 2014; Wendon, 2014) uses a story approach with pictograms representing the characters involved. Alliteration in the characters' names (e.g. Robber Red, Hairy Hatman, Munching Mike) helps to reinforce the learning of letter-to-sound relationships. Both programmes are supported fully by a wide range of teaching materials. *Phonics International* (Hepplewhite, 2011) is a very comprehensive and systematic approach to teaching decoding that can be used with beginners or with older students with literacy difficulties. Full details can be found on the website referenced under Online Resources for this chapter. These programmes have undergone evaluation by the Department of Education in the UK and are recommended among the resources for use in schools and early childhood settings (DfE, 2014c).

Simple word-building experiences

It is important that word-building activities involving sounding out letters and blending them to make words are introduced alongside teaching of the common vowel sounds (V) and consonants (C). For example, at the simplest level, adding the /a/ sound to the sound /m/ makes *am*; adding /a/ to /t/ produces *at*; adding /o/ to /n/ makes *on*; and adding /u/ to /p/ makes *up*, etc. Later, when CVC words (e.g. *rub*, *sat*) are being introduced for sounding and blending, particular attention should be paid to the middle vowel. Children with learning difficulties often pay inadequate attention to vowels when trying to identify words, instead guessing too quickly from the initial letter. As well as attending to and reading these units in print, children should also learn to write them unaided when the teacher dictates the sounds.

As simple as this basic work may appear, for many students with learning problems it is often the first real link they make between spoken and written language. It is vital that children who have not recognized the connection between letters and sounds be given this direction early. The only prerequisite skills required are good phonemic awareness and adequate visual perception so that the differences between letters can be perceived easily.

Selecting early text materials

Opinions differ on whether children at this stage should use graded reading books that contain a high proportion of 'regular' words (words that can be decoded easily by sounding and blending their letters). During the 1980s and 1990s such books were utterly shunned by whole-language practitioners because they often presented rather stilted and unnatural language patterns – for example, 'Pat has a bat', 'A dog and a frog sit on a log.' Instead, children were exposed from the start to 'real' books, with no attempt to control vocabulary or sentence length. Times have changed and many publishers have returned now to producing some graded books and programmes that help children build their confidence and automaticity by applying phonic skills successfully. With this confidence they are soon ready to read books that are not controlled for vocabulary. The use of graded readers has also been found useful when working with students learning English as a second or additional language (Rabbidge & Lorenzutti, 2013).

Moving beyond simple phonics

Obviously, to become a skilled and automatic decoder a child must soon learn far more than single letter-to-sound relationships. It is important that he or she begins to recognize and use *groups of letters* that represent a sound unit. Simple word-building activities will be extended first to the teaching of digraphs (two letters representing only one speech sound, as in sh, ch, th, wh, ph) and blends (two or three consonants forming a functional unit in which each letter contributes a sound, such as br, cl, sw, st, str, scr).

Later, for the highest level of proficiency in recognizing and spelling unfamiliar words, children need experience in working with longer and more complex letter strings (orthographic units) such as -eed, -ide, -ite, -ight, -ound, -ate, -own, -ous, -ough, -tion. As students become proficient in identifying larger units represented by clusters of letters they can decode and spell many more words. When children equate these letter groups with pronounceable units such as syllables in spoken words, many inconsistencies in English spelling patterns are removed. The aim of word study activities at this level is to help students recognize orthographic units and to seek out these pronounceable parts of words. The criticism is sometimes made that phonic knowledge is of little value (or even a hindrance) because of the irregularity of English spelling. This is true only if children's phonic knowledge is limited to *single* letter-to-sound correspondences.

It is essential to point out at this stage that all word-building activities are used as a supplement to reading and writing for real purposes, not as a replacement for authentic literacy experiences. For example, words used to generate lists containing important orthographic units for young children to learn can be taken from words encountered in the shared-book approach, guided reading activities (described later) and from their daily writing.

Building sight vocabulary

Alongside explicit instruction in phonics, children also need to acquire as rapidly as possible a mental bank of words they know automatically by sight. Much of a child's learning in this area arises naturally from their daily reading and writing experiences. The more frequently a child reads a word, the more likely it is that the word will be retained in long-term memory. During early reading experience the more often a word is decoded from its letters, the more rapidly it becomes known instantly by sight, without the need for further decoding. Immediate recognition of commonly occurring words contributes very significantly to fluent reading and easy comprehension of text.

Teachers often remark that children with learning difficulties can recognize a word on Monday but appear to have forgotten it completely by Tuesday. These students need to practise recognition of key words more frequently and systematically in order to build their 'sight vocabulary'. Use of flashcards can be of great value for this purpose. Playing games or participating in other activities involving the reading of important words on flashcards can provide the repetition necessary for children to store these words in long-term memory. Among the many other available resources, computer software has also proved to be effective in increasing children's word recognition skills (Karemaker *et al.*, 2010).

Many writers have produced lists of words, arranged in frequency of occurrence beginning with the most commonly used words. The list below contains the first 60 most commonly occurring words derived from various lists.

a	I	in	is	it	of	the	to	on	and	he	she
was	are	had	him	his	her	am	but	we	not	yes	no
all	said	my	they	with	you	for	big	if	so	did	get
boy	look	at	an	come	do	got	girl	go	us	from	little
when	as	that	by	have	this	but	which	or	were	would	what

Some words that occur very frequently are often confused and misread by beginning readers and students with reading difficulties. Basic sight words often confused include:

were	where	when	went	with	want	which	what
who	how						
here	there	their	they	them	then	than	

Comprehension

Woolley (2014, p. 108) describes reading comprehension as: '...a constructive practice that is influenced by factors within the learner and by external factors such as text readability, task difficulty, and socio-cultural purposes and practices'. Comprehension is not something that comes *after* learning the mechanics of reading. Reading for meaning must be the focus of any language and literacy programme from the very beginning. For example, when teachers read stories they always encourage children to think about and evaluate ideas in the story, clarify meaning, explain details, look for cause and effect, interpret, make predictions of what may happen next, and summarize main points. The teaching of reading must also encourage critical and creative thinking.

Children who comprehend effectively draw upon prior knowledge and use many cognitive processes as they read. For example, they may visualize images associated with narrative material, they may pose questions to themselves, they may reflect upon the relevance of what they are reading, they may challenge the accuracy of stated facts, and (most importantly) they monitor their own level of understanding.

It is observed that in many primary school classes formal comprehension activities linked to the reading of text rarely demand responses beyond recall of factual information as stated directly on the page (literal level). A curriculum that sets out to develop children's thinking and comprehension should include other more challenging questions and activities that demand reflection, interpretation, prediction and critical thinking (interpretive, inferential and creative levels). The example below illustrates how questions can be designed to evoke different levels of thinking following the reading of a short story about the crash of a passenger aircraft:

* How many passengers escaped the crash? (factual)
* Did failure of cabin pressure lead to the crash? (interpretation)
* From the way he behaved before the crash, what kind of man do you think the pilot was; and could his judgement be trusted? (inferential)
* A newspaper report later gave information obtained from eyewitness accounts of the crash. Is this information likely to be entirely accurate and trustworthy? Why? (critical)
* How could air travel be made even safer than it is now? (creative)

Difficulties with comprehension

Some students can be reasonably accurate and fluent in their reading performance at word level but still have problems in comprehending. They may be weak at inferring meaning beyond the words on the page, and they tend not to read critically or attend to detail. In order to improve students' comprehension, it is important to consider the possible underlying difficulties.

Sometimes comprehension problems stem from a student's limited vocabulary knowledge or lack of fluency. A student may be able to read a word correctly on the page but not know its meaning. If a student has difficulty understanding what is read, it is worth considering whether there is a serious mismatch between the student's own vocabulary and the words used in the book. Remember, the Simple View of Reading stresses that language comprehension is a fundamental component in the reading process. In this situation there is a need to devote more time in class to word study and to vocabulary building. There is also a need sometimes to pre-teach difficult vocabulary before the text is read.

Matching the *readability level* of books to students' current reading ability level can do much to increase comprehension and confidence. Readability of text is a major factor influencing whether or not material can be read easily with understanding. Difficult text – in terms of concepts, vocabulary, sentence length and complexity – is not easy for any reader to process, and can cause frustration and loss of motivation for those with learning difficulties (Petscher, Wanzek & Otaiba, 2014; Scott & Balthazar, 2013). Difficult text leads to slow reading and a high error rate.

There appears to be an optimum rate of fluency in reading that allows for accurate processing of information. Automaticity in reading, based on smooth and effortless word identification and contextual cueing, allows the reader to use all available cognitive capacity to focus on meaning. Children who read very slowly (or much too fast) often have great difficulty comprehending. Slow word-by-word reading makes it difficult for the reader to retain information in working memory long enough for meaning to be maintained. Slow reading also tends to restrict cognitive capacity to the low-level processing of letters and words, rather than allowing full attention to higher-order ideas and concepts within the text. Fast reading may result in important detail being overlooked. Sometimes modifying rate of reading needs to be a specific focus in children's intervention programmes.

Some children have difficulty recalling information after reading. Recall is dependent partly upon such factors as vividness and relevance of the information in the text; but it is also dependent upon a student giving focused attention to the reading task and knowing that it is important to remember details. Recall is best when readers connect passage content to their own previous knowledge and experience, and when they discuss or rehearse key points from the text. These factors may provide clues to help identify why a particular child is having problems in remembering what he or she has read.

Improving comprehension

The reading comprehension skills of all children can be increased when teachers spend time demonstrating effective strategies for processing and reflecting upon text. These strategies must encompass:

- previewing the material before it is read to gain an overview;
- locating the main idea in a paragraph;
- generating questions about the material by thinking aloud;
- predicting what will happen, or suggesting possible causes-and-effects;
- summarizing or paraphrasing the main content.

The explicit teaching of comprehension strategies requires direct explanation, modelling, thinking aloud and abundant guided practice. Strategies such as self-questioning, self-monitoring, rehearsing information, constructing graphic organizers, and creating mnemonics to assist recall have all proved valuable.

Students with reading difficulties benefit greatly from strategy training, and tend to make significant gains in reading comprehension. However, they usually take very much longer than other students to master reading strategies, so training and practice must be continued longer than many teachers expect. Wendt (2013) has strongly recommended that all subject teachers in secondary schools should make a planned effort to integrate reading for meaning into their own subjects, so that students continue to develop comprehension and study skills beyond those achieved in primary school.

A successful programme for the development of comprehension should include at least these components:

- large amounts of time devoted to reading;
- teacher-directed instruction in comprehension strategies;
- using text as one source from which to obtain new information;
- frequent occasions when students can talk with the teacher and with one another about their response to a particular text.

It is important that readers are exposed to a wide range of texts, and are not limited to interpreting a simple narrative genre (stories). Deriving meaning from different forms of text – narrative, expository and informational – helps students acquire a broader range of cognitive strategies (Woolley, 2014).

One example of a simple reading comprehension strategy is *PQRS*, where each letter in the mnemonic signifies a step in the strategy. The four steps are:

1   **P** = *Preview*. First scan the chapter or paragraph, attending to headings, subheadings, diagrams and illustrations. Gain a very general impression of what the text is likely to be about. Ask yourself, 'What do I know already about this topic?'
2   **Q** = *Question*. Next generate some questions in your mind: 'What do I expect to find out from reading this material? Will I need to read the text very carefully or can I skip this part?'
3   **R** = *Read*. Then read the passage or chapter carefully for information. Read it again if necessary. 'Do I understand what I am reading? What does this word mean? Do I need to read this section again? Are my questions answered? What else did I learn?'
4   **S** = *Summarize*. Finally, identify the main ideas, and state briefly the key points in the text in your own words.

The teacher models the application of PQRS strategy several times using different texts, demonstrating how to focus on important points in the chapter or article, how to check one's own understanding, how to back-track or scan ahead to gain contextual cues, and how to select the key points to summarize. This modelling helps students appreciate the value of having a plan of action for gaining meaning from text, and the value of self-questioning and self-monitoring while reading. The students are helped to practise and apply the same approach with corrective feedback from the teacher. To aid generalization, it is important to use different types of reading material used for different purposes and to remind students frequently to apply the strategy when reading texts in different areas of the curriculum.

Reading and study-skill strategies are best taught through dialogue between teacher and students working together to extract meaning from a text. Dialogue allows students and teachers to share their thoughts about the process of learning and to learn from the successful strategies used by others. Dialogue also serves a diagnostic purpose by allowing a teacher to appraise the students' existing strategies used for comprehending and summarizing texts. Peers can facilitate each other's learning of reading strategies in small groups.

An approach known as *reciprocal teaching* has proved extremely useful in a group situation to facilitate dialogue and to teach specific cognitive strategies (Rosenshine & Meister, 1994). In this approach, teachers and students work together, sharing and elaborating ideas, generating questions that may be answered from a specific text, predicting answers, checking for meaning and finally collaborating on a summary. The teacher's role initially is to demonstrate effective ways of processing the text, to ask relevant questions and to instruct the students in strategic reading; the long-term aim is to have students master these strategies for their own independent use across a variety of contexts.

Another approach to improving students' comprehension in mixed-ability classes is to devise differentiated reading assignments that contain questions of four types (Chien, 2013). Type 1 questions are straightforward, and simply ask for information that is presented clearly within the text (literal level). Type 2 questions require 'thinking and searching'. In other words, the reader must put together pieces of information in the text to arrive at an answer. Type 3 asks for information that is not specifically stated, but can be inferred by the reader. Type 4 questions require the reader to go beyond the text to link his or her prior knowledge and experience in order to interpret a story, article or report at a deeper and more personal level. The approach has been found helpful for ESL students as well as others.

To summarize, the following general principles help to facilitate development of comprehension skill for all students, including those with learning difficulties.

- Ensure that reading material is varied and interesting to the students and at an appropriate readability level.
- Always make sure students are aware of the purpose in reading a particular text.
- Apply comprehension strategy training to real texts; do not rely on contrived comprehension exercises for strategy training.
- Prepare students for entry into a new text. Ask: What might we find in this chapter? What do the illustrations tell us? What does this word mean? Let's read the subheadings before we begin.
- Read comprehension questions *before* the story or passage is read so that students enter the material knowing what to look for in terms of relevant information.
- After reading the text, encourage students to set comprehension questions for each other; then use these questions to discuss what is meant by factual level information, critical reading, inferring, predicting. This type of activity lends itself to the reciprocal teaching format described above.
- Devote time regularly to discussing how a particular sample of text can be summarized. Making a summary is an excellent way of ensuring that students have identified main ideas.
- Make frequent use of advance organizers such as a list of key points to look for. Use graphic organizers or story maps to summarize relationships among key points after reading the text.
- Use newspapers, magazine articles and online documents sometimes as the basis for classroom discussion and comprehension activities.
- In general, aim to *teach* comprehension skills and strategies, rather than simply *testing* comprehension.

Teaching approaches

Two Tier 1 teaching approaches that can be used effectively alongside and after phonics instruction to develop children's language comprehension, vocabulary, word recognition and reading with understanding are the *shared-book approach* and *guided reading*.

Shared-book approach

The shared-book approach is highly appropriate for kindergarten and for children in the early stages of learning to read, but the basic principles can also be applied to older children with learning difficulties if age-appropriate books are used. As a beginning-reading method, the shared-book approach has proved equal or superior to other methods and produces very positive attitudes towards reading, even with slower children (Allington, 2012). The scaffolding provided in shared-book sessions creates opportunities for thinking, discussion, reflection and writing (Milburn *et al.*, 2014). *Reach Out and Read* (ROR) is a well-established programme that helps parents engage in shared-book reading with their own children (Pelatti *et al.*, 2014).

The shared-book approach aims to develop:

- children's enjoyment and interest in books and stories;
- thinking and comprehending;
- concepts about books and print;
- awareness of English language patterns;
- word-recognition skills;
- phonic skills.

In a typical shared-book session children encounter stories, poems, jingles and rhymes read to them by the teacher using a large-size book with enlarged print and colourful pictures. Sitting in a group close to the teacher, all children can see the 'big book' easily. They can see the pictures and words, and can follow the left-to-right direction of print as the teacher reads aloud. The book should have the same visual impact from several feet away as a normal book would have in the hands of a child. The children's attention is gained and maintained by the teacher's enthusiastic presentation of the story and discussion of the pictures. Familiarity with the language patterns in the story is developed and reinforced in a natural way. Stories that children may already know and love are useful in the early stages because they present an opportunity for the children to join in even if they cannot read the words. The first time the story is read, the teacher does not interrupt the reading with questions or teaching points. The main aim is to understand and enjoy the story.

The basic steps for implementing the shared-book approach include:

Before reading:
- read together the story title;
- refer to the cover picture or other pictorial material;
- stimulate some brief discussion about the topic and title;
- praise children's ideas.

During reading the teacher:
- reads the story aloud;
- maps the direction of print with finger or pointer;
- thinks aloud sometimes: 'I wonder if she is going to…'
- pauses sometimes at predictable words to allow children to guess;
- sometimes asks children, 'What do you think will happen next?'

After first reading:
- children and teacher discuss the story;
- recall main information.

Second reading of the story the teacher:
- aims to reinforce some word–recognition skills;
- covers certain words to encourage prediction from context;
- increases children's phonic knowledge by asking them to sound out certain words;
- encourages writing (spelling) of a few of the words.

Follow up:
- writing and drawing activities;
- word families;
- individual and partner reading of small books (same story);
- children make up some questions about the story.

The shared-book approach, when implemented efficiently, embodies all the basic principles of effective teaching, particularly the elements of motivation, demonstration by the teacher, student participation, scaffolding, feedback and successful practice. It also encourages sharing of ideas between children and adults in a small group situation. The discussion of each story should not simply focus on low-level questions of fact and information, but rather should encourage children to make personal connections, think, feel, predict and extend ideas. The study of the text should also facilitate vocabulary growth. The method can serve a valuable compensatory role for children with special needs who enter school lacking rich language and literacy experiences in the home. Mueller and Hurtig (2010), for example, provide advice on how to conduct shared reading with deaf and hard-of-hearing students, using supplementary sign language and audio-visual technology. Similarly, Liboiron and Soto (2006) describe the application of shared-book activities incorporating alternative and augmentative communication.

Guided reading

In the literature on reading, 'guided reading' is most often presented as an approach for use with children after the third school year (Lyons & Thompson, 2012). Most of the suggestions for providing guidance are, however, merely extensions of what should have been occurring from an early stage during the shared-book approach. It is an excellent way to develop a strategic, reflective and critical approach in children who are now beyond the beginner stage (Fountas & Pinnell, 2013).

Guided reading is an approach in which the teacher supports each child's acquisition of effective reading strategies for unlocking text at increasingly challenging levels. For this reason guided reading is considered an essential part of any balanced approach to literacy teaching. It addresses the need to help students become efficient in comprehending various genres of text. The guidance provided for the students may focus at times on sub-skills such as word identification and decoding, but its main emphasis is the development of a strategic approach to comprehension.

The guided reading sessions are usually conducted by the teacher, but with heavy emphasis placed on students' active participation through discussion, cooperative learning and sharing of ideas. As with the shared-book approach, there are three main stages at which guidance from the teacher is provided: *before* reading the text, *during* the reading and *after* reading the chosen text.

• *Before reading*
  Guidance before reading prepares the readers to enter the text with some clear purpose in mind. At this stage the teacher may, for example, focus children's attention on their prior knowledge related to the topic, encourage them to generate questions, raise issues, or make predictions about information that may be presented in the text, remind them of effective ways of reading the material, alert them to look out for certain points, and pre-teach some difficult vocabulary to be encountered later in the text.

• *During reading*
  The guidance during reading may encourage the students to generate questions, look for cause–effect relationships, compare and contrast information, react critically, check for understanding and highlight main ideas.

• *After reading the text*
  The guidance provided by the teacher may help children summarize and retell, check for understanding and recall, and encourage critical reflection and evaluation.

The processes involved in guided reading sessions, while primarily serving a teaching function, also allow the teacher to observe and assess the students' comprehension strategies. This is a very important diagnostic function, enabling a teacher to adapt reading guidance and questioning to match students' specific needs.

Reading aloud

Although almost all the reading that children will do eventually is carried out silently, there is great value in having children who are still working their way towards proficiency read aloud on a fairly regular basis. The book should be at a suitable readability level to ensure success; and if a student is to read aloud to the whole class, it is advisable to give an opportunity to practise the material first, for example as homework.

Reading aloud serves a number of purposes. First, it can give the child a feeling of competence and can help develop expression and fluency. Second, it can give a clear indication to the teacher or tutor the extent to which the child has developed a sight vocabulary, is applying decoding skills when encountering unfamiliar words, is making use of contextual cues and is self-correcting when necessary. Third, reading ability can be further enhanced during the reading as the teacher provides appropriate scaffolding, feedback and support (Pentimonti & Justice, 2010).

When tutoring individuals, the child and adult could take turns in reading each paragraph or a page. This 'reading together' enables the adult to model good phrasing and expression and takes some of the pressure off the child. The momentum of the reading is maintained and more of the story is read during the session. Reading aloud during a tutoring session should not go on for too long or the child will become fatigued and error rate will rise.

Sustained Silent Reading

Sustained Silent Reading (SSR) is a specific period of classroom time set aside each day for students and teacher to read material of their personal choice. Often the first 15 minutes of the afternoon session are devoted to SSR across the whole school. When SSR is implemented efficiently, all students engage in much more reading than previously. In doing so they increase their ability to concentrate on reading tasks and develop greater interest in books. In some cases the students increase the range and quality of what they choose to read, and are seen to become more discriminating as readers.

If SSR is implemented inefficiently, it can result in some students wasting time. A problem emerges when students with reading difficulties select books that are too difficult for them to read independently. Teachers need to guide the choice of books to ensure that all students can read the material successfully during these periods. Children with ADHD often find SSR sessions difficult to cope with because of the demands on sustained attention to task.

The following chapter deals in more detail with strategies and specific programmes designed to help students overcome reading difficulties. The approaches described can be regarded as appropriate for use in Tier 2 and Tier 3 teaching within the Response to Intervention model.

Online resources

- A policy paper from the Academy of the Social Sciences in Australia (*Learning to Read in Australia* by Coltheart and Prior; 2007) provides an excellent overview of the research that supports early teaching of phonic skills. It can be found at: http://earlyreadingcentre.com/LearningToReadInAustralia_Coltheart_Prior.pdf.
- A fund of information on the phonic approach for early reading can be found on the National Literacy Trust website at: www.literacytrust.org.uk/resources/practical_resources_info/1035_phonics-methods_of_teaching.
- The Department for Education in the UK has issued a useful set of suggestions for teaching the higher levels of phonic skill. Available at: www.gov.uk/government/publications/teaching-the-higher-levels-of-phonics.
- Also issued by the DfE in the UK is a sample recording sheet for the *Phonics Screening Check*. Available at: www.gov.uk/government/uploads/system/uploads/attachment_data/file/299970/phonics_screening_check_sample_materials_-_Answer_sheet.pdf.
- The *Phonics International* programme by Debbie Hepplewhite can be located at: www.phonicsinternational.com/.
- The *National Literacy Trust* has prepared a list of books that can support a phonics approach. Available online at: www.literacytrust.org.uk/resources/practical_resources_info/5448_booklist_books_that_support_the_teaching_of_phonics.

- Details of the phonics programme *Jolly Phonics* can be found at: http://jollylearning. co.uk/overview-about-jolly-phonics/.
- Additional information on implementing the shared-book approach can be located at: www.hubbardscupboard.org/shared_reading.html.
- Examples of activities for guided reading are provided at: www.tes.co.uk/article. aspx?storycode=354516.
- The Florida Center for Reading Research provides some useful information on differentiating and grouping for reading instruction. Available online at: http://opi. mt.gov/pub/RTI/EssentialComponents/RBCurric/Reading/RTITools/Differentiated%20Reading%20Instruction.pdf.

Further reading

Cohen, V.L. & Cowen, J.E. (2011). *Literacy for children in an information age: Teaching reading, writing and thinking*. Belmont, CA: Wadsworth Cengage.

Ellery, V. (2014). *Creating strategic readers*. Newark, DE: International Reading Association.

Fox, B.J. (2013). *Phonics and structural analysis for the teacher of reading* (11th edn). Boston, MA: Pearson.

Klinger, J., Vaughn, S. & Boardman, A. (2015). *Teaching reading comprehension to students with learning difficulties* (2nd edn). New York: Guilford Press.

O'Connor, R.E. (2014). *Teaching word recognition: Effective strategies for students with learning difficulties* (2nd edn). New York: Guilford Press.

Oczkus, L. (2014). *Just the facts! Close reading and comprehension of informational text*. Newark, DE: International Reading Association.

Saunders-Smith, G. (2009). *The ultimate guided reading how-to book* (2nd edn). Thousand Oaks, CA: Corwin Press.

Woolley, G. (2014). *Developing literacy in the primary classroom*. London: Sage.

Chapter 10

Intervention for reading difficulties

Under the Response to Intervention model described in Chapter 1 children who are struggling with reading during the first year of school, even though they are receiving high-quality teaching, are soon given regular additional intensive tuition in small groups of up to five students. These groups are often referred to as 'booster classes'. The supplementary methods of instruction used at this Tier 2 level are research-based and of proven efficacy. The students' progress is closely monitored, and when a child begins to read at or above the standard expected for his or her age the additional support is phased out. Those who do not respond well are provided with Tier 3 individual instruction, as described later. These students require ongoing highly intensive support if they are to make any real progress (Vaughn & Wanzek, 2014).

General principles for reading intervention (Tier 2)

- Struggling readers need to be identified as early as possible and given additional teaching in small groups.
- Daily instruction for approximately 30 minutes is recommended because it achieves very much more than twice-weekly intervention.
- Children experiencing reading difficulties must spend considerably more active learning time in developing decoding skills, word recognition, comprehension and fluency.
- Frequent practice at a high rate of success is essential to build skills to a high level of automaticity and to strengthen children's confidence to learn.
- Texts used with struggling readers must be carefully selected to ensure a very high success rate. Books with repetitive and predictable vocabulary and sentence patterns can be particularly helpful in the early stages.
- Children should be explicitly taught the knowledge, skills and strategies they lack for identifying words and extracting meaning from text.
- Writing should feature in each session because this helps to strengthen concepts about print and spelling. A great deal of phonic knowledge, as well as word analysis and blending skills, can be developed by helping children work out the sounds they need when spelling the words they want to use.
- Children must perceive genuine and realistic reasons for engaging in reading and writing activities. There is a danger that struggling readers may simply receive a remedial programme comprising routine skill-building exercises.
- Multisensory and multimedia approaches often help children with learning disabilities attend to and remember letter-to-sound correspondences and sight words.

- Early intervention must also focus on the correction of any negative traits the children may display that impair their progress, such as disruptive behaviour, poor attention to task or task avoidance.
- Maximum progress occurs when parents or others provide additional support and practice outside school hours. For this reason, children should also be provided with appropriate books they can read independently at home.
- Withdrawing students for tuition in small groups can achieve a great deal, but it is also essential that the regular classroom programme also be adjusted (that is, differentiated in terms of reading materials, skills instruction and assignments) to allow weaker readers a greater measure of success in that setting. Failure to adapt the regular class programme frequently results in loss of achievement gains when the students no longer receive extra assistance.

Teaching procedures at Tier 2 draws on what is already known about effective instruction that results in optimum learning. In particular, the following components are required:

- creation of a supportive learning environment;
- presentation of learning tasks in easy steps;
- resource materials provided at an appropriate level of difficulty;
- direct teaching, with clear modelling and demonstration of skills and strategies by the teacher or tutor;
- provision of much guided practice with feedback;
- efficient use of available instructional time;
- close monitoring of each child's progress, and re-teaching where necessary;
- independent practice and application;
- frequent revision of previously taught knowledge and skills.

Using tutors

Given the heavy workload and crowded timetable that most teachers face each day, it is becoming increasingly common in schools to find that the additional support needed by some children at Tier 2 is provided by other personnel, working under direction from the teacher. Such personnel include volunteer helpers, parents and paraprofessionals (e.g. classroom aides). These tutors must always implement learning activities that have been designed or selected by the teacher, and must follow the teacher's precise advice. It is essential that unqualified tutors also be provided with a great deal of guidance on how to function in their role of tutor-supporter (Sanetti et al., 2012). In particular, they usually need help in breaking a learning task down into easier steps, giving positive corrective feedback, listening more and talking less, praising and encouraging the tutee, and being supportive rather than overly critical or 'didactic'. Particular attention must be given to ensuring that these tutors are knowledgeable and skilled in teaching phonic decoding; there should be no assumption that they already know how to do this.

The tutoring approach known as 'Pause, Prompt, Praise' (PPP) should be taught to all tutors. In this approach, when a child encounters an unfamiliar word the tutor, instead of stepping in immediately and supplying the word, waits for about 5 seconds to allow time for the child to recognize or decode it. If the child is not successful, the tutor provides a prompt, perhaps suggesting that the child attend to the initial letter, sound out the letters, or read to the end of the sentence and think of the meaning of the passage. When the child succeeds in identifying the word, he or she is praised very briefly. If the child cannot read the word after prompting, the tutor quickly supplies the word. The child is also praised for self-correcting while reading.

Another teaching strategy that should be taught to all tutors is *constant time delay* (CTD) (Browder *et al.*, 2009). This strategy is useful for teaching and consolidating basic sight vocabulary, letter or numeral recognition, number facts and naming shapes, but can also be used in most situations where a student is asked a question. An example of time delay is when a tutor displays a word on a card and asks the child to 'Please say this word', then waits for up to 5 seconds to allow the child to think and respond. If the response is correct, the teaching sequence moves on. If incorrect, the teacher provides the correct answer, and asks the question again. The child then responds with the correct answer.

Within the classroom context support can also be provided by peer tutors (other students). The effectiveness of peer tutoring for academic improvement is well documented (Woolley, 2014). The use of a partner or peer tutor has beneficial effects for students with learning difficulties by increasing time-on-task, facilitating practice with feedback and improving reading performance.

Specific programmes for intervention (Tier 3)

In recent years, several specific intervention programmes have emerged. These programmes include *Reading Recovery®*, *Success for All*, *QuickSmart*, *MULTILIT* and *Reading Rescue*.

Reading Recovery®

Reading Recovery® is an early intervention programme first developed by Marie Clay in New Zealand. It is now used in many other parts of the world, including America, Canada, Australia and England. In the UK, the 'Every Child a Reader Project' (2005–08) utilized *Reading Recovery®* as the main intervention. It can be regarded as a Tier 3 intervention as it involves intensive individual tutoring.

Children identified as having reading difficulties after one year in school are placed in the programme to receive daily tuition tailored to their needs by a teacher specifically trained in *Reading Recovery®* methods. The children receive this individual support for approximately 15–20 weeks (100 hours).

A typical *Reading Recovery®* lesson includes seven activities:

*   re-reading of familiar books;
*   independent reading of a new book introduced the previous day;
*   letter-identification activities, using plastic letters in the early stages;
*   writing of a dictated or prepared story;
*   sentence building and reconstruction from the story;
*   introduction of a new book;
*   guided reading of the new book.

The texts selected are designed to give the child a high success rate. Frequent re-reading of the familiar stories boosts confidence and fluency. Optimum use is made of the available time and students are kept fully on task. Teachers keep detailed records of children's oral reading errors and use these to target accurately the knowledge or strategies a child still needs to learn. It is probable that volunteer helpers would improve the quality and impact of their assistance to individual children if they utilized teaching strategies similar to those in *Reading Recovery*®, under the teacher's direction.

Reading Recovery®, when correctly implemented, can be effective in raising young children's reading achievement and confidence (IES, 2013). It is claimed that the programme is highly successful with many children in Year 1, and that at least 80 per cent of children who undergo the full series of lessons can then read at the class average level or better. It must be noted, however, that data from the Ministry of Education in New Zealand indicate that 9 per cent of children still do not make adequate progress and have to be referred for longer and even more intensive specialist support (Tunmer *et al.*, 2013a). Children's responses to *Reading Recovery*® therefore vary, and there are indications that the approach fails to meet the needs of children with the most severe reading problems (Serry *et al.*, 2014). It is possible that these children have a genuine learning disability or some other disorder that causes a problem in learning.

Reading Recovery® is not without its critics (e.g. Tunmer *et al.*, 2013a; Wheldall, 2013). For example, it is felt that far too little attention is devoted to explicit instruction in phonics and decoding for children with major weaknesses in this area. In part, this is due to the fact that *Reading Recovery*® was created during the era when 'whole language' approach held sway and phonics was regarded as having only a minor role in reading proficiency (Serry *et al.*, 2014). Tunmer *et al.* (2013b) claim that little or no progress has been made over the past decade in reducing the literacy achievement gap in New Zealand, because the Ministry of Education there still advocates use of a constructivist 'multiple cues model' of reading. Other observers question the sustainability of the success rate of those who complete all sessions, suggesting that gains made during the programme are not always maintained. It has also been noted that skills and motivation acquired in the *Reading Recovery*® lessons do not necessarily spill over into better classroom performance. This is possibly because the reading materials provided in the regular setting are not so carefully matched to the child's ability level and the child receives much less individual support. Other difficulties associated with *Reading Recovery*® include the need to organize time in the school day for some children to be taught individually; and the need to provide appropriately trained personnel to give the daily tuition. Criticisms also relate to the labour-intensive nature of one-to-one intervention, and cost effectiveness remains an unresolved issue. However, Iverson *et al.* (2005) provided evidence to show that children can be taught in pairs without any detrimental effect on their progress. Teaching children in pairs needs a little more time, but by increasing instructional time by about a quarter, *Reading Recovery*® teachers can double the number of students served without compromising the outcome.

Research data on the effectiveness of *Reading Recovery*® can be located on the Reading Recovery Council of North America website at: www.readingrecovery.org/research/effectiveness/index.asp.

Success for All

Success for All is a comprehensive whole-school programme intended to improve literacy teaching and prevent reading failure. It was designed in the US by Robert Slavin and his associates (Slavin *et al.*, 2009; Slavin & Madden, 2012). The programme spans school years from kindergarten to Grade 8, and also provides training and follow-up support for teachers and tutors. *Success for All* is widely used in the US, where the Common Core Standards are now incorporated into the approach (Slavin & Madden, 2013), and has also been adopted for use in several other countries, including England where positive results are reported (Tracey *et al.*, 2014). The intervention involves intensive one-to-one teaching, using teachers or specially trained paraprofessionals to help improve the learning rate for at-risk and socially disadvantaged children.

Tutoring in *Success for All* places emphasis on students reading meaningful texts, combined with phonics instruction. Although instruction in segmenting and blending phonemes was included in the programme from its inception, recent years have seen the amount of attention given to explicit synthetic phonics increase. Importance is also placed on demonstrating strategies to monitor comprehension. These reading and language lessons operate daily for 90 minutes, thus providing for intensive instruction and practice. One unique feature of *Success for All* is that junior classes throughout the school usually group for reading at the same time, with children going to different classrooms based on their ability level. This arrangement necessitates block timetabling which some schools find difficult to implement.

In an attempt to avoid the lack of generalization and transfer of skills sometimes found with *Reading Recovery*®, the *Success for All* teacher also participates in the mainstream reading programme and assists with reading lessons in the regular classroom. This helps ensure that one-to-one tutoring is closely linked to the mainstream curriculum, not divorced from it.

Research evidence in general has supported *Success for All* as an effective intervention model (IES, 2009b). The *Best Evidence Encyclopedia* states that: '*Success for All* has strong evidence of effectiveness for struggling readers. Across nine qualifying studies, the weighted mean effect size was +0.55' (0.55 represents a significant positive effect). A comprehensive review of evaluation studies can be found in an online report by Slavin and Madden (2012) at: www.successforall.org/SuccessForAll/media/PDFs/Summary_of_Research_September_2012.pdf.

QuickSmart

QuickSmart is a Tier 3 intervention programme implemented in Australia. It targets middle years students (ages 10–13 years) who exhibit ongoing difficulty in acquiring functional literacy. The reading component focuses on improving students' automaticity in word recognition, and on increasing fluency in reading connected text. Teaching focuses on mastery of sets of words organized in units of 9–12 lessons. The sets begin with high usage three- and four-letter words, and move later to more complex and demanding words. The focus words are incorporated in two or more passages of connected text relevant to the topic. Typical activities used in the sessions include:

- flashcard activities;
- vocabulary building;
- repeated readings of a target text to improve fluency;
- comprehension strategies;
- reading games;
- regular testing.

The total programme is extremely comprehensive and includes preparation sessions for school principals, teachers and instructors, professional follow-up, resource materials for teachers and students, a computer-based assessment and monitoring component, and the use of data from formal standardized measures of attainment for objective evaluation of students' progress. The programme has undergone regular evaluation and revision. Results from several studies indicate that *QuickSmart* students are able to narrow the gap between their performance standard and that of their higher-achieving peers (NCSiM-ERRA, 2009).

The lesson format for *QuickSmart* is designed to ensure maximum engagement in learning and a high success rate for students during each 30-minute session. Students are taught in pairs and the programme is normally implemented three times a week for 30 weeks. The guiding principle is that building fluency and confidence in the most basic skills enables students to devote much more cognitive effort to the higher-order processes involved in reading for meaning.

QuickSmart learning and teaching strategies are drawn from research evidence identifying effective methods for students with learning difficulties. These include explicit strategy instruction, modelling, discussion, questioning, feedback, scaffolding, guided and independent practice, and frequent reviews. Each lesson involves brief revision of work covered in the previous session, a number of guided practice activities featuring overt self-talk, discussion and practice of memory and retrieval strategies, and games and worksheet activities followed by timed and independent practice activities. Strategy instruction and concept development are seen as key components of each lesson.

The professional development component of *QuickSmart* focuses on training teachers and tutors to provide effective instruction to maximize students' engagement in learning activities during the available time, embodies abundant guided and independent practice to develop fluency and confidence, and gives positive feedback for success.

Details of *QuickSmart* literacy and numeracy intervention can be found online at: http://simerr.une.edu.au/quicksmart/pages/qsreading-intervention.php.

MULTILIT

The name *MULTILIT* stands for 'Making up Lost Time in Literacy'. This comprehensive Tier 2/Tier 3 approach to teaching low-progress readers (aged 7 or above) addresses five key areas necessary for effective reading instruction – namely, phonemic awareness, phonic decoding, fluency, vocabulary and comprehension. It has three strands covering *word attack* (phonics), *sight words* and *reinforced reading* (reading of meaningful text).

The teaching approach within *MULTILIT* draws on evidence from research into the most powerful strategies to help readers who are significantly behind their peers. The student is given a placement test at the beginning of intervention to ensure that he or she is placed at the correct level within the programme. It is claimed that a child undertaking *MULTILIT* can make 15 months' progress in word recognition in two terms of instruction. As well as providing programme and materials development, *MULTILIT* also incorporates a strong component of professional training for teachers and tutors. The designers conduct ongoing research into the overall effectiveness of the approach (e.g. Buckingham *et al.*, 2012).

The programme is tutor or teacher led and should be delivered at least three to four times a week. The tutor and student work through each of several levels of instruction for tackling unfamiliar words, progressing to the next level once the student has mastered the current level. Sight vocabulary is targeted at the same time, with particular reference to a list of 200 key words. Rapid automatic recognition of sight words helps to develop reading fluency. The other component in the programme is termed 'reinforced reading'. During this part of each session the student is able to transfer and generalize knowledge and skills by reading books chosen carefully to be at an instructional level.

The designers of *MULTILIT* suggest that *Reading Recovery*® fails to provide the least able students with sufficient explicit training in phonemic awareness and decoding. To address this need they have also devised *MINILIT* (Meeting Individual Needs in Literacy) (Reynolds *et al.*, 2007). This involves a 15-week tutoring programme with groups of three to six students working for one hour daily with a tutor. Each session involves time spent on phonemic awareness, sight vocabulary, word-attack skills, text reading and story time. The intervention paves the way for smooth entry into the classroom reading programme, or into *MULTILIT* for those still needing support. Full details of MULTILIT can be found online at: www.multilit.com/.

Reading Rescue®

This intervention provides intensive training for teachers and paraprofessionals in methods suitable for individual tutoring of children with literacy difficulties in Year 1 and Year 2. The programme was developed by the University of Florida and the Literacy Trust (US). A study by Ehri *et al.* (2007) suggests that adults who have undertaken the training become as effective as reading specialists in improving children's word reading skills and comprehension. *Best Evidence Encyclopedia* considers the approach to be as effective as *Reading Recovery*®. Details of *Reading Rescue*® can be found online at: http://literacytrust.org/.

Supplementary tutoring strategies and activities

In the early stages of intervention it is helpful to incorporate materials and activities that will hold a child's attention effectively and provide additional opportunities for practising important skills. Hand-held communication devices and e-learning apps have added considerably to the non-print media that can be incorporated into a literacy programme. These activities should always be linked with the main theme of the lesson or topic and not simply be provided as unrelated time-fillers or 'busy work'.

Games and apparatus

Games and word-building equipment can be used as adjuncts to any early literacy programme. For example, games and activities provide enjoyable ways of discovering and reinforcing letter-sound relationships and word recognition (McDougall *et al.*, 2009). Games provide an opportunity for learners to practise and over-learn essential material that might otherwise become boring and dull. Such repetition is essential for children who learn at a slow rate or who are poorly motivated. Concrete and visual materials such as flashcards, plastic letters and magnet boards can be very effective in holding a student's attention and ensuring active involvement in the lesson. The use of games and equipment may also be seen as non-threatening, thus serving a therapeutic purpose within a group or individual teaching situation.

There can be little doubt that well-structured games and apparatus perform a very important teaching function. Games and apparatus should contribute to the objectives for the lesson, not detract from them. A game or apparatus must have a clearly defined purpose and be matched to genuine learning needs in the children who are to use it.

Multisensory approaches

For students with severe learning difficulties who cannot easily remember letters or words, it is helpful to use methods that engage them more actively with material to be studied and remembered (Birsh, 2011). The abbreviation VAKT is often used to indicate that multisensory methods are visual, auditory, kinaesthetic and tactile. The typical VAKT approach involves the learner in finger-tracing over a letter or word, or tracing it in the air while at the same time saying the word, hearing the word and seeing the visual stimulus.

The best-known multisensory method is the Fernald VAK Approach, which involves the following steps. First, the learner selects a particular word that he or she wants to learn, and the teacher writes the word in blackboard-size cursive writing on a card. The child then finger-traces over the word, saying each syllable as it is traced. This is repeated until the learner feels capable of writing the word from memory. As new words are mastered, they are filed away in a card index for later revision. As soon as the learner knows a few words, these are used for constructing simple sentences.

It can be argued that multisensory approaches using several channels of input help a child integrate, at a neurological level, what is seen with what is heard, whether it be a letter or a word. On the other hand, VAKT approaches may succeed where other methods have failed because they cause the learner to focus attention more intently on the learning task. Whatever the reason for its effectiveness, this teaching approach involving vision, hearing, articulation and movement usually does result in improved assimilation and retention. It is obviously easier to apply the VAKT approach with young children (or children with intellectual disability), but in a private one-to-one tutoring situation it is still a viable proposition with older students.

Language-Experience Approach

The Language-Experience Approach (LEA) has been used very effectively in mainstream literacy programmes and as an individualized approach within remedial or intervention contexts. It forges a clear connection between speech and print. From the student's point of view, the principle underpinning the method is summed up as:

> *What I know about, I can talk about.*
> *What I say can be written down by someone.*
> *I can read what has been written.*

The Language-Experience Approach uses the child's own thoughts and language patterns to produce carefully controlled amounts of personalized reading material. In some ways, it can be described as a form of 'dictated-story' approach, with young children (or older children with literacy problems) being helped to write material that is personally meaningful and relevant to them. With assistance and practice they can read what they have written and can begin to store some of the words and spelling patterns in long-term memory. Reading their own material several times also contributes to confidence and fluency (Bixler, 2009). From the daily writing, and from activities conducted in parallel with the writing, the children can also be taught important phonic knowledge and skills (Brugelmann & Brinkmann, 2013).

The Language-Experience Approach combines two major advantages that are of great benefit to struggling readers. First, the approach uses the child's own interests to generate topics and material for reading and writing in the child's own language-experience book. This tends to be more intrinsically motivating for the child than attempting to read difficult material in published texts. Second, the teacher is able to work within the child's current level of oral language competence in terms of vocabulary and sentence length. This is of great help for children who are well below average in general language ability, due perhaps to restricted preschool language experience, hearing impairment, intellectual disability or a language disorder. The basic principles of the Language-Experience Approach can also be used within intervention programmes for non-literate adults or those learning English as a second language.

The steps involved in implementing this approach are summarized below.

- The child and tutor talk together about the chosen topic.
- A simple statement, using the child's own words, is then written by the teacher on the first page in the child's language-experience book – for example, 'My new bike' (to accompany a drawing or photo); or 'I go to school by bus.'
- They read the statement together at least twice.
- The child copies the sentence from the teacher's model.
- Older children can be encouraged to type or word process the same sentence on a strip of paper, and that version is then pasted into the book.
- The teacher then writes out the child's statement again on a card, and the card is cut into separate words.
- The child engages in an activity to rebuild the sentence, using the word cards in the correct left-to-right sequence. He or she reads the statement again, pointing to each word.
- The cards can then be presented in random order to practise word recognition and to identify initial sounds.

In each new lesson, a topic is selected related to the child's personal interests and the procedure described above is repeated. Each day the child revises the sentence from the previous lesson, and engages in word recognition using the separate word cards. The teacher's control over what is written each day ensures that not too much new vocabulary is added. If too much material is written, the overload will result in failure to learn.

Important sight words will occur naturally during the daily writings. When the child can recognize these easily, they can be highlighted on a vocabulary list in the front cover of the child's book. If certain common words seem to present particular problems for the child, additional activities such as flashcard quiz or Word Lotto can be introduced to practise and overlearn these words.

Gradually the amount written each day can be increased and the child will need less and less direct help in constructing sentences. The use of Language-Experience Approach in this way is highly structured and is based on mastery learning principles at each step. The approach may sound slow and tedious but it does result in progress in even the most resistant cases of reading failure. The growth in word recognition skills is cumulative.

Although every opportunity is taken to teach and apply phonic decoding skills during the daily language-experience activities, it is also necessary to set aside additional time in the early stages to teach the child all basic letter-sound correspondences thoroughly, and to practise sounding and blending. LEA used alone is not sufficient to ensure complete mastery of essential decoding skills. Once a child has made a positive start using the Language-Experience Approach and learning the alphabetic code, he or she can be introduced to a graded reading book. It is wise to prepare the way for this transition by including in the child's language-experience material some of the vocabulary that will be met in the first reader.

The activity of 'sentence building' is an essential component in this approach. At any age level a learner who is beginning to read should be given the opportunity to construct and reconstruct sentences from word cards. This sentence-building procedure is valuable as a teaching technique and for informal assessment. The child's ability to construct, reconstruct and transform sentences reveals much about his or her language competence, sequencing ability and memory for words. Sentence building is particularly helpful to students with impaired hearing and those with language disorders. It is also a valuable approach for learners of English as a second language (Landis *et al.*, 2010).

Cloze procedure

Cloze procedure is a simple technique designed to help a reader become more skilled in using context to support recognition of unfamiliar words (Woolley, 2014). The procedure merely requires that certain words in a sentence or paragraph be deleted and the reader asked to read the paragraph and supply possible words that might fill the gaps. Variations on the cloze technique involve leaving the initial letter of the deleted word to provide an additional clue; or at the other extreme, deleting several consecutive words, thus requiring the student to provide a phrase that might be appropriate.

> It was Monday morning and Leanne should have been going to sch———. She was still in ———. She was hot, and her throat was ———.
> 'I think I must take you to the d———,' said her ———. 'No school for you t———y.'

The use of the cloze procedure can be integrated easily into the shared-book approach and guided reading activities described in Chapter 9. Cloze activities can be used with individuals, or with small groups of students. For groups the prepared paragraphs are duplicated on sheets for the children or displayed on an overhead projector. As a group, the children discuss the best alternatives for the missing words and then present these to the teacher. Reading, vocabulary and comprehension are all being developed by a closer attention to logical sentence structure and meaning.

Repeated Reading and the Impress Method

Oral reading fluency (ORF) is a useful aspect of reading performance that can be measured reasonably accurately and can be used as one indicator of improvement over time. Repeated Reading is a procedure designed to increase fluency, accuracy, expression and confidence in children who are already under way with reading (Staudt, 2009). The procedure can be particularly useful with secondary school students with reading difficulties.

Repeated Reading simply requires readers to practise reading a short passage aloud until their accuracy rate is above 95 per cent and the material can be read aloud fluently. The teacher first models the reading while the student follows in the text and then spends a few minutes making sure that the student fully understands the material. The student practises reading the same material aloud, with corrective feedback from the teacher if necessary. The student continues to practise reading the text until nearly perfect, and finally records the reading on audiotape. When the recording is played back, the student hears a fluent performance, equal in standard to the reading of even the most competent student in class. This provides an important boost to the student's confidence. Greater fluency also leads to improved comprehension because the reader is expending less mental effort on identifying each word.

The Impress Method (also known as the Neurological Impress Method: NIM) is a variation of Repeated Reading using a unison reading procedure in which the student and tutor read aloud together at a natural rate (Flood et al., 2005). It may be necessary to repeat the same sentence or paragraph several times until the student becomes fluent at reading the material with low error rate. The Impress Method is particularly useful when a child has developed a few word-recognition skills but is lacking in fluency and expression. It is recommended that sessions should last no more than 5–10 minutes but be provided on a very regular basis for several months.

The Impress Method is very appropriate for use in peer tutoring, where one child who is a better reader provides assistance for a less able friend. In such cases the peer tutor usually needs to be shown how to act effectively as a model reader, and how to be supportive and encouraging to the tutee, as suggested above. A quick search online for Neurological Impress Method will provide many links, some with video examples.

Technology, ICT and reading

Information and communication technology has created many new and interesting ways for children to engage in literacy activities for authentic purposes – for example, using e-readers, interactive reading websites, texting, emails, surfing the Internet, social networking and creating blogs. Evidence is accumulating to support the value of ICT as a contemporary medium for language and literacy development (e.g. Bromley, 2013; Genlott & Grönlund, 2013; Hutchison & Woodward, 2014; Wright et al., 2013). A study found that a structured use of the Internet as a medium for applying and practicing reading skills was very effective in middle school, with improvements in reading achievement, engagement rates and attitude (Cooney & Hay, 2005). Studies have indicated that children with reading difficulties can gain much from using text-to-speech (TTS) software, with its combined visual and auditory presentation. Gibson (2009) has reported that a computer program, Read Naturally, was effective in increasing oral reading fluency and comprehension standard in First Grade children. This study also provided added support for the value of repeated reading. A study by Walcott et al. (2014) indicates that computer-based reading activities can significantly increase the on-task engagement of students with learning difficulties and produces gains in reading skills.

The use of technology for literacy also covers computer-assisted learning (CAL). At the most basic level, computer programs exist that will help students improve letter recognition, alphabet knowledge, word recognition, decoding, sentence-completion, cloze and spelling skills (Chambers et al., 2008; Karemaker et al., 2010). Spelling and word study may be presented through age-appropriate programs in which a target word is displayed on the screen and the student is required to copy (retype) the word. The word is then embedded in a sentence for the student to read and again copy. Gradually the cues are removed until the student is reading, writing and using the word correctly in context with a high degree of automaticity. Examples of literacy games apps can be found at: www.ictgames.com/literacy.html.

The main benefit of CAL is that programs usually make use of well-established principles of instruction such as clear presentation, modelling in easy steps, active participation and practice to mastery level. Students are active throughout the learning session and have high levels of motivation. Computers are infinitely patient, allow for self-pacing by the student and provide immediate feedback. Many programs also provide scaffolding and feedback to the learner while at the same time ensuring practice with high success rate. Programs often have an in-built system that can show at a glance a student's progress and error rate. Whether used by one student alone, or by two students working together, the computer is an excellent tool for learning in the regular classroom.

At higher levels, programs may focus more on comprehension, application and 'reading to learn' rather than 'learning to read'; but students with reading problems are often limited in their ability to use ICT to research information for classroom projects. Close monitoring by the teacher, and judicious use of peer tutoring, can help to reduce this problem and at the same time help the student acquire computer skills.

In the home situation, the computer can also aid literacy development because children can work alone or with a parent on early reading and writing skills. Parents who are computer literate can also help their children search for, read and interpret information from the Internet for homework or personal interest.

Online resources

- A useful summary of intervention methods and resources is available on the National Literacy Trust website: www.literacytrust.org.uk/Database/resources2. html#intervention.
- The Dyslexia-SpLD Trust has useful material on intervention and support at: www. interventionsforliteracy.org.uk/schools/guidance/.
- For detailed information on RTI visit Response to Intervention Network at: www.rtinetwork.org/learn.
- A detailed description of the teaching strategy known as constant time delay can be found at: http://nycdoeit.airws.org/pdf/Constant%20Time%20Delay%20in%20 Math.pdf.
- Research data on the effectiveness of *Reading Recovery*® can be located on the Reading Recovery Council of North America website at: http://readingrecovery. org/reading-recovery/research/effectiveness.
- Teachers can obtain information on *Success for All* from the Success for All Foundation at: www.successforall.org/What-Is-SFA/.
- Details of *QuickSmart* literacy and numeracy intervention can be found online at: http://simerr.une.edu.au/quicksmart/pages/qsreading-intervention.php.
- The Language-Experience Approach is clearly described at: www.education.com/ reference/article/language-experience-approach/.

Further reading

Bursuck, W.D. & Damer, M. (2015). *Teaching reading to students who are at risk or have disabilities* (3rd edn). Upper Saddle River, NJ: Pearson.

Caldwell, J.S. (2014). *Reading assessment: A primer for teachers in the Common Core era.* New York: Guilford Press.

Cockrum, W. & Shanker, J.L. (2013). *Locating and correcting reading difficulties* (10th edn). Boston, MA: Pearson-Allyn and Bacon.

DeVries, B.A. (2014). *Literacy assessment and intervention for classroom teachers* (4th edn). Scottsdale, AZ: Holcomb Hathaway.

Gipe, J.P. (2014). *Multiple paths to literacy: Assessment and differentiated instruction for diverse learners* (8th edn). New York: Pearson Education.

McCormick, S. and Zutell, J. (2014). *Instructing students who have literacy problems* (6th edn). Boston, MA: Pearson-Allyn and Bacon.

Mesmer, H.A., Mesmer, E. and Jones, J. (2014). *Reading intervention in the primary grades.* New York: Guilford Press.

Chapter 11

Problems with written language

In recent years there has been much more attention paid to improving students' ability to write clearly and accurately. Since 2013, the revised National Curriculum in the UK has specified precisely the grammar and writing competencies that students are expected to achieve year by year. These competencies are also a focus of attention in the mandated testing that accompanies the curriculum (Myhill & Watson, 2014). A similar situation exists within the new Australian Curriculum and testing programme (ACARA, 2014a). In the US, the Common Core State Standards now specify what is expected in terms of English grammar and writing outcomes (CCSS, 2014a).

Writing is one of the most complex skills that students must learn, and it is not surprising that some have difficulty in achieving proficiency. While reading and writing are separate processes, and in some respects draw upon different areas of knowledge and skill (and different brain areas), there is also some overlap between reading and writing. For example, automaticity in recognition of common words in reading is fairly closely linked with automaticity in writing those words easily and correctly; knowledge of phonics helps both reading and spelling; familiarity with grammar and sentence structure is important in writing and is also one of the supportive semantic cueing systems used in fluent reading.

The active creation of written text involves two key areas of competence: (i) lower-order transcription skills such as handwriting (or keyboarding) and spelling; and (ii) self-regulated thinking and planning involved in creating, sequencing and expressing ideas. The more automatic the lower-order skills become, the greater will be the cognitive capacity available to the writer for thinking, composing and revising. Studies have clearly indicated that students with learning difficulties can be helped to improve in these areas (Datchuk & Kubina, 2013; Hansen & Wills, 2014; Peterson, 2014; Wright & O'Dell, 2013). It is important therefore to identify as early as possible any children who are beginning to have writing problems (Ritchey & Coker, 2014).

Areas of difficulty

Many of the most basic problems that students with learning difficulties experience occur first in the lower-order skills of handwriting and spelling. To illustrate this point, a study in the UK found that at age 11–12 years at least 33 per cent of children could not meet the age-appropriate standard for spelling, and 95 per cent could not meet the standard for speed of writing (25 words per minute) (Montgomery, 2008). On the issue of slow handwriting, one study has suggested that the problem is not with the physical act of writing but is caused by the student pausing too frequently (Sumner *et al.*, 2013).

These researchers concluded that this may be due to the cognitive load imposed by having to cope concurrently with the demands of spelling and composing.

Moving beyond lower-order skills, the higher-order demands of written expression are even more difficult for some children to acquire. Written expression involves much more than adding or combining discrete skills in a linear sequence. Competence in expression draws heavily upon an individual's background experiences, general knowledge, vocabulary, imagination and sense of audience, as well as possession of effective cognitive strategies for planning, encoding, reviewing and revising written language (Peterson, 2014).

Students with learning difficulties often lack a basic knowledge of how best to approach the writing process. They often display the following weaknesses:

- limited ability to plan, execute and revise written work;
- difficulties in formulating goals and generating ideas;
- inability to organize an appropriate structure for a composition;
- a tendency to spend too little time in thinking before writing;
- slowness and inefficiency in executing the mechanical aspects of writing;
- limited output of written work in the available time.

In addition, weak writers often use either very simple sentence structures, or tend to produce long and rambling sentences with repetitive use of conjunctions. They favour simple words with known spellings over more interesting and expressive words – but still make many spelling errors. Above all else, they do not enjoy writing and would prefer to avoid it.

Losing confidence and motivation

A student who has problems writing will experience no satisfaction pursuing the task and will try to avoid writing whenever possible. Avoidance reduces opportunities for practice, and lack of practice results in no improvement. The student loses confidence and self-esteem in relation to writing, as well as developing an even more negative attitude. The problem for the teacher is to motivate these students to write and to provide them with enough support to ensure increased success. It is clear that these students need to be taught effective strategies for approaching writing tasks.

It is fortunate that contemporary approaches to the teaching of writing have done much to alleviate the anxiety and frustration that many of the lower-ability students experienced in years gone by whenever 'composition' appeared on the timetable (Bayat, 2014). To them it meant a silent period of sustained writing, with little or no opportunity to discuss work with others or ask for assistance. Great importance was placed on accuracy and neatness at the first attempt, and many children felt extremely inhibited. Even when the teacher was not a severe judge of the product, the children themselves sometimes carried out self-assessment and decided that they could not write because their product was not perfect. It is therefore important to consider approaches to teaching that may prevent loss of confidence and motivation, and instead make students feel successful as writers.

Teaching approaches

There are two main approaches to teaching writing – the traditional *skills-based approach* with a focus on instruction in basic skills of writing and grammar, and the *process approach* with a focus on how best to generate ideas and express them clearly through a process of drafting, revising and polishing (Bayat, 2014).

Skills-based approach to writing

The skills-based or traditional approach usually involved fairly tight control imposed by the teacher. Writing skills were expected to develop mainly through structured exercises and practice. The teacher usually selected an essay topic about which all students were expected to write. Often a teacher simply set a topic but provided no instruction or feedback on how best to attempt the writing task. Without this guidance the activity became more an assessment procedure rather than a teaching and learning experience.

This traditional skills-based approach eventually fell out of favour in many schools because it was believed to be less motivating for students than having them working on topics they have chosen for themselves. There is also some doubt that skills taught in routine exercises ever transfer, and it is argued that component skills of writing and editing should be taught in an integrated way as part of feedback given to children as they write on their own chosen topics (Peterson & Portier, 2014). Beginning in the 1980s and extending until recently, the accepted wisdom became a view that teachers should never teach isolated skills but instead should scaffold and support students' own developing strategies as they write for authentic purposes. This view underpins the 'process approach' that was part of 'whole-language' pedagogy, and became popular in primary and secondary schools in many countries. The process approach places emphasis not upon the mechanics of writing but on the thinking and creativity that are involved in composing, editing and revising written work. Variants of the process approach are described later, and include writing workshop, shared writing and guided writing.

With the renewed attention being given to improving students' grammar and writing accuracy in Britain, Australia and the US, it is likely that some aspects of the skills-based approach may return to classroom teaching. This is likely to occur by giving more time to explicit instruction as part of the time spent in process writing, writers' workshop and guided writing, as described below.

Process approach to writing

The process writing approach helps young children understand that a first attempt at writing rarely constitutes a finished product. Writing usually has to pass through a number of separate stages, from the initial hazy formulation of ideas to the first written draft, through subsequent revisions and editing to a final product (although not *all* writing should be forced to pass through all stages). Teachers themselves should model this writing process in the classroom and demonstrate the planning, composing, editing and publishing stages in action. In the process approach, children confer with the teacher and with peers to obtain opinions and feedback on their written work as it progresses (Peterson & Portier, 2014). Although process writing is very much a student-centred approach it still provides abundant opportunities for a teacher to give individualized direct instruction to advance a student's writing abilities. Students' responses are deliberately shaped and refined through a natural process of feedback and reinforcement. In addition, children are taught specific aspects of drafting, editing, grammar and style through the provision of appropriate 'mini lessons' from time to time. It is possible that too little attention was devoted to this aspect in the past, which may account for the reported decline in students' writing accuracy.

Since the process approach depends upon student-writers having someone with whom to confer (it is often referred to as the writing conference approach), it is important to consider possible sources of assistance in the classroom beyond the teacher and classmates. Teacher aides, older students, college and university students on teaching practice and parent volunteers can all provide help within the classroom programme. In all cases, these helpers must understand their role and they require some informal training by the teacher if they are to adopt an approach that is supportive rather than critical or didactic.

Writing workshop

Writing workshop is a whole-class session where all children are engaged in various forms of writing activity and are supported by classmates and teacher (Conroy *et al.*, 2009). Children in writing workshop are helped through the complete prewriting, drafting, revising and 'publishing' cycle, and their products become part of the reading material available in the classroom. The underlying principle is that of 'writers working together', cooperating and providing feedback to one another. A friend or partner can be used as a sounding board for ideas and can read, discuss and make suggestions for written drafts. Group sharing and peer editing are essential elements in the sessions.

Motivation during writing workshop comes mainly through the freedom that children are offered in terms of topics and genre. Choice of topic is usually (but not always) made by the writer rather than the teacher. It is believed that selecting a personal topic reduces the problem of generating new ideas necessary for a teacher-chosen topic. A familiar topic reduces cognitive load in the initial planning and drafting stages. Students work independently on their own writing or work in small groups, with support available from the teacher. During this time, access to information technology and word processing is usually appropriate (Thornton, 2013). Finally, children share their writings with their peers. Comments, advice and feedback come not only from teacher but also from peers.

During the session the teacher should confer with almost every student about his or her writing. This conference with the student involves far more than dispensation of general praise and encouragement. The conference between teacher and individual students should represent the 'scaffolding' principle whereby the teacher supplies the necessary support to help students gain increasing control over their own writing strategies. Differences in abilities among the students will determine the amount of time the teacher spends with each individual.

The teaching of specific language skills during writing workshop takes place in three ways:

- a mini-lesson may be conducted for 5–10 minutes, covering a specific grammar rule, spelling, or use of adverbs and adjectives;
- individual children receive guidance and feedback during the session;

- principles of grammar, usage, style and spelling are an important part of whole-class sharing at the end of the session.

Shared writing

Shared writing emerges naturally within writing workshop, or can be made part of any other lesson that involves students in writing. By middle primary school, most children are capable of evaluating the quality of their own writing, but they still need guidance from the teacher and peers on how best to revise and improve their work. Teachers must spend time modelling positive and helpful critiquing before expecting students to do this spontaneously – for example, how to give descriptive praise, how to highlight good points in a piece of writing, how to detect what is not clear, how to help with shaping of new ideas and how to assist with polishing the final product. 'Peer critiquing' is often written about as if it is a simple strategy to employ in the classroom; but in reality it needs to be done with great sensitivity. Children with learning difficulties in the class may not cope well with negative and critical feedback from their peers, because it may seem to draw public attention to their weaknesses.

Guided writing

Guided writing is also an element within the process approach. Guided writing involves demonstrations by the teacher of specific writing strategies, styles or genres, followed by guided and independent application of the same techniques by the students. Using a whiteboard, a teacher might begin by demonstrating, for example, how to generate ideas for a new topic, how to create and structure an opening paragraph and how to develop the remaining ideas in logical sequence. Later, students take it in turns to present their own material to the group, receiving constructive feedback from peers. The guided approach is thought to be more effective in fostering students' writing skills than either the traditional teacher-direct method or unstructured use of the process method.

Students can be given guidelines or checklists to help them evaluate and revise their written work. For example, the checklist might contain the following questions.

- Did you begin with an interesting sentence?
- Are your ideas easy to understand?
- Are your ideas presented in the best sequence?
- Did you give examples to help readers understand your points?
- Is your material interesting? Can you make it more interesting?
- Have you used paragraphs?
- Have you checked spelling and punctuation?

Strategy training

The weaknesses in writing described earlier indicate that students need to be taught effective plans of action for approaching writing tasks. This type of strategy training was discussed previously in Chapter 6, where its value for students with learning difficulties was stressed. In the same way that strategy training can improve reading comprehension, it can also be effective in improving writing, particularly the aspects of planning, drafting, revising and self-correcting (Joseph & Konrad, 2009). Students begin to exhibit more sophisticated writing once they develop effective strategies for planning and revising text, and as they learn to self-regulate.

An appropriate starting point for strategy training is for the teacher to demonstrate, step by step, an effective plan for tackling a particular writing topic. The teacher uses 'thinking aloud' to reveal the way he or she goes about planning, generating ideas, drafting, revising and editing the piece of writing. This can be demonstrated on the whiteboard, overhead projector or computer screen. The students then apply the steps in the strategy to a similar topic, and receive support and feedback from the teacher.

During strategy training students are typically taught to use self-questioning or self-instruction to assist with the process of planning, writing, evaluating and improving a written assignment. Questions similar to those listed above under 'Guided writing' can be used as prompts within the strategy. Emphasis is placed on metacognitive or self-regulating aspects of the writing process (self-checking for clarity in what is written, self-monitoring, self-correction). In the early stages the students may be required to verbalize the steps or questions as they work through the plan of action. Later, as the student becomes more confident in using the strategy independently, overt verbalization is unnecessary.

It is always necessary to maximize the possibility that a strategy will generalize beyond the training sessions into students' everyday writing. This may be achieved by:

- continuing with instruction and practice until students have thoroughly internalized the strategy and can use it automatically;
- leading students to consider when and where a particular strategy can be used;
- discussing how to modify a strategy for different situations.

Many low-achieving students have, in the past, written very little during times set aside for writing. This is part of the vicious circle which begins with 'I don't like writing so I don't write much, so I don't get much practice, so I don't improve...' Use of strategies such as LESSER can help reduce this problem ('LESSER helps me write MORE'). The strategy guides students to organize their thoughts and to write a longer and more interesting assignment than they would otherwise produce. Writing strategies that involve mnemonics have proved to be helpful to students with learning difficulties (Wright & O'Dell, 2013).

L = List your ideas.
E = Examine your list.
S = Select your starting point.
S = Sentence one will tell us about this first idea.
E = Expand on this first idea with another related sentence.
R = Read what you have written. Revise if necessary. Repeat for the next paragraph.

Intervention for individuals and groups

Students who exhibit difficulties in written expression fall into one of two groups, but there is overlap in terms of their instructional needs. The first group comprises students of any age level who have learning difficulties or who have a learning disability. For these students, the teacher needs to structure every writing task carefully in the beginning, and provide appropriate support to ensure the students' successful participation. In general, students with difficulties need help in two basic stages of the writing process: (i) planning and (ii) revising and polishing the final product. The teaching of each of these stages should embody basic principles of effective instruction – namely, modelling by the teacher, guided practice with feedback, and independent practice and application.

The second group of problem writers comprises the reluctant and unmotivated students who can write, but do not like to do so. These students appear not to appreciate the relevance of writing and have not experienced the satisfaction of producing good written communication. Some of these students may have encountered negative or unrewarding experiences during the early stages of becoming writers. They may have acquired what has been termed 'writing apprehension' which now causes them to avoid the task whenever possible. Their problem leads to habitually low levels of practice and productivity. Here the teacher must try to regain lost interest and build confidence.

Ideally, a student receiving extra assistance will choose his or her own topics for writing; if not, it is essential to give the student an appropriately stimulating subject. The topic must be interesting and relevant, and within the student's range of experience. The student must see a purpose in transferring ideas to paper. Regardless of whether the activity involves writing a letter or email to a friend, preparing notes for a class report or composing a science-fiction fantasy story, the student should perceive the task as enjoyable and worthwhile.

Paving the way to success

The first important step in improving a student's writing skills is to allocate sufficient time for writing within every school day. To some extent the introduction of 'literacy hour' in many schools has addressed this issue. If writing occurs daily, there is much greater likelihood that writing skills, motivation and confidence will all improve.

A classroom atmosphere that encourages students to experiment with their writing without fear of ridicule is a very necessary condition for the least able students. In many cases, particularly with the upper primary or secondary student with a history of bad experiences in writing, simply creating the supportive atmosphere is not enough. Much more than the ordinary amount of guidance and encouragement from the teacher will also be needed. Students with writing difficulties benefit from being given a framework they can use whenever they write (see 'Strategy training' and 'Guided writing' above). They need specific guidance in how to begin their writing, how to continue and how to complete the task. In this context, they can be taught a script of questions to ask themselves which will facilitate the generation of ideas and will assist with the organization and presentation of the material across different writing genres.

Students with difficulties need to be helped *daily*. For low-achieving students or those lacking in confidence, the teacher must structure each writing assignment very carefully – for example by:

- talking through the topic first, encouraging the student to think of a sequence of ideas;
- posing some relevant questions to stimulate thinking;
- writing down some key vocabulary on the whiteboard;
- suggesting a few possible sentence beginnings.

In the early stages, it is important not to place undue stress upon accuracy in spelling since this can stifle the student's attempts at communicating ideas freely. If the student is using a word processor it is best not to stop to check spellings until the writing is complete. This gives students the freedom to compose with full attention to content and sequence. Open-ended questions can be used to extend the student's thinking and to build upon the writing so far produced.

Small booklets are usually better than exercise books for students who are unskilled and reluctant writers. The opportunity to make a fresh start every week is far better than being faced with the accumulation of evidence of past failures which accrue in a thick exercise book. For students of all ages, a loose-leaf folder with work samples and computer printouts is a useful replacement for the traditional exercise book.

Paired writing

In the same way that working with a partner can improve reading skills, having a partner for writing is also beneficial. Paired writing can be used with cross-age tutoring, peer tutoring, parent and child tutorial groupings, and in adult literacy classes. The pairing comprises a helper and a writer. The helper's role is to stimulate ideas from the writer that the helper notes down on a pad. When sufficient ideas have been suggested, the helper and writer review the notes on the pad and discuss the best sequence for presenting these. A story planner format could be used (see below). The writer then begins first draft writing, based mainly on the notes. In the case of students with severe learning difficulties, the helper may act as scribe as the 'writer' dictates. The helper then reads aloud the draft that has been written. The writer then reads the draft. Working together, the pair will edit the draft for clarity, meaning, sequence, spelling and punctuation, with the writer taking the lead if possible. The writer then revises the material by writing or word processing a 'final copy'. Helper and writer discuss and evaluate the finished product.

Suggestions for reluctant writers

The following sections describe various activities and teaching strategies that can be used with struggling writers.

The skeleton story

Getting started is the first obstacle faced by many students who find writing difficult. To address this problem some teachers use 'writing frames' in the form of templates and rubrics designed to scaffold and make simple the task of composing. One version is to provide some stem sentences that must be completed using the student's own ideas and words. Example:

> Something woke me in the middle of the night.
> I heard...
> I climbed out of the bed quietly and...
> To my surprise I saw...
> At first I...
> I was lucky because...
> In the end...

With groups of low-achieving students it is useful, through collaborative effort first, to complete one version of the skeleton story on the whiteboard or screen. This completed story is read to the group. Each student is then given a sheet with the same sentence beginnings, but he or she must write a different story. The stories are later shared in the group. Students of limited ability find it very much easier to complete a story when the demands for writing and sequencing are reduced in this way, and when a structure has been provided.

Patterned writing

For students with limited writing ability, a familiar story with repetitive and predictable sentence patterns can be used as a stimulus for writing a new variation on the same theme. The plot remains basically the same but the characters and the details are changed. For example, the children write a new story involving a 'Big Grey Elephant' instead of a 'Little Red Hen'; and the Big Grey Elephant tries to get other animals to help him move a log from the path: 'Who will help me move the log? 'Not I', said the rat. 'Not I', said the monkey, 'Not I', said the snake', and so forth.

Sentence combining

Activities involving the reconstruction of several simple sentences into longer and more interesting sentences have proved valuable for weaker writers. The activities provide an opportunity for writers to construct more interesting and varied sentences within their stories or reports. For example:

> The giant was hungry.
> The giant ate the meat pie.
> The meat pie was huge.
> = The hungry giant ate the huge meat pie.

The main benefit from the experience of sentence combining is that the process can be revisited every time a student is asked to read, edit and improve a piece of writing.

Story planner

A story planner is a form of graphic organizer that provides struggling writers with a starting point for generating ideas for writing. A 'story web' is created by writing the main idea or title in the centre of a sheet of paper, then branching off from the main idea into different categories of information. These ideas and categories might include: the setting for the story, the type of action that takes place, the characters involved, the outcome, etc. Prompts and cues could be used to stimulate the students' thinking as the web is constructed. Students brainstorm for ideas that might go into the story. In random order, each idea is briefly noted against a spoke in the web. The class then reviews the ideas and decides upon an appropriate starting point for the story. Number One is written against that idea. How will the story develop? The children determine the order in which the other ideas will be used, and the appropriate numbers are written against each spoke. Some of the ideas may not be used at all and can be erased. Other ideas may need to be added at this stage, and numbered accordingly. The students now use the bank of ideas recorded on the story planner to start writing their own stories. The brief notes can be elaborated into sentences and the sentences gradually extended into paragraphs.

By preparing the draft ideas and then discussing the best order in which to write them, the students have tackled two of the most difficult problems they face when composing – namely, planning and sequencing.

Expanding an idea

Begin by writing a short, declarative sentence.

We have too many cars coming into our school parking area.

Next, write two or three sentences that add information to, or are connected with, the first sentence. Leave two lines below each new sentence.

We have too many cars coming into our school parking area.
The noise they make often disturbs our lessons.
The cars sometimes travel fast and could knock someone down.
What can we do about this problem?

Now write two more sentences in each space.

We have too many cars coming into our school parking area.
The noise they make often disturbs our lessons. The drivers sound their horns and rev the engines. Sometimes I can't even hear the teacher speak. The cars travel fast and could knock someone down. I saw a girl step out behind one yesterday. She screamed when it reversed suddenly.
What can we do about this problem? Perhaps there should be a sign saying 'NO CARS ALLOWED'. They might build some speed humps or set a speed limit.

Edit the sentences into appropriate paragraphs and combine some short statements into longer, complex sentences. Use of a word processor makes these steps much faster and the process of editing and checking spelling easier. The teacher demonstrates this procedure, incorporating ideas from the class. Students are then given guided practice and further modelling over a series of lessons, each time using a different theme.

Writing a summary

Students with learning difficulties often have problems when required to write a summary of something they have just read. Specific help is needed in this area and one or more of the following procedures can be helpful to such students.

• After the reading, the teacher provides a set of 'true/false' statements based on the text. The statements are presented on the sheet in random order. The student must read each statement and place a tick against those that are true. The student then decides the most logical sequence in which to arrange these true statements. When copied into the student's exercise book these statements provide a brief but accurate summary of the text.

- The teacher provides some sentence starters in a sequence that will provide a framework for the summary. For example: 'The first thing most travellers notice when they arrive at the airport is…'; 'When they travel by taxi to the city they notice…'. The student completes the unfinished sentences and in doing so writes the summary.
- The teacher provides a summary but with key words or phrases omitted. The words may be presented below the passage in random order, or clues may be given in terms of initial letters of word required. The student completes the passage by supplying the missing words.
- Simple multiple-choice questions can be presented. The questions may deal with the main ideas from the text and with supporting detail. By selecting appropriate responses and writing these down the student creates a brief summary.

All the suggestions above are designed to simplify the task demands for writing, and at the same time motivate the reluctant student to complete the work successfully. In most cases, the use of a word processor will also add interest and an important element of control by the learner.

Word processors

There is now clear research evidence supporting the benefits of using word processors with learning-disabled students (e.g. Graham, 2008; Hetzroni & Shrieber, 2004; University of Washington, 2012). Undoubtedly, the arrival of word processors in the classroom heralded a new opportunity for students of all levels of ability to enter the realm of writing and composing with more enthusiasm and enjoyment. Using a word processor makes the task of writing far less arduous. Word processing seems to be of great benefit to students who do not usually write very much, and to those with the most severe spelling problems. In particular, students with learning difficulties gain confidence in creating, editing, erasing and publishing their own unique material through a medium that holds attention and is infinitely patient.

Students with learning difficulties need first to develop some basic keyboard skills if the word processing is to be achieved without frustration. It is usually necessary to teach only the most essential skills to enable the student to access the program, type the work and save the material at regular intervals. Even this simple level of operation can give some students a tremendous boost to confidence and can encourage risk-taking in writing and composing. Using a computer regularly can enhance students' written work significantly in terms of organization and control over the writing process.

For students with learning difficulties, word processing de-emphasizes physical aspects such as handwriting and letter formation, and allows more mental effort to be devoted to generating ideas. Students tend to work harder and produce longer essays, of better quality, when using word processors for writing. Polkinghorne (2004, p. 26) stated:

> Computers can change the whole writing process [making] it easier to plan and record ideas. It is much easier to edit, change and work with those ideas and publish and share the final product. Computer access helps alleviate hesitancy caused by poor spelling, lack of grammar skills, poor handwriting, and inability to proofread and edit hand written work easily.

Similarly Graham (2008, p. 6) observed that word processing is:

...typically packaged together with other software or hardware that provides additional support for writers. This includes supports that help writers with the mechanical demands of writing, such as spelling, capitalization, punctuation, and usage. Computers tools, such as spelling and grammar checkers, speech recognition (writer can hear written text) and speech synthesis (writer's speech is converted to typed text), all have the potential to compensate for problems in these areas.

Online resources

- Issues associated with difficulties in writing are discussed online by Dr Mel Levine at: www.pbs.org/wgbh/misunderstoodminds/writingdiffs.html.
- Some useful information on assisting students with writing difficulties can be located on the National Center for Learning Disabilities (NCLD) website at: iwww.ncld.org/types-learning-disabilities/dysgraphia/seven-important-facts-about-supporting-students-with-writing-learning-disability.
- The NCLD website also has a very useful summary of the current computer apps to help students with writing difficulties, online at: http://ncld.org/students-disabilities/assistive-technology-education/apps-students-ld-dysgraphia-writing-difficulties.
- A brief article by Ann Logsdon (2014) on writing disabilities is available at: http://learningdisabilities.about.com/od/learningdisabilitybasics/p/ldbasicwriting.htm.
- The National Institute of Neurological Disorders and Stroke has information about *dysgraphia* (a specific learning disability affecting writing): www.ninds.nih.gov/disorders/dysgraphia/dysgraphia.htm.

Further reading

Cunningham, P.M. (2010). *What really matters in writing: Research-based practices across the elementary curriculum.* Boston, MA: Allyn & Bacon.

Curtis, C. & Hake, M. (2014). *Grammar and writing Grade 5: Teacher's* (2nd edn). Chicago, IL: Houghton Mifflin/Steck-Vaughn.

Graham, J. & Kelly, A. (2010). *Writing under control* (3rd edn). London: Routledge.

Graham, S., MacArthur, C.A. & Fitzgerald, J. (Eds). (2013). *Best practices in writing instruction* (2nd edn). New York: Guilford Press.

Litt, D.G., Martin, S.D. & Place, N.A. (2014). *Literacy teacher education: Principles and effective practices.* New York: Guilford Press.

Polette, K. (2011). *Teaching grammar through writing: Activities to develop writer's craft in all students in Grades 4–12* (2nd edn). Boston, MA: Pearson.

Chapter 12

Difficulties with spelling

For many students with learning difficulties, spelling continues to be a problem long after reading skills have improved. In part, this arises because in English language it is impossible to spell every word by a simple translation of sound to letter. But children's difficulties can also result from too little time and attention devoted in schools to explicit teaching of spelling skills and strategies. Insufficient instruction and corrective feedback in the early years are major causes of poor spelling.

For several decades from the 1970s, teaching spelling ceased to feature prominently in the primary school curriculum, due mainly to the influence of the whole-language approach to literacy. Under that approach students were expected to acquire spelling skills simply through daily immersion in the writing process. Teachers were encouraged to ignore spelling mistakes and accept 'invented' spellings in order not to focus attention too much on the mechanical aspects of writing. This integrated approach was deemed to be a 'natural' way of acquiring spelling skill and therefore regarded as preferable to any form of direct teaching. This unsystematic approach proved inadequate for many children and they failed to become proficient spellers.

In recent years, the systematic teaching of spelling has enjoyed something of a renaissance, due to a growing awareness that accurate spelling is important, and children will not necessarily become adequate spellers if they are left to discover spelling principles for themselves. The current view is that a systematic approach to spelling and word study is absolutely essential and leads to measurable improvement in spelling ability. If young writers are provided with direct guidance, scaffolding and feedback in the early stages, their emergent spelling skills can be improved very significantly (Reed, 2012; VanNess et al., 2013). Current teaching approaches aim to help students become more independent, and capable of detecting and self-correcting errors. Guidelines for curriculum in the US, Britain and Australia now require that due attention be given to ensuring that all students can spell and can use appropriate resources to check the spelling of complex words (ACARA, 2014a; CCSS, 2014a; Gov.UK, 2014b).

Best practices in spelling instruction

Research studies in recent years (e.g. Kemper et al., 2012; Moats, 2009; Treiman et al., 2013) have led to the firm conclusion that best practice in spelling involves teaching directly the essential knowledge, skills and strategies required. Direct teaching requires clear modelling by the teacher, imitation, corrective feedback and practice. However, it is also recognized that spelling should not be taught in a totally decontextualized manner, through unrelated exercises or drills. The instruction provided must help children learn techniques for tackling any words they require for authentic writing purposes. Under this form of instruction, children are taught efficient methods for learning and remembering unfamiliar words and for generating correct spelling patterns. Learning is not left to chance, and error correction is encouraged. Monitoring and checking students as they write provides teachers with an opportunity for giving constructive advice to spellers, tailored to the needs of each individual. Without instruction most children begin to develop their own strategies for spelling difficult words, but many of these strategies are not effective and contribute to ongoing problems.

There are specific principles that should guide a teacher's approach to spelling and that delineate an effective programme. These principles are:

- allocating specific time for instruction and practice (15 minutes daily in the early and middle primary school years);
- arousing children's genuine interest in words, and in accurate spelling; cultivating a positive attitude;
- teaching a core vocabulary of common words;
- matching materials and activities to students' stage of development;
- teaching effective cognitive strategies for tackling words, proofreading, checking and self-correcting;
- making classroom self-help resources readily available (dictionaries, common core word lists, topic-specific word lists, word walls, electronic speller checkers, computer access).

Best practice also indicates that instruction in spelling must take due account of the stage of linguistic development children have reached. Attempting to teach children words too far above their current expressive and receptive language level is counterproductive. It is therefore important for teachers to be aware of the stages of development through which children pass on their way to becoming proficient spellers.

The stages have been described in the following way – although the exact name for each stage has differed among the various researchers (e.g. Bissex, 1980; Scharer & Zutell, 2003):

Stage 1: Prephonetic. This stage represents the first step towards 'invented spelling' as a component of emergent writing. In the kindergarten years the child 'plays' at writing (often using capital letters) in imitation of the writing of others. There is no connection between these scribbles and speech sounds or real words. Studies with preschool children have indicated that if developmentally appropriate feedback is provided during this stage, invented spelling encourages children to begin to pay closer attention to associations between oral and written language (Ouelette *et al.*, 2013).

Stage 2: Phonetic. At this stage the child relies mainly upon phonemic awareness and some knowledge of letter-to-sound correspondences picked up through incidental learning. The words children invent at this stage are often quite recognizable to others because they are beginning to apply phonic principles when they spell. Many inaccuracies still exist – for example, a phoneme may be equated incorrectly with a letter *name* rather than the sound, as in 'rsk' (ask), 'yl' (while), 'lfnt' elephant).

Towards the end of the phonetic stage, approximations move much nearer to regular letter-to-sound correspondences, as in 'sed' (said), 'becos' (because) or 'wotch' (watch). Some children still have difficulty identifying the second or third consonant in a letter-string, and may write 'stong' (strong) or 'bow' (blow). Or they may fail to identify correctly a phoneme within the word and may write incorrect letters, as in 'druck' (truck), 'jriv' (drive), 'sboon' (spoon), 'dewis' (juice). These are normal inaccuracies on the way to proficiency.

It should be noted that the majority of individuals with poor spelling have reached this phonetic stage but have not progressed beyond it. Their problem is a tendency to be over-dependent on phonic information and therefore to write irregular words as if they have perfect letter-to-sound correspondences. These students now need to be taught to use strategies, such as visual checking of words and spelling by analogy, in order to move to the next stage. Activities involving word analysis are also useful in helping the student recognize letter patterns within words (orthographic units) (Templeton *et al.*, 2015). The process of building up orthographic images in memory is also facilitated by the study of word families with common letter sequences – for example, *gate, date, late, fate, mate*.

Stage 3: Transitional. At this stage there is clear evidence of a more sophisticated understanding of word structure. The child becomes aware of within-word letter strings and syllable junctures. Common letter sequences such as *str-, pre-, -ough, -ious, -ea-, -ai-, -aw-, -ing* are used much more reliably. The children who gain real mastery over spelling at this stage also begin to use words they know already in order to spell words they have never written before (spelling by analogy).

Stage 4: Independence. At this stage the child has mastery of quite complex grapho-phonic principles, and also uses visual imagery more effectively when writing and checking familiar words. A growing awareness of word meanings and derivations (morphology) also signals an increase in control over spelling (Wolter & Dilworth, 2014). Flexible use is made of a wide range of spelling, proofreading, self-help and self-correcting strategies.

In general, the spellings produced by children provide a useful window into their current thought processes related to encoding written language. Examination of the written work produced by students with difficulties can reveal a great deal about their existing skills and specific needs in spelling. Observation and assessment should be the starting point for planning instruction.

Spelling as a complex behaviour

Spelling can be regarded as a very complex behaviour because it involves coordination of ear, eye, hand and brain, and also relies to a significant degree on accurate pronunciation of words (Westwood, 2014). The strategies used to teach spelling need to be based on the contribution of each of these five modalities.

Auditory skills and phonic knowledge

In order to spell, young children in the first years of schooling rely on auditory perception to a much greater extent than older children, simply because they have not yet had as much visual exposure to words through daily reading and writing experiences. Building a memory bank of words and letter strings takes time and experience. The extent to which early attempts at spelling rely upon attention to sounds is evident in children's early attempts at inventing the words they want to use in their writing.

For many years, teachers regarded the encoding of words as a *visual* skill. If students were fortunate enough to receive any guidance at all in spelling, they were mainly taught ways of improving whole-word visual memory – for example, the 'look-cover-write-check' strategy, discussed later. Much less importance was attached to listening (auditory processing) due to the erroneous belief that sounding out words leads to too many errors because of the irregularities in English spelling. It was argued that because many words are not written precisely as they sound, with perfect letter-to-sound translation, it is not beneficial to teach children to use phonic information when spelling. But to counter this argument, it should be noted that more than 80 per cent of English words can be encoded as they sound if attention is given not just to single letters but to *letter clusters* (e.g. pre-, acc-, -ain, -ite, -ight, str-, -tion). Only some 4 per cent of English words are truly irregular and must be learned through repeated writing. The conclusion must be that knowledge of phonic units enhances early spelling because it enables children to relate the sounds they can hear in a spoken word to the letter or letters required to represent that sound in the written form.

Research has indicated that in the early stages of learning to spell it is important that a child has adequate phonemic awareness, a concept already discussed in Chapter 9 (Cordewener *et al.*, 2012; Sanchez *et al.*, 2012). The basic knowledge upon which successful spelling develops seems to depend upon knowing that spoken words can be broken down into smaller units, and that these units can be represented by letters. This process is referred to as *orthographic mapping* (Ehri, 2014).

Visual skills

Of course, visual skills are also very important. Proficient spellers make great use of visual information when writing and checking words, and for detecting errors. Strategies that involve deliberate use of visual imagery, such as look–say–cover–write–check, are very effective for the learning of what are termed 'irregular' words – those with unpredictable letter-to-sound correspondences. The effective use of visual perception in learning to spell helps a student build a memory bank of visual images of common letter strings (orthographic awareness), and the knowledge in this store can be called upon whenever the student attempts to write an unfamiliar word. The process requires the child first to identify the sound units within the word and to match these sound units with appropriate letter clusters stored as visual images in orthographic memory. Having identified the sound values in the word, and having represented these units on paper by writing the specific letters in sequence, visual perception is used to check that what the student writes on paper also 'looks right' – for example, *brekfirst* should be recognized as an incorrect visual pattern for the word *breakfast*.

Learning to spell by eye does not mean that learners simply acquire the ability to spell by seeing words as they read – just 'looking' at words does not seem to be enough for most learners. It is necessary to examine a word very carefully, with every intention of trying to commit its internal configuration to memory. As this behaviour does not come naturally, it is important that students are given the necessary instruction and practice. By implication, this means devoting specific time and attention to *word study*, over and above any help given to individual students as they write (Templeton *et al.*, 2015). It is most unlikely that such an important skill as word analysis could be adequately developed through incidental learning alone.

Spelling by hand

Spelling is also a motor skill, as well as a combined visual and auditory skill. The spelling of a word is produced by the physical action of writing or keyboarding, and *kinaesthetic memory* (or motor memory) is therefore involved in learning to spell. Indeed, the rapid speed and high degree of automaticity with which a competent speller encodes a very familiar word directly from meaning to its graphic representation supports the view that motor memory is involved. The frequent action of writing may be one of the powerful ways of establishing the stock of images of words and letter strings in orthographic memory.

It is clear that poorly executed handwriting and uncertain letter formation inhibit the easy development of spelling habits at an automatic response level. This has implications for the way in which we teach handwriting in the early years of schooling. It is essential that a swift and easy style of writing should be taught and practised from the early years of schooling. Most experts now recommend that cursive (joined) handwriting has benefits over manuscript style (each letter written separately). According to Montgomery (2012) handwriting supports spelling; and the advantage of cursive style is that each written word consists of one continuous line or pattern, with all elements flowing together.

Spelling and the brain

Obviously the brain plays the central role in thinking about words, and in generating and checking plausible spelling alternatives. The learning of new words and the analysis of unfamiliar words prior to writing are both brain-based (cognitive) activities. The brain coordinates and integrates various sources of perceptual information to help predict the spelling of a word. Working out the most probable way to spell an unfamiliar word also requires the writer to consider the meaning of the word, and the separate *morphemes* (small units of meaning such as prefixes, suffixes, plural endings) that make up the word. It is also the brain that makes the decision whether to apply auditory, visual, or some other strategy to encode the word. The ability to recall and apply spelling rules and strategies, or to recognize when a word is an exception to a rule, reflects a cognitive aspect of spelling. Similarly, devising some form of mnemonic to help one recall a particularly difficult word illustrates a cognitive solution to a problem.

Pronunciation

Accurate pronunciation of a word plays an important role in spelling (Papen *et al.*, 2012; Rosenthal & Ehri, 2011). This issue is particularly relevant when teaching English as a second language, but it also applies to students from restricted language backgrounds, those using a strong regional dialect and students with hearing impairment. In cases of serious spelling difficulty it is always wise to check if the student is actually hearing and saying a target word correctly. For example, you are unlikely to spell *library* or *escape* correctly if you say '*libry*' and '*excape*'.

Teaching spelling

The majority of students do not learn to become good spellers simply by being immersed in reading and writing activities, so adequate time must be devoted to spelling instruction, particularly in the primary school years. The starting point for enhancing spelling development is the arousal of children's genuine interest in words. This requires that teachers and tutors display personal enthusiasm for all forms of word study and application. In the early years, children benefit from guided experience in listening carefully to words, stretching words out and segmenting them into pronounceable subunits (Murray & Steinen, 2011).

Effective instruction does not set out to teach students how to spell each and every individual word they may need in their writing; rather, it should teach students how to think about constructing words by drawing on the multiple linguistic factors that underpin spelling. Students make most progress in spelling when they are explicitly taught strategies for working out how words are constructed, so effective instruction must help students understand the phonological and morphological principles in English spelling. These principles apply equally to teaching students with or without spelling difficulties, but in addition students with difficulties need more individualized attention, systematic error correction, more frequent practice, and sometimes the use of teaching methods that involve multisensory input, such as tracing, writing and keyboarding (Kast et al., 2011).

Applying a visual approach

A visual approach is most appropriate for the learning of irregular words. It requires students to memorize the overall appearance of a word and the correct sequence of letters. Rather than attending to sounds and syllables within the word, the student attempts to store a visual image of the word, or key parts of the word, in long-term memory. Research has suggested that children can be trained to focus more attentively on words and to improve their visual imagery for letter sequences (Roberts, 2012). One method for achieving this is called Look-Say-Cover-Write-Check. This approach is better than any rote learning or recitation procedure for learning to spell a word. It gives the student an independent system that can be applied to the study of any irregular words set for homework or for correction from free writing. Students can work in pairs, where appropriate, to check that the procedure is being followed correctly by the partner.

The look-say-cover-write-check approach is based on the principle of learning words by giving attention to their visible sequences of letters, rather than using letter-to-sound correspondences. A similar approach is simply called 'Copy-Cover-Compare' (Konrad & Joseph, 2014).

The visual spelling strategy in action involves the following steps:

- look very carefully at the word;
- say the word clearly while looking closely at the details;
- cover the word so that it cannot be seen;
- write the word from immediate memory, pronouncing it quietly as you write;
- check your version of the word with the original – if it is not correct, go back through the steps again until you can produce the word accurately;

- for some students with severe problems, tracing over the word with a finger may help with attention to detail and retention of the letter sequence;
- check for recall a week later.

To improve visual processing of words, one of the simplest aids to make and use is the flashcard. These cards are particularly useful for teaching irregular words and for students who need to be weaned away from over-dependence on a purely phonetic approach to spelling – for example, students who have reached a developmental plateau at the phonetic stage. Each target word is introduced to the student on a card about 30 cm × 10 cm. The word is pronounced clearly and attention is drawn to any particular features in the printed word that may be difficult to recall later. The child is encouraged to make a 'mental picture' of the word and examine it. Some teachers say, 'Use your eyes like a camera. Take a picture of the word. Close your eyes and imagine you can still see the word.' With the eyes closed, the child is then told to trace the word in the air. After a few seconds the student writes the word from memory, articulating it clearly as he or she writes. The word is then checked against the flashcard. The rapid writing of the whole word using cursive style avoids the inefficient letter-by-letter copying habit that some students have developed.

Several computer programs designed to develop spelling skills using a visual approach are available, and some studies have indicated that these can be quite effective if implemented correctly (e.g. Cekaite, 2009; Kast et al., 2011; Mayfield et al., 2008). Teachers should ensure that the way in which the words are presented on the screen causes the students to attend carefully to the sequence and clusters of letters and requires the student to *type the complete word* from memory each time. Programs that focus too much attention on spelling letter-by-letter, unscrambling jumbled words or inserting missing letters into spaces are far less effective.

Applying phonic principles

It is unnecessary and inappropriate to use Look-Say-Cover-Write-Check if the target word could be written correctly from its component sounds. The phonemic approach encourages students to attend carefully to sounds and syllables within regular words and to write the letters most likely to represent these sounds. As stated previously, while it is true that some 20 per cent of English words are not completely regular (and 4 per cent are very unpredictable), some 80 per cent of words do correspond reasonably well with their letter-to-sound translations, particularly if small groups of letters are recognized as representing larger sound units. The phonic knowledge necessary for effective spelling thus goes well beyond knowing the sound associated with each single letter (Berninger et al., 2013).

Spelling and meaning: morphemic approach

Children often need to be shown explicitly that words related in meaning are frequently related also in spelling pattern. To facilitate the study of words related by meaning, students can be helped to compile word families sharing a common root or base (e.g. *certain, uncertain, certainly, uncertainty, certainty, ascertain*). Dictionary skills can be used to identify such words. This type of activity is valuable because it helps make spelling more predictable by relating it to meaning.

An approach that specifically capitalizes on linking spelling with meaning is the morphemic approach. In this approach, children are taught to apply knowledge of sub-units of meaning within a word. The smallest unit of meaning is termed a 'morpheme', and the written equivalent of a morpheme is known as a 'morphograph'. For example, the word *throw* contains only one morpheme, but *throwing* contains two. The word *unhappiness* (un-happ[y]-ness) contains three morphemes. The latter example also illustrates the use of a rule (changing y to i) when combining certain morphemes. When using a morphemic approach, these rules need to be taught.

Perhaps the best-known programme using a morphemic approach is *Spelling through Morphographs* (Dixon & Englemann, 2006). The materials are appropriate for students from Year 4 upwards and can be used with adults. In 140 lessons, the students learn all the key morphographs and the basic rules of the spelling system. *Spelling through Morphographs* has proved particularly valuable for able students with specific learning difficulties.

In general, teaching basic morphological principles through word study has proved helpful for improving spelling and for raising children's interest in words (Apel *et al.*, 2013; Devonshire & Fluck, 2010; Goodwin *et al.*, 2012; Wolter & Dilworth, 2014). Word study is particularly valuable to those exhibiting specific language disorders and learning difficulties (Wolter & Green, 2013). Students learning English as a second language can also benefit from this approach as part of vocabulary development (Diaz, 2010).

All the above strategies for teaching spelling should be regarded as complementary, not mutually exclusive. It has been shown that, used together in appropriate ways, these strategies can help students with even the most serious spelling disabilities (Narang & Gupta, 2014; What Works Clearinghouse, 2014).

Spelling rules

Some experts advocate teaching spelling rules to students as a key part of any spelling programme; but students with learning difficulties find most rules too obscure to be of help when they are faced with a particular word to spell. In many cases, rather than drilling complex rules, it is easier to help students spell the specific words they need for their immediate writing and to teach them strategies to use when learning and checking new words.

Rules may be of some value for older students, and for students of above average intelligence (Kemper *et al.*, 2012), particularly if incorporated into a morphemic approach such as *Spelling through Morphographs*. These intelligent students can often understand the rule or principle fully and can apply it appropriately. But even with these students, the rules should be simple and have few exceptions (e.g. 'i' before 'e' except after 'c'; words ending with 'e', drop the 'e' when adding an ending that begins with a vowel – *hope, hoping*; words ending in a single vowel, double the consonant before adding an ending that begins with a vowel – *stop, stopped, stopping*).

Activities such as Word Sorts (see below) can be used to help students discover some rules and principles for themselves. This process is much more effective than any attempt at rote memorizing a taught rule.

Dictation

Although the regular use of dictation has fallen out of favour in many schools, it is sometimes suggested that dictation develops listening skills and concentration, and at the same time gives students experience of spelling words in context. Dictation still enjoys an accepted place in teaching English as a second or additional language. When dictation is used, the material should first be presented for children to study *before* it is dictated. In this way, there is an opportunity to clarify meaning and to point out any difficult words.

Another approach encourages proofreading and self-correction. An unseen passage at an appropriate level of difficulty is dictated for students to write. They are then given a period of time to check and alter any words that they think are incorrect, perhaps using a different colour pen. The teacher then checks the work and can observe two aspects of the student's performance. First, it is useful to look at the words the child has been able to self-correct (or at least knows to be wrong). Second, the teacher can record words that were in fact wrong but were not noticed by the student. If these are basic words that should be known by the student, activities can be devised that will help the student master them.

Spelling lists

It is known that rote learning of words from a standard all-purpose list does not generally result in any transfer of spelling skill to everyday writing. The limitation of formal lists is that they usually fail to supply a particular word at the time when the student needs to use it for writing or proofreading. In addition, having one common word list for all students in the class ignores the fact that children are at different stages of spelling development and therefore have different learning needs. For this reason, teachers remain unsure when and how to use spelling lists, if at all.

There is a place for judicious use of spelling lists if they are tailored to students' needs. From the point of view of the weakest spellers, the most useful list will be one compiled according to personal writing needs and common errors. A copy of this list can be kept in the back of the student's exercise book or folder, and used when he or she is writing a rough draft or proofreading a final draft of a piece of work. Other lists might contain words grouped by visual, phonemic or morphemic similarity (word families). The value of lists comprising word families is that they represent yet another way of helping students establish awareness of common orthographic units. This awareness will help a student take a more rational approach to tackling an unfamiliar word – for example, by *using analogy* to move from the known to the unknown. The decision to use such lists with an individual student or group of students must be made in the light of their specific learning needs.

Another useful list will be of new vocabulary that is introduced during the study of each new classroom topic in any subject area. This applies to secondary schools as well as primary schools. Students may not need to learn all the words on such a list, but they can refer to it when writing. 'Word Walls' represent an excellent method of ensuring that words children need in their daily writing are readily to hand. Words are written in blackboard-size writing on poster sheets on the classroom wall so that children can locate and use them as necessary. Vocabulary is added regularly to the Word Wall as each new topic is studied.

Developing strategic spellers

Students have become truly independent in spelling when they can look at an unfamiliar word and select the most appropriate strategy for learning that word. For example, they need to be able to look at a word and decide for themselves whether it is phonemically irregular or regular. For an irregular word, they may need to apply the Look-Cover-Write-Check strategy, coupled perhaps with repeated writing of the word. If the word is phonemically regular, they need to recognize that they can spell it easily from its component sounds. When students can operate at this level, the shift is from rote learning to an emphasis on approaching words rationally.

This level of independence does not come easily to all students. Many individuals need to be taught how to learn new material. Some students, if left to their own devices, fail to develop any systematic approach. They may just look at the word. They may recite the spelling alphabetically. They may copy letter-by-letter rather than writing the whole word. They may use no particular strategy at all, believing that learning to spell the word is beyond them. Any serious attempt to help children with spelling difficulties must involve determining *how* they set about learning a word or group of words. Where a student has no systematic approach, it is essential that he or she be taught one.

Cognitive and metacognitive approaches to spelling are designed to teach students specific self-regulatory strategies to use when learning new words or checking spelling at the proofreading stage of writing (Westwood, 2014). For example, they are taught to ask themselves:

- How many syllables do I hear in this word?
- Do I have the right number of syllables in what I have written?
- Do I know any other words that sound like this word?
- Does this word look correct? I'll try it again.
- Does this look better?

As with all examples of strategy training described in this book, the teacher's role is to model effective strategies, to 'think aloud' and to demonstrate ways of going about the task of spelling, checking and self-correcting. Most effective teachers of spelling help children to develop a variety of spelling strategies and also draw their attention to spelling patterns by analogy with other known words.

Remedial strategies

In addition to the general teaching activities described above, several specific approaches have been developed to help struggling spellers. Most of these approaches involve intensive one-to-one instruction.

Simultaneous Oral Spelling

Simultaneous Oral Spelling (SOS) was first developed by Gillingham and Stillman (1960). It has been applied very successfully for remediation of spelling problems in individual tutorial settings and is appropriate for any age level beyond beginner. The approach involves five steps:

- teacher selects the target word and pronounces it clearly;
- student pronounces the word clearly while looking at it very carefully;
- student says each syllable in the word, or breaks a single-syllable word into onset and rime;
- student *names* the letters in the word twice;
- without reference to the model, the student writes the word while naming each letter.

Note that the letter *name* is used, not its common sound. This makes the method particularly appropriate for older students, who may be embarrassed by 'sounding out' words.

Repeated writing

The practice of having a student correct an error by writing the correct version of the word several times is believed by some teachers to serve no useful purpose. They consider that it is a purely mechanical performance that can be carried out without conscious effort on the part of the learner, and that words practised in this way are not remembered.

It is true that if the student is thinking of other things or is distracted by noise or activity while carrying out the repeated writing, the procedure is of little or no value. *However,* repeated writing of a target word can be very helpful indeed if (i) the learner has every intention of trying to remedy an error and (ii) if he or she is attending fully to the task. Writing is one way in which kinaesthetic images of words can be more firmly established. Only a few words (usually *no more than three*) should be practised in any one session.

Old Way/New Way method

Lyndon (1989) identified the psychological construct of 'proactive inhibition' as a possible reason for the failure of many conventional remedial methods to help a student 'unlearn' incorrect responses, such as habitual errors in spelling. Proactive inhibition (or proactive interference) is the term used to describe the situation where previously stored information interferes with one's ability to remember new information or to acquire a new response. What the individual already knows, even erroneous information, is protected from change.

Lyndon's approach, called 'Old Way/New Way', uses the student's error as the starting point for change. A memory of the old way of spelling of the word is used to activate later an awareness of the new (correct) way of spelling the word. The following steps and procedures are used in 'Old Way/New Way':

- student writes the word in the usual (incorrect) form;
- teacher and student agree to call this the 'old way' of spelling that word;
- teacher shows student a 'new way' (correct way) of spelling the word;
- attention is drawn to the similarities and differences between the old and the new forms;
- student writes word again in the old way;
- student writes word in the new way, and points out the differences;
- repeat five such writings of old way, new way and statement of differences;

- write the word the new way six times, using different colour pens or in different styles; older students may be asked to write six different sentences using the word in its 'new' form;
- revise the word or words taught after a two-week interval;
- if necessary, repeat this procedure every two weeks until the new response is firmly established.

Word Sorts

Students are provided with word cards containing the words to be studied and compared. The words might be *sock, black, truck, lock, rack, luck, trick, track, block, lick, sack, stick, flock, flick, suck*. The students are asked, 'What is the same about these words?' The response might be that the words all end with /ck/. The words might now be categorized in other ways by sorting the cards into groups (for example, words ending in /ock/; words ending in /ack/). At a more advanced level, Word Sorts can involve words that are grouped according to the meaning–spelling connection, as discussed above under the morphemic approach – for example, *played, playfully, replay, player, playground, horseplay*.

Word Sorts represents a valuable investigative and active approach to help children discriminate among orthographic features within and across words. Comparing and contrasting words in this way helps older students (including adults) discover basic some spelling rules.

Programming for individual students

When planning an individualized programme in spelling, the following points should be kept in mind:

- analyse some samples of the students' written work and use appropriate spelling tests to discover their existing skill levels and areas of weakness;
- set some clear objectives for teaching and learning – discuss these with the student;
- collect a list of words frequently needed by the students to whom you are giving special help, and use this list for regular review and assessment;
- in secondary schools, obtain vocabulary lists for word study from specific subject areas – for example, *ingredients, temperature, chisel, theory, science, hydrochloric, equation, gymnasium*;
- within each tutorial session, students must work on specific words misspelled in free writing lessons as well as on more general word lists or word families;
- when making a correction to a word, the student should rewrite the whole word, not merely erase the incorrect letters;
- repetition and overlearning are important, so use a range of games, word puzzles and computer tasks to reinforce the spelling of important words;
- games and activities must be closely matched to the objectives of the intervention programme;
- daily attention will be needed for the least able spellers, with weekly revision and regular testing for maintenance;
- requiring students to spell words aloud without writing them down is of very little value for learning, because the visual appearance of the word as it is being written provides important feedback to the speller;

- a neat, careful style of handwriting that can be executed swiftly and easily is an important factor associated with good spelling.

Online resources

- Some simple tips for explicit teaching of spelling can be found at: http://rwd1. needham.k12.ma.us/program_dev/documents/curriculumbinder/spelling/explicitinst strategies.pdf.
- A paper titled *Research-based Tutoring of English Spelling* by Rosevita Warda is available online at: www.learnthat.org/pages/view/whitepaperenglishspelling.html.
- Activities for word study and spelling can be found on the Literacy Connections website at: www.literacyconnections.com/WordsTheirWay.php.
- More useful hints are available at: www.primary-education-oasis.com/how-to-teach-spelling.html.
- A useful online interactive programme using LCWC principles and suitable for the early primary school years and for older poor spellers: www.ictgames.com/lcwc. html.
- Beating Dyslexia.com website has an item titled *Spelling help: How to spell any word.* www.beatingdyslexia.com/spelling-help.html.
- A PowerPoint presentation on spelling strategies can be located at: www.slideshare. net/joannerudling/slideshare-spelling-strategies-memory-tricks.

Further reading

Benjamin, A. & Crow, J.T. (2010). *Vocabulary at the centre.* Larchmont, NY: Eye on Education.

Ganske, K. (2013). *Word journeys: Assessment-guided phonics, spelling and vocabulary instruction* (2nd edn). New York: Guilford Press.

Morris, H. & Smith, S. (2011). *33 ways to help with spelling.* London: Fulton.

Raymond, S. (2014). *Spelling rules, riddles and remedies.* London: Routledge.

Stone, L. (2014). *Spelling for life.* London: Routledge.

Templeton, S.R., Bear, D.R., Invernizzi, M.A., Johnston, F.R., Flanigan, K., Townsend, D.R., Helman, L. & Hayes, L. (2015). *Vocabulary their way: Word study with middle and secondary students* (2nd edn). Boston, MA: Pearson.

Westwood, P. (2014). *Teaching spelling: Exploring commonsense strategies and best practices.* London: Routledge.

Chapter 13

Numeracy and basic mathematical skills

In this age of information and communication technology, the importance of numeracy has increased – not decreased – and it now ranks alongside literacy in importance (Tout, 2014a). Literacy and numeracy are recognized as vital foundations for children's overall achievement in school; and both areas of competence are also crucial for transition into further education, training and employment.

Many children, with and without disabilities or learning difficulties find mathematics a difficult subject to learn, and failure rates are often quite high in this important subject. In the UK, standards in mathematics have tended to decline in recent years. Data published by the Organisation for Economic Co-operation and Development indicate that 16–24-year-olds in Britain are ranked close to the bottom for numeracy in the league tables for developed countries (OECD, 2013). Concern has also been expressed in Australia, where it is stated that: 'A significant number of 15-year-old Australians do not have access to sufficient numeracy and mathematical skills to be able to cope equitably with life in the 21st century and are, potentially, disempowered' (Tout, 2014b, p. 1). Results from the *Program for International Student Assessment* (PISA) show that Australian students' performance in mathematics has declined in absolute terms since 2003. The same picture has emerged in the US, where Peterson *et al.* (2011, p. 4) remark: 'When more than two-thirds of students fail to reach a proficiency bar [in mathematics], it raises serious questions: Are U.S. schools failing to teach their students adequately?' In this chapter, some of the possible reasons for this situation are suggested, and appropriate teaching methods to help overcome learning difficulties are described.

Contemporary perspectives on mathematics teaching

As a result of reforms in mathematics education that started in many countries in the late 1980s, schools were encouraged to implement a *constructivist* teaching approach, often referred to as activity-based or problem-based mathematics. When using this approach, teachers are expected to create learning situations that provide opportunities for students to *discover* mathematical relationships and number skills by engaging in problem solving, rather than through explicit instruction and practice in arithmetic skills. A constructivist approach places emphasis on helping students move beyond rote learning of routine calculations to a much deeper understanding of mathematical concepts. It has been said that too often in the past, students have been expected to remember algorithms, rules and facts without grasping the underpinning concepts or making real sense of mathematics.

In theory at least, constructivist approaches appear to have much to offer; but the notion that mathematics can be learned entirely by immersion in problem solving has been challenged (e.g. Doabler *et al.*, 2014; Latterell, 2005; Westwood, 2011). There is little doubt that most students make much better progress in mathematics when they are directly taught, particularly in the early stages (Bellert, 2009; Doabler *et al.*, 2014; Graham & Pegg, 2010; Swain *et al.*, 2010). Direct teaching is certainly essential for students with learning difficulties (Doabler & Fien, 2013; Farkota, 2013).

Critics suggest that constructivist theory makes unreasonable assumptions concerning children's ability to discover, conceptualize and remember mathematical relationships for themselves. There is also major concern over the reduced attention given in activity-based mathematics to developing children's fluency and automaticity in fundamental number skills. Evidence seems to indicate that not all children make good progress under an approach that relies on the acquisition of vital skills through incidental learning; and this is certainly not the approach used to teach mathematics in countries that currently rank highest in student achievement. In these countries (e.g. Japan, Korea, Singapore, Hong Kong, Finland), teachers have not moved wholeheartedly into student–centred activity methods (Andrews, 2013). Their most effective teachers provide systematic instruction in mathematics in such a way that genuine understanding accompanies mastery of number skills and problem solving. The emerging perspective is that effective teaching and learning in mathematics requires a careful combination of investigative activities and teacher-directed explicit instruction and practice (Doabler *et al.*, 2014; Slavin *et al.*, 2009). This important principle is now officially recognized in the US, where it is clearly stated that procedural skills and mathematical understanding are equally important and should be the focus of attention (CCSS, 2014b).

It is clear that to be an effective teacher of mathematics one has to have good subject knowledge and a sound understanding of how best to teach concepts and skills to students. Typically, mathematics lessons in countries with the highest achievements reveal that teachers maintain close control over curriculum and learning process. However, they ensure that all students are engaged fully during interactive whole–class lessons that involve thinking mathematically, problem solving and applying new skills. The emphasis is certainly upon constructing meaning, but not through the medium of unstructured activities. The teacher takes an active role in imparting relevant information, teaching specific skills and stimulating students' thinking. In countries such as Britain and Australia, the recommendation is for daily intensive lessons using an interactive whole–class teaching approach (see Chapter 15). Lessons are conducted at a reasonably fast pace and incorporate a high degree of student participation and practice.

Whole-class teaching and group work

The use of a direct teaching approach does not mean that teachers should abandon the use of group work and collaborative learning in the classroom. Lessons with a well-planned component of group activities can facilitate students' interest, motivation and achievement. Group tasks that involve students in discussion, sharing of ideas and peer assistance appear to help them negotiate a better understanding of key concepts and processes (James & Steimle, 2014). These lessons also allow for some degree of differentiation of curriculum content according to students' ability levels. Use can also be made of computer-assisted learning, statistical spreadsheets and Internet searches as part of group and pair assignments in the mathematics lesson.

Learning difficulties in mathematics

It has been found that children's achievements in numeracy are affected by many influences, including gender, socio-economic background, family characteristics and quality of instruction (Daraganova & Ainley, 2012; OECD, 2013). Gender, in particular, appears to be a very strong influence on achievement in mathematics, with boys tending to outperform girls in most countries (de Bartoli, 2014). This is likely to be a culturally determined phenomenon, rather than a genetic difference between males and females in aptitude for mathematics.

While many students find mathematics a difficult subject to study, it is suggested that between 5 and 7 per cent of students have very significant problems in learning even the most basic mathematical concepts and skills. A few of these students may have a specific learning disability related to mathematics (*dyscalculia*) (Williams, 2013); but most have simply encountered difficulty in the early stages and have lost confidence in their own ability. They quickly develop a poor attitude towards the subject, and this destroys their motivation.

Some students exhibit high levels of anxiety in situations where they are expected to demonstrate competence in applying mathematical skills (Pearn, 2014). 'Math anxiety' is now a well-recognized phenomenon, and has attracted research interest over the years. There is evidence from neuroscience (using functional magnetic resonance imaging) that a high anxiety level is not only emotionally draining but also seriously impedes learning processes in the brain (Buckley, 2013; Buckley & Reid, 2013). A major challenge for teachers of mathematics is to present the subject in such a way that students *enjoy it*, and experience success rather than failure (Pappano, 2014). One way of stimulating the interest of low achievers is to avoid making textbook exercises the only material used in lessons. While practice exercises are important for students with learning difficulties, greater use should also be made of first-hand experiences and topics outside the classroom that can involve calculating (e.g. sports events in the news, television data, transport, newspaper reports, the natural environment, the built environment) (NCETM, 2014). Clear links should be also made explicit between mathematics and other school subjects such as geography, science, history and PE (cross-curricular maths).

Based on information summarized by several writers (e.g. Farkota, 2005; Toland *et al.*, 2014), major factors associated with learning difficulty in mathematics include:

- insufficient or inappropriate instruction;
- students falling behind and becoming discouraged;
- little or no differentiation of learning activities or assessment tasks to match students' differing abilities;
- too little structuring of activity-based tasks, with students failing to learn anything from them;
- teacher's use of complex language when explaining mathematical relationships or when posing questions;
- students' weak reading skills contributing significantly to difficulties in mathematics;
- too little teaching time devoted to ensuring students achieve conceptual understanding.

In terms of specific weakness in basic number skills:

- abstract symbols may have been introduced too early in the absence of concrete materials or real-life examples;

- students' grasp of simple relationships in numbers to 20 may not be fully developed before larger numbers involving complications of place-value are introduced;
- students may misunderstand the relationship between rational and whole numbers (e.g., thinking that ¼ is larger than ½ because 4 is larger than 2);
- too little time spent in developing automaticity with number facts, leading later to slowness and inaccuracy in calculations.

It is important that any student with learning difficulties in mathematics should be identified early and given appropriate support. Several early intervention programmes for children with learning difficulties exist, and focus on such fundamental skills as counting, numeral recognition, grouping, solving simple addition and subtraction problems, and place value.

It is clear that mastery of basic number facts and development of sound 'number sense' must be given high priority in any intervention programme (Gobel et al., 2014; Powell & Fuchs, 2012; Sood & Jitendra, 2013). A report issued by the Australian Council for Educational Research (ACER, 2013) reviewed almost a dozen such programmes and recommended that a specific intervention should only be adopted if the content aligns with learning objectives of the mathematics curriculum, and if it has credible evidence of effectiveness. Examples of useful programmes include *Mathematics Recovery* (Wright, 2003), *QuickSmart Numeracy* (Bellert, 2009) and *Numeracy Recovery* (Dowker, 2005). *Mathematics Recovery* involves 30 minutes a day of individualized assessment-based instruction for low-achieving children aged 6–7 years. *QuickSmart Numeracy* targets students in the middle school years and is effective in building up fluency and confidence in basic arithmetic and in strategy use. *Numeracy Recovery* targets 6–7-year-old children and involves 30 minutes instruction per week over a period of approximately 30 weeks.

Assisting students who struggle with mathematics

Several educators have identified important components in programmes that are effective for helping weaker students improve in mathematics (Dawes, 2014; Maccini & Gagnon, 2006; Zheng et al., 2013). Their suggestions apply equally to both primary and secondary school students in need of Tier 3 assistance. The most important components include:

- providing individualized help that is matched to the child's current level of understanding;
- giving additional practice to achieve mastery of basic facts and procedures;
- sequencing curriculum material carefully and controlling task difficulty;
- providing extended time to complete assignments and to work on problems;
- encouraging the use of concrete materials where necessary and helpful;
- reading word-problems aloud to the student to avoid any reading difficulty;
- permitting use of a calculator;
- using cue cards to display the steps to take in carrying out a specific process;
- facilitating individual support by using a classroom assistant or by adopting peer tutoring.

What should be taught?

In recent years, the content of mathematics courses in the UK and Australia has generally been delineated in the guidelines that accompany national curricula (ACARA, 2014b; DfE, 2014d). In both countries there has been a tendency to introduce more demanding mathematics content in recent years, in order to raise students' standards of proficiency. The importance of fluency in mental arithmetic and in using efficient written methods for basic calculations is being stressed. In the US, the *Common Core State Standards* now describe the 'varieties of expertise' (skills and concepts) that must be mastered from kindergarten through high school mathematics (CCSS, 2014b).

Traditionally, students with learning problems were usually placed in the lowest-ability group and given a watered-down version of the mainstream curriculum. Sometimes (particularly in special schools and secondary special classes) a 'functional' curriculum would be developed with a title such as 'real-life math'. The belief was that students with special needs required an alternative to the mainstream programme, with the content significantly reduced in both quantity and complexity. However, it is generally agreed now that all students should be helped to engage with the core mathematics curriculum. It is argued that students with special needs, like all other students, are entitled to engage in interesting and relevant mathematics. For this reason, coverage of the mathematics course in mainstream schools should be reduced as little as possible for lower-ability students, in order to maintain sufficient interest and challenge. It is also acknowledged, however, that some adjustment may need to be made to the curriculum content and objectives for children with intellectual disabilities.

Alongside practice in basic skills, relevant mathematical elements and problems should also be integrated into other school subjects and related to real-life situations. A reality-based approach is more likely to enhance students' motivation and involvement, and also increases the likelihood that mathematical skills will generalize to other situations and uses (Dawes, 2014).

A diagnostic approach

There are many reasons why students experience difficulty mastering the facts, concepts and operations in arithmetic and applying these successfully to problem solving. The first steps towards intervention should be to: (i) ascertain what the student can already do in this area of the curriculum; (ii) locate any specific gaps in knowledge which may exist; (iii) determine precisely what he or she needs to be taught next; and (iv) gain an impression of the student's attitude toward mathematics and level of confidence.

Assessment at an appropriate level will help a teacher answer the questions, 'What can the student do independently in mathematics?' and 'What can he or she do if given a little help and guidance (scaffolding)?' Examining the student's workbooks and conducting some informal testing will determine the level at which he or she is functioning. Children's errors tend to reveal much about their level of knowledge and skill and can thus serve a useful diagnostic function for programming. The nature of a student's errors can help identify gaps in understanding, faulty procedural knowledge, or misconceptions. Appropriate follow-up testing can then be used. For this purpose teachers can construct their own informal 'mathematical skills inventory' containing items covering key concepts, knowledge and skills presented in earlier years, together with essential material from the current year. Observing a student working through the items can help a teacher discover what the student can do, and how confident he or she is. Gaps in existing knowledge can be identified, and this will assist in ordering priorities for instruction.

There are three levels at which diagnostic work in mathematics can be conducted – concrete, semi-concrete and abstract. At the *concrete level*, the student may be able to solve a problem or complete a process correctly if allowed to manipulate objects (e.g. counters). At the *semi-concrete level*, pictorial representation of objects, together with symbols or tally marks will provide sufficient visual information to ensure success. At the *abstract level*, a student can work successfully with symbols only. During the diagnostic work with a student, the teacher may move up or down within this continuum from concrete to abstract in an attempt to discover the level at which the student can succeed with each concept.

Assessment should not be confined to the basic arithmetic processes. The main goal in teaching mathematics to students is the development of problem-solving skills, and therefore assessment of a student's current ability in this domain is important. Close investigation of strategies used by a student when solving a problem can be achieved in a *diagnostic interview*. Using a set of appropriate problems as a focus, discussion between teacher and student can reveal much about the student's flexibility in thinking, underlying knowledge, number skills and level of confidence. Teachers may probe for understanding in the following areas when appraising problem-solving abilities:

- detecting what is called for in a problem;
- identifying relevant information;
- selecting correct procedure;
- estimating an approximate answer;
- computing the solution;
- checking the answer.

It may be helpful to keep the following thoughts in mind when investigating a student's functional level. When the student explains or demonstrates how he or she tackles a problem, the teacher can identify the exact point of confusion and can intervene from there. By referring to any items the student fails to solve in a test or during deskwork, consider:

- Why did the student get this item wrong?
- Can he or she carry out the process if allowed to count on fingers, or use a number line or calculator?
- Ask the student to work through an example step by step. Can he or she explain the mathematical process? At what point does the student misunderstand?

Learning at the concrete and semi-concrete levels

Real and structural materials

When working with young or intellectually disabled children it is essential to use real objects to illustrate quantitative relationships. In intervention programmes, and in remedial teaching contexts, real objects can be supplemented by materials such as counters, picture cards, Multibase Arithmetic Blocks (MAB), Cuisenaire Rods and

Unifix. Using structural material of this type provides a bridge between concrete experience and abstract reasoning. It takes learners from experiences at the semi-concrete stage (not the real object but something used to represent it) through to the semi-abstract (use of the first stages of symbolic representation, such as tally marks). Using concrete material appears to help children construct deeper mathematical understanding (Baroody et al., 2009; Dawes, 2014). For example, structural material can be used to illustrate conservation of number, place value, grouping, re-grouping, multiplication and so forth. It can also be used to represent visually the variables and quantities contained within word problems.

Structural material is particularly important for students with learning difficulties and learning disabilities as it helps them understand and store *visual representations* of number relationships. It must be recognized, however, that concrete materials have to be used effectively if students are to form necessary connections between the material and the underlying concepts and processes they are designed to illustrate (Moscardini, 2009). Problems arise if students simply play with the apparatus or if they come to rely on it too much and do not progress to the next level of processing number relationships mentally.

Counting

Counting is perhaps the most fundamental of all early number skills. Developing competence in counting and comparing groups is an important milestone in the early school years (Kolkman et al., 2013). Counting assists with the development of *conservation of number* because it facilitates comparison of groups. Conservation refers to awareness that rearranging a set of objects into a different pattern does not change the number of items in the set.

If a child has not acquired accurate counting of real objects, the skill must be taught by direct instruction. The problem is often that very young students (or older students with intellectual disability) fail to make a correct one-to-one correspondence between the spoken number and each object touched in a sequence. If the physical act of counting a set of objects appears difficult for a student with a physical disability, manual guidance of his or her hands may be needed.

Counting of actual objects will eventually be extended to encompass the 'counting-on' strategy for addition and the 'counting-back' strategy for subtraction, in the absence of real objects. These important strategies will need to be taught directly to some students.

Recognition of numerals

The cardinal value of number symbols should be related to a wide variety of sets of objects. Teachers can make numeral-to-group matching games (for example, the numeral 11 on a card to be matched with 11 birds, 11 kites, 11 cars, 11 dots, 11 tally marks, etc.). Teacher-made lotto cards containing a selection of number symbols (1–10; 1–20; or 25–50, etc.) can also help in developing speed of recognition. When the teacher holds up a card and says the number, the student covers the numeral on the lotto card. At the end of the game, the student must read each number aloud to the teacher as it is uncovered on the card. Later these same lotto cards can be used for basic addition and subtraction facts, the numerals on the cards now representing correct answers to some simple question from the teacher (5 add 4 =...? The number 1 less than 8 is...?). Activities with number cards can also be devised to help students sort and arrange numerals in correct sequence from 1 to 10, 1 to 20, etc.

The writing of numerals should be taught in parallel to the above activities. Correct formation of numerals should be established as thoroughly as correct letter formation in handwriting. This will reduce the incidence of reversals of figures in written recording.

Written recording

There is a danger that some young students or those with moderate learning difficulties will be expected to deal with symbolic number and recording too early. Pictorial recording, tally marks and dot patterns are all acceptable forms of representation for the young or developmentally delayed child. Gradually, the writing of number symbols will accompany picture-type recording and then finally replace it, by which time the cardinal values of the numerals are understood. It is important that written recording should evolve naturally from concrete experiences.

Number facts

Functional knowledge in arithmetic involves two major components: mastery of number facts that can easily be retrieved from memory (up to $9+9$ and 9×9) and a body of knowledge about computational procedures. Both components are required in typical problem-solving situations. For example, number facts (e.g. $5+4=9$; $3\times6=18$) are involved within sub-routines carried out in all computations, and for this reason they need to be recalled with a high degree of automaticity. Number facts only become automatic after a great deal of practice and application. Many students with learning disabilities have difficulty learning and recalling number facts and tables so require extra attention devoted to this key area. Being able to recall number facts easily is important for two main reasons: it makes calculation easier, and it allows time for the deepening of understanding.

Knowing number facts is partly a matter of learning through repetition (constant exposure and practice) and partly a matter of grasping a rule and developing insight (e.g. that zero added to any number does not change it: $3+0=3$, $13+0=13$, etc.; or if $7+3=10$, then $7+4$ must be 'one more than ten', etc.). It is also essential to ensure that young children grasp the interrelationships involving given number combinations (e.g. that 5 is $4+1$, $3+2$, $2+2+1$, $6-1$, etc.) (Jung et al., 2013).

Teaching computational skills

Once young students have evolved their own meaningful forms of recording in the early stages, one must move on to the introduction of conventional forms of vertical and horizontal computation. For example, a student should be able to watch as a 'bundle of ten rods and two extra ones' are added to a set already containing a 'bundle of ten rods and three extra ones' and then write the operation as:

$12+13=25$

or

```
  12
 +13
  25
```

The reverse of this procedure is to show the student a 'number sentence' ($20-13=7$) and ask him or her to demonstrate what this means using some form of concrete materials. MAB blocks are particularly useful for this purpose. Unifix blocks (larger in size) are more appropriate for children with poor manipulative skills.

This stage of development is likely to require careful structuring over a long period of time if students with learning difficulties are not to become confused. The careful grading of examples, combined with adequate amounts of concrete practice at each stage, is crucial for long-term mastery. Clear examples of methods for carrying out written computation in the four processes can be found in Appendix 1 of the guidance document for the National Curriculum in mathematics in the UK (DfE, 2014d).

It has been traditional to teach students verbal self-instructions (scripts) for carrying out the steps in a particular calculation. Verbal cueing is only required during the time a child is first mastering a new algorithm. Once mastered, the algorithmic procedure becomes automatic and verbal cueing is phased out. For example, using the decomposition method for the following subtraction problem, the student would be taught to verbalize the steps in some way similar to the wording below.

```
 5 7 8 1 1
 -1 3 9
   4 4 2
```

The child says:

> 'Start with the units. I can't take 9 from 1 so I must borrow a ten, and write it next to the 1 to make 11.
>
> Cross out the 8 tens and write 7 tens. Now I can take 9 from 11 and write 2 in the answer box.
>
> In the tens column, 7 take away 3, leaves 4 tens.
>
> In the hundreds column, 5 take away 1 leaves 4. Write 4 in the answer space.
>
> My answer is 442.'

A support teacher, tutor or parent who attempts to help a student in this area of school work should liaise closely with the class teacher in order to find out the precise verbal cues that are used in teaching the four processes so that exactly the same words and directions are used in the remedial programme to avoid confusion. The 'scripts' are phased out as soon as the student can perform routine calculations automatically.

With the advent of the constructivist approach, the teaching of these verbal scripts fell into disrepute. It is felt by some experts that these cues inhibit the thinking of the more able students and may prevent them from devising insightful methods of completing a calculation. It is argued that mindlessly following a memorized script may represent nothing more than rote learning. However, without such verbal cues in the early stages lower-ability students are likely to remain totally confused and frustrated.

It is important that students also be taught other strategies for solving addition and subtraction problems, preferably those which will help develop insight into the structure and composition of the numbers involved. For example, if the student is faced with $47 + 17 = ?$, he or she is encouraged to think of this regrouped as a set of $(40 + 7)$ added to a set of $(10 + 7)$. The tens are quickly combined to make 50, and the two 7s make 14. Finally, 14 combined with 50 produces the result 64. Once children have grasped the principle, fewer errors seem to occur with this method than with the traditional vertical addition. This is almost certainly because the approach is meaningful and does help to develop insight into the structure of numbers. The steps can also be easily demonstrated using MAB blocks or similar concrete materials.

With subtraction the procedure may be illustrated thus:

$(53 - 27 = ?)$
53 can be regrouped as $40 + 13$
27 can be regrouped as $20 + 7$
Deal with the tens first: $40 - 20 = 20$
Now the second step: $13 - 7 = 6$
We are left with 26.

Calculators

Clearly, calculators have an important role to play in extending mathematics for older students – more than simply acting as a tool to avoid tedious calculations (Goos, 2012). However, guidelines for the use of calculators in mathematics teaching within the revised National Curriculum in the UK suggest that they should not be introduced formally until upper Key Stage 2 (DfE, 2014d). It is also required that students not be allowed to use calculators during standard tests of mathematical ability in the primary school years. Previously, the use of calculators had been encouraged in mathematics lessons; but a review in 2011 concluded that this had resulted in a decline in students' skills in mental and written calculation. There has now been a swing back to acknowledging that children in the primary years need to develop these fundamental cognitive skills without relying on a calculator.

In the Australian Curriculum, calculators are included under the general description of 'technology' recommended to support graphical, computational and statistical aspects of mathematics lessons. As early as Year 3, the curriculum guidelines state that students should be able to use a calculator to check the solution and reasonableness of an answer. By Year 7 students should be able to investigate problems and calculate with and without digital technologies (ACARA, 2014b). The Common Core State Standards in the US do not provide specific guidance about when students should use a calculator; however, when taking the new tests linked to the Common Core, the use of calculators appears to be delayed until the secondary school.

In terms of students with special needs, a calculator provides a means of temporarily bypassing computational weaknesses. There is a valid argument that time spent drilling mental and mechanical arithmetic is largely wasted if students still cannot remember the steps later when working through a calculation. The use of the calculator as a supplement is defensible in such cases. The instructional time saved can then be devoted to helping students think carefully as they select the operation needed to solve particular problems. However, only as a last resort should a teacher decide to abandon completely the teaching of paper and pencil computational skills.

Developing problem-solving skills and strategies

The whole purpose of mathematics education is to acquire information, skills and strategies that enable an individual to solve problems they may encounter during school time, working life, at home and during leisure. Children need therefore to be taught how and when to use computational skills and problem-solving strategies for authentic purposes. Mathematical problem solving is particularly challenging for children because it involves reading (or careful listening), integration of information, interpretation, selection of appropriate computational processes, and self-checking (Krawec, 2014). From the learner's perspective, solving a problem involves much more than simply applying a pre-taught algorithm. Non-routine problems need to be analysed and explored, and possible procedures must be checked for appropriateness.

Students with learning difficulties commonly display helplessness and confusion when faced with mathematical problems in printed word form. They may begin by having difficulty reading the words, or with comprehending the exact meaning of specific terms. Often they do not really understand what they are being asked to find out, and this compounds their difficulty in selecting a process to use. Their inability and lack of success leads to loss of confidence and undermines self-esteem and motivation. Their most obvious weakness is a total lack of any effective strategy for approaching a mathematical problem. Most students with these difficulties need to be directly taught a range of effective problem-solving and task-approach strategies (Krawec, 2014). The aim is to teach them how to process the information in a problem without a feeling of hopelessness. They need to be able to sift the relevant from the irrelevant information and impose some degree of structure on the problem. From a teacher's point of view, instructing students in problem solving is more difficult than teaching them basic arithmetic processes, and not all teachers are particularly skilled in teaching problem-solving strategies.

It is generally accepted now that there are recognizable and teachable steps through which an individual needs to pass when solving mathematical problems. These steps can be summarized as:

- interpretation of the problem to be solved;
- identification of processes and steps needed;
- translation of the information into an appropriate algorithm (or algorithms);
- careful calculation;
- checking of the result.

It is also recognized that in addition to cognitive skills involved in the five steps there are also significant metacognitive components. These components include the self-monitoring and self-correcting while working through a problem. For example, the student must think:

- What needs to be worked out here? (identify the problem)
- How will I do this? (select or create a strategy)
- Can I picture this problem in my mind? Can I draw it? (visualization)
- Is this working out OK? (self-monitoring)
- How will I check if my solution is correct? (reflection, reasoning, evaluation)
- I need to correct this error and then try again (self-correction)

When teaching a problem-solving strategy the teacher needs to:

- model and demonstrate effective use of the strategy for solving routine and non-routine problems;
- 'think aloud' as various aspects of the problem are analysed and possible procedures for solution identified;
- reflect upon the effectiveness of the procedure and the validity of the result obtained.

A problem-solving strategy might, for example, use a particular mnemonic to aid recall of the procedure. For example, in the mnemonic 'RAVE CCC', the word RAVE can be used to identify the first four possible steps to take:

R = Read the problem carefully.
A = Attend to words that may suggest the process to use (*share, altogether, less than, how many*).
V = Visualize the problem, and perhaps make a sketch, diagram or table.
E = Estimate the possible answer.

The letters CCC suggest what to do next:

C = Choose the numbers to use.
C = Calculate the answer.
C = Check the answer against your estimate.

Once students have been taught a particular strategy they must have an opportunity to apply the strategy themselves under teacher guidance and with feedback. Finally they must be able to use the strategy independently, and generalize its use to other problem contexts. The sequence for teaching problem solving to students with learning difficulties therefore begins with direct teaching, followed by guided practice and ending with independent control.

Since there is evidence that students can be helped to become more proficient at solving problems (Montague & Dietz, 2009), teachers of students with learning difficulties need to devote adequate time to this important aspect of mathematics. Studies have shown that strategy use can be beneficial for students with learning difficulties, provided the steps and processes involved do not place excessive demands on working memory (Lussier *et al.*, 2014). As mentioned above, encouraging these students' use of a calculator will enable teachers to spend more time on exploring problems, rather than restricting them to a diet of mechanical arithmetic. Supplementary use of a calculator need not inhibit the development of students' computational skills; and children who are permitted to use calculators often develop a better attitude towards mathematics.

Additional teaching points to consider when improving the problem-solving abilities of students with learning difficulties include:

- pre-teaching any difficult vocabulary associated with a specific word problem so that comprehension is enhanced;
- providing cues (such as directional arrows) to indicate where to begin calculations and in which direction to proceed;

- linking problems to the students' life experiences;
- providing more examples than usual to establish and strengthen the application of a particular strategy;
- giving children experience in setting their own problems for others to solve;
- stressing the value of self-checking and self-correction;
- using appropriate computer-aided instruction (CAI).

Students with specific talents in mathematics

Mathematics is one area of the curriculum where some gifted students may display a high degree of aptitude. It is all too easy for these students to become bored and frustrated in mathematics lessons where the material is pitched at the average standard for the age group and the pace of progress is slow. Often too much time is devoted to routine problems involving concepts and skills that the student has already mastered (Engel *et al.*, 2013). To meet the special needs of talented mathematicians some form of differentiation is absolutely essential to offer higher levels of challenge, enrichment and application. Such differentiation may be accomplished partly by selecting curriculum content, resource materials and computer software at a level appropriate for the student's higher abilities, and partly by grouping students by ability for mathematics. In both cases, teachers need to have a good depth of subject knowledge to be able to select relevant content to include in such programmes.

Judging by the number of pleas for practical advice appearing in teachers' online chatrooms and websites, many primary school teachers feel inadequately prepared for teaching mathematics to students of very high ability. Without adequate depth of subject knowledge, teachers may simply put together a hotchpotch of cute activities and puzzles that lack real scope, purpose and wider application. What are needed instead are projects that require talented students to use initiative and advance their mathematical skills through investigation, application and problem solving in a meaningful and interesting context.

On the matter of organization, some schools with a sufficient number of students with talents in mathematics have found it valuable to withdraw them for special group work for certain periods each week or to offer extra-curricular activities with a focus on mathematics. This arrangement works well because the students can interact with equally able peers and the teacher can operate a more advanced programme incorporating acceleration, extension and enrichment.

Of course, it must also be noted that a few gifted and talented students, while high achievers in most school subjects, may actually exhibit a specific learning disability in the area of mathematics (*dyscalculia*). The advice on teaching presented in this chapter is applicable to these students. They may also need personal counselling and advice if their disability in mathematics is causing them undue worry or anxiety.

Online resources

- The Common Core State Standards for mathematics in the US can be found at: www.corestandards.org/Math/Practice/.
- The 2014 guidelines for mathematics in the revised National Curriculum in England can be found at: www.gov.uk/government/publications/national-curriculum-in-england-mathematics-programmes-of-study/national-curriculum-in-england-mathematics-programmes-of-study.

- National Centre for Excellence in Teaching Mathematics. (2015). The England-China Mathematics Project: Interim Report. *NCETM Newsletter, January 2015*. Available online at: https://www.ncetm.org.uk/public/files/20660892/Shanghai_teachers_special_report_Nov_2014.pdf.
- Mathematics in the Australian Curriculum can be located at: www.australiancurriculum.edu.au/mathematics/Curriculum/F-10?layout=1.
- General teaching advice can be found in the online publication *Mathematics for children with SEN* at: www.deni.gov.uk/10_maths_for_ch_with_sen.pdf.
- Important considerations when adapting the mathematics curriculum for students with special needs are discussed in an online document from the Board of Studies in New South Wales (2014) at: http://syllabus.bos.nsw.edu.au/mathematics/mathematics-k10/supporting-special-education-students/.
- PowerPoint material on *Teaching the Common Core to students with significant disabilities* (Browder, D., Lee, A. & Wood, L., 2014) can be located online at: www.signetwork.org/file_attachments/304/download.
- The website *About.com: Learning Disabilities* discusses difficulties some students have in mastering basic mathematics. Online at: about.com/od/learningdisabilitybasics/p/ldbasicmath.htm.
- A staff training module on teaching mathematics with gifted students prepared by the Lancashire Grid for Learning can be found at: www.lancsngfl.ac.uk/secondary/math/download/file/PDF/Mathematics%20for%20Gifted%20Pupils.pdf.

Further reading

Chinn, S. (2011). *The trouble with maths*. London: Routledge.

Gaffney, M. & Faragher, R. (Eds). (2014). *Leading improvements in student numeracy*. Melbourne: ACER Press.

Li, Y. & Huang, R. (2012). *How Chinese teach mathematics and improve teaching*. London: Routledge.

Nelson, G. (2014). *Fostering children's number sense in Grades K-2*. Boston, MA: Pearson Educational.

Storygard, J. (2012). *Count me in! K-5*. Thousand Oaks, CA: Corwin Press.

Chapter 14

Differentiating the curriculum and adapting instruction

Meeting students' special educational needs successfully in mainstream classrooms usually requires that subject matter, learning activities, teaching procedures, resource materials and patterns of classroom organization must often be adapted or modified. This strategy of adapting to students' needs and abilities to make classrooms more inclusive is known as *differentiated instruction* – previously it was referred to as 'mixed-ability teaching'. In simple terms, differentiated instruction can be defined as teaching things differently according to certain important differences among learners. In principle, effective differentiation means that the educational needs of almost all children with disabilities, learning difficulties, language differences and with gifts and talents can all be met in the regular classroom, and within a common curriculum.

In the UK, official policy guidelines have endorsed a differentiated approach as a necessary component for inclusive education, and as a way of giving almost all learners access to the National Curriculum (DfE, 2013c, 2013d; NCSE, 2011). The Department for Education in England has stated:

> We know that how some pupils access the national curriculum will be different from others. This may mean that their rate of progress is different and will be dependent on adapting teaching approaches to meet their needs but does not mean that they are unable to participate fully. In practice this means ensuring that the national curriculum is taught in ways that enable all pupils to have an equal opportunity to succeed.... [T]eachers must determine the support and teaching interventions their pupils need to participate fully in all parts of the school curriculum.
>
> (TES Connect, 2014)

However, in England it is still possible for schools to 'disapply' the requirements of the National Curriculum for students with special needs if their disability or disorder means that following the curriculum is clearly inappropriate for their needs. These students are now assessed under what are termed the 'P Scales' (DfE, 2014a).

The Australian Curriculum Assessment and Reporting Authority (ACARA, 2013a, 2013b) offers teachers and school principals specific guidance on how the new Australian Curriculum can accommodate the learning needs of almost all students with disabilities and difficulties. These sources basically give advice on *personalizing* students' learning by making any necessary adjustments to teaching methods, resources, learning activities and classroom environments to enhance access. Adjustments include:

- providing alternative representations of teaching materials for curriculum topics (e.g. using multimedia, Braille, fully illustrated texts, simplified texts, captioned videos); this is entirely compatible with the concept of Universal Design for Learning, as discussed later;
- using more direct teaching, more modelling of skills and cognitive strategies, more frequent guided practice, and more support for some students;
- scaffolding students' learning through prompting, feedback and correction;
- varying time allocation for classroom tasks to take account of students' differing rates of responding;
- providing alternative ways for students to demonstrate their learning (e.g. using augmentative and alternative communication systems; oral rather than written assignments);
- improving access (e.g. seating arrangements; wider aisles for wheelchair access; modified furniture; larger writing on the whiteboard);
- organizing flexible groupings of students, and facilitating more peer assistance and peer tutoring;
- providing easy access to equipment, assistive technology and alternative communication systems;
- utilizing additional support personnel such as classroom assistants, parents, volunteer helpers;
- adjusting the timetable to accommodate a disabled student's out-of-classroom therapy or training sessions.

In this chapter, some generic principles and practices for differentiation are discussed, with specific suggestions for adapting curriculum content, resources, teaching approaches and assessment procedures. Some problems associated with differentiation are also highlighted.

Keep it simple

Although effective differentiated instruction has become a yardstick of best practice in inclusive schools, it must be acknowledged that implementing differentiation is never simple. Sustaining a differentiated approach in mixed-ability classes invariably places very heavy demands on teachers' time, knowledge, ingenuity and organizational skills. It is no easy task to teach and manage a class in which many types of activity are occurring simultaneously (Parsons & Vaughn, 2013). Studies have suggested that teachers often claim to use differentiation to a much greater degree than they actually do when observed in practice (William *et al.*, 2014).

From the beginning it is essential to stress the *simplicity principle*. Differentiation does not mean that every single lesson and every topic must be planned and presented through content adjusted to each individual – to attempt to do this is totally unrealistic and largely unnecessary (Glass, 2011). Adaptations and modifications should not be made unless absolutely unavoidable. Whenever possible, a student with special needs should be helped to use mainstream materials and participate in regular learning activities. Adaptations to curriculum are most effective and most easily sustained when they are simple, easy to design and implement, and based on typical assignments and activities. Differentiation should be less about drastically changing the content of the curriculum for some individuals and more about providing alternative pathways and additional support to achieve common goals in learning a particular topic (Dettmer *et al.*, 2013).

Adapting curriculum content

Curriculum content to be studied may be increased or decreased for some students in terms of depth and complexity. The core concepts and skills within a topic are still covered, but at different depths. Key aspects of the curriculum may be reduced to manageable units and presented in smaller steps for students with learning difficulties. Modifying curriculum content usually implies that students with learning difficulties are required to cover less material in the lesson, and the tasks or activities are usually easier to accomplish. In the case of gifted or more able students, the reverse would be true – they might cover more content and in greater depth. For these students, lesson content would be extended and made more challenging.

Several potential problems exist when modifying the curriculum. For example, reducing the complexity and demands of tasks, and setting easier objectives for some students, may sound like very good advice, but watering down the curriculum in this way can have the long-term effect of increasing the achievement gap between students with learning difficulties and other students (Westwood, 2013). By reducing the demands placed on students of lower ability, we may be exaggerating the effect of individual differences and perpetuating inequalities among students. The ideal to be aimed for is that all children experience basically the same curriculum as far as possible, but receive varying amounts and types of support to ensure success.

As stated above, differentiation is most easily implemented where it does not involve drastic changes to the curriculum. Obviously this argument cannot be extended to cover students with moderate to severe intellectual disabilities who are integrated in inclusive classrooms. In such cases, it will be necessary to modify significantly the demands of the mainstream curriculum to match more closely the students' cognitive level and self-help skills. In many countries, this is achieved through the medium of an individual education plan (IEP) and the provision of additional services. The IEP specifies precisely any modifications to curriculum content that are necessary, and may also suggest alternative activities.

Modifying activities and learning tasks

Learning activities are obviously closely associated with curriculum content. The difficulty level of tasks and activities that students are required to undertake in the lesson can be varied. Activities can be completed via different pathways (e.g. using a computer program, discussions with a partner, tackling a textbook exercise, watching a video, playing a game). It is important that activities set for less able students are not simply 'busy work' that is less demanding and less interesting.

One approach to differentiating activities and tasks is termed *tiered assignments*, with work on a topic planned and provided at three or four levels of challenge. Students are first allocated tasks at a level that matches their own ability and rate of learning. They can progress to higher levels over time. Hodgson (2013) presents some excellent examples of tiered reading comprehension and writing activities around the theme of 'motorcycles'. These examples have the great advantage of using a format that does not immediately label the worksheets (in the eyes of the peer group) as being for a specific ability level. Students do not like to be given simplified materials because this practice marks them out as different, and undermines their status in the peer group. Adolescents in particular are acutely sensitive to peer-group reactions and deeply resent being overly treated as if they are lacking in ability.

Teachers can use various ways of grouping students within the class to allow for different tiered activities to take place, under differing amounts of teacher direction. At various times, the classroom can be set up to support individualized projects or for cooperative group-work, and use may be made of learning centres, computer-aided instruction or resource-based learning (see Chapter 15).

Instructional materials

Another area where modifications can be made to improve access to the curriculum is that of instructional resources. The resource materials used within a lesson (texts, worksheets, exercises, whiteboard notes, computer software) may need to be modified, and additional or different equipment may need to be provided for some students (e.g. a calculator with audio output for a student with impaired vision; counting materials in a simple mathematics lesson; a pencil with a thick grip for a student with poor hand coordination). A variety of texts and instructional materials at various levels of complexity and readability should be made available for students to use. Some materials will be designed for use in cooperative learning situations, while other material may be for use for individual assignments. Differentiation through materials is often attempted by providing *graded worksheets*. There may be occasions where graded worksheets are appropriate and helpful, but if used too frequently in class can produce boredom.

Listed below are some suggestions for preparing instructional materials for students with literacy weaknesses. Often these simple adjustments enable a student to access text without the need for further assistance. When preparing print materials (worksheets, assignment cards, study notes, independent learning contracts) teachers might:

- simplify the language – use short sentences, substitute simple words for difficult terms;
- pre-teach any important new vocabulary;
- modify sentence construction to facilitate comprehension – active voice is easier to process than passive voice: *The teacher reads a story*, rather than *A story was read by the teacher*;
- make printed instructions or questions very clear and simple;
- present information in small blocks of text rather than dense paragraphs;
- use bullet points and lists rather than paragraphs;
- improve legibility of print and layout: if necessary, enlarge the size of print;
- highlight important information by using underlining or printing the words in bold type or colour;
- provide clear illustrations or diagrams;
- give cues or prompts where written responses are required from the students – for example, provide the initial letter of the answer, or use dashes to show the number of words required in the answer.

Products from lessons

Often the output from a lesson will be tangible products such as written work, graphics or models; but sometimes the product is another form of evidence of learning, such as an oral report, a performance, a presentation to the group, participation in discussion or the answering of oral questions. Differentiating the products of learning may mean that:

- each student is not expected to produce exactly the same amount or quality of work as every other student;
- a student may be asked to produce work in a different format: for example, an audio recording, a drawing or poster, scrapbook, a multiple-choice exercise rather than a formal essay;
- individual students may negotiate what they will produce and how they will produce it in order to provide evidence of their learning in a particular topic.

The potential danger in setting out from the start to accept less work from some students or of an inferior quality is that this strategy represents a lowering of expectations that can result in a self-fulfilling prophecy. These students produce less and less, and the teacher in turn expects less and less of them. A different perspective suggests that teachers need to help students achieve more, not less, in terms of work output than they would have achieved without support. Differentiation of product should never be seen as offering certain students a soft option. It should never lead to a student consistently managing to avoid tasks he or she does not like to complete.

Homework assignments

Differentiated homework assignments are an important way of meeting the needs of gifted and able students as well as those of students with difficulties. Some students may be given homework that involves additional practice at the same level of difficulty while others may have extension tasks involving more challenging applications, critical thinking and reflection. It is usually helpful to discuss with a student's parents the purposes of homework assignments so that they can give appropriate help and encouragement.

Teaching strategies

When teaching procedures and processes are differentiated some of the following strategies may be used:

- greater use of explicit and direct forms of instruction when introducing new topics; and later with certain groups within the classroom;
- re-teaching some concepts or information to some students using simpler language and more examples;
- the questions asked during a lesson should be pitched at different levels of difficulty for different individuals;
- much closer monitoring of the work of some students throughout the lesson;
- the teacher may use particular tactics to gain and maintain the interest of poorly motivated or distractible students;

- corrective feedback and descriptive praise may be given in more detail or less detail, according to the students' needs;
- the teacher may give more assistance or less assistance to individual students;
- extra practice may be provided for some students, often via differentiated home-work assignments;
- extension work may be set for the most able students, requiring independent study, investigation and application.

There is evidence to suggest that teachers are much better at using modifications to the teaching processes described above than they are at modifying curriculum content (Chan *et al.*, 2002). They appear to find teaching process modifications more natural and much easier to accomplish within their personal teaching style. For example, skilled teachers already provide additional help to students when necessary, by using prompting and cueing and guidance. They differentiate their questioning, and they make greater use of praise, encouragement and rewards during lessons. These are all strategies that can be applied while the teacher is still following a common curriculum with the whole class – and for this reason they are regarded as the most feasible adaptations for teachers to make.

Varying the pace

The rate at which new information is presented and activities are carried out during lessons can be varied. The speed at which students are required to complete tasks, answer questions and produce outputs can be adjusted to individual needs. The nature of learning tasks set for students will be matched to their learning rate and abilities, with some tasks taking longer to complete than others.

Amount of assistance

Teachers can vary the amount of direct help given to individuals during a lesson. They may also encourage peer assistance and collaboration among students. The services of a classroom assistant can also be used. Giving extra individual assistance as and when necessary is one of the relatively easier strategies for teachers to employ to enable a mixed-ability class to study the core curriculum.

Assessment

Assessment refers to any process used to determine how much learning, and what quality of learning, has occurred for each student in the class. Assessment provides an indication of how effective a particular episode of teaching has been. Outcomes from assessment also highlight anything that may need to be taught again, revised or given additional practice time for some students. Petscher, Kershaw, Koon & Foorman (2014, p. 1) have remarked that: 'Monitoring student progress is central to accountability systems in general and is useful for measuring how well students respond to instruction or intervention.'

Descriptions of differentiation usually include reference to modifying assessment pro-cedures for a student with a disability or learning difficulty. This form of differentiation is deemed necessary because these students may have problems demonstrating what they know (or can do) if the assessment method requires them to use language, literacy, numeracy or motor skills they do not possess.

Modifications to assessment processes include such options as:

- simplifying the instructions for tests, or for questions embedded within assessment tasks;
- shortening tests and tasks;
- allowing longer time for some students to complete the work;
- allowing a student with special needs to have some assistance in performing the task (e.g. questions read aloud to the student; student dictating answers to a scribe);
- enabling the student to present the work in a different format (e.g. notes rather than an essay).

Classroom tests are one of the ways in which teachers routinely assess the progress of their students. Students with special needs may require modification to test formats or additional time to complete the test. Some may need a variation in the mode of responding. Standard adaptations for test formats include:

- enlarging the print;
- leaving more space for the student to write the answer;
- using different types of questions (e.g. short answer, multiple-choice, sentence completion, gapped paragraphs, matching items format);
- rewriting instructions in simple language and highlighting key points;
- keeping directions brief and simple;
- providing prompts such as *Begin the problem here. Answer in one sentence only.*

Modifications to test administration procedures include:

- using oral questioning and accepting oral answering;
- using a scribe to write down a student's answers;
- giving short rest breaks during the test without penalty;
- allowing extra time to complete the test;
- avoiding penalties for poor spelling or handwriting;
- allowing a student to use a laptop to undertake the test;
- giving credit for drawings or diagrams if these help to indicate that the student knows the concept or information;
- administering the test in a quiet environment other than the classroom to reduce distractions for some students (e.g. social worker's office, withdrawal room).

Starting points

An appropriate place to begin planning differentiated instruction is by identifying essential core information, concepts or skills associated with the curriculum topic to be taught. All students in the class will be expected to master this core content to the best of their individual abilities. Differentiating the topic then becomes a process of creating different ways that students with difficulties can achieve this goal through engaging in a variety of coherent experiences matched to their abilities. For example, some students may encounter new ideas through reading about them in books; some may need to encounter them through direct experience or via video or role play; others will gain most from discussing the issues or problems with teacher and peers; and some will acquire the concepts most easily through direct teaching. As a general rule, all students in the group will learn best if provided with a variety and combination of activities and pathways.

Planning needs to include consideration of strategies for delivering additional help to certain students during the lesson (e.g. via peer assistance, a learning support assistant or from the teacher). It is also important to consider how students will be grouped, and how the available time will be used most effectively. When planning differentiated objectives for a lesson it is helpful to keep in mind the three stem statements:

- All students will...
- Some students will...
- A few students may...

In other words, *all students* will be expected to master the essential core knowledge and skills, but possibly through engaging in different learning activities. *Some students* will achieve more than this core; and *a few students* may achieve one or two higher-order objectives through extension and enrichment activities.

Accommodations for students with disabilities

Within the domain of inclusive education, the term *accommodation* usually conveys the notion of making sure that students with disabilities can participate fully or partially in the mainstream curriculum. This is achieved, as indicated above, by varying the type of activities or the method of instruction, providing additional human and technical resources, giving extra support, modifying the ways in which the student can respond, or adapting the classroom environment. Many of the modifications and adaptations already described are equally appropriate for students with disabilities. For example, simplifying tasks, re-teaching important concepts and skills frequently, allowing more time for students to complete work, encouraging different outputs from students and facilitating peer assistance are all strategies that reduce or remove barriers to learning. Some students will also need additional support and modified equipment. The specific needs of students with disabilities are usually identified within their individual education plans and the IEP should be seen as the main source of advice for the types of differentiation and adaptation needed by a students.

Technological accommodations often involve the use of assistive devices to help a student communicate or to produce work (e.g. modified keyboard, computer with a visual display and touch screen or with voice synthesizer, Braillers for blind students, enlarged text on computer screen for a student with partial sight, radio-frequency hearing aids for students with impaired hearing). Less sophisticated aids might include communication boards or picture-card systems for students without speech. It is beyond the scope of this book to discuss assistive technology in great detail, but some additional information was provided in Chapter 3 and Chapter 4.

Universal Design for Learning

In recent years, much has been written about the notion of Universal Design for Learning (UDL). The assumption behind UDL is that it should be possible to prepare and present information and skills to students in multiple ways that match their aptitudes and enable them to express themselves and demonstrate their learning. In principle, UDL caters for the needs of all students, ranging from those with difficulties through to those with gifts and talents. Under this principle, it should be possible for students of differing abilities in any classroom to have equal access to the curriculum and to achieve the planned learning objectives by taking different pathways tailored to their abilities and needs (Turnbull *et al.*, 2012).

Gargiulo and Metcalf (2010) state that the three essential features of UDL that must be considered when designing curricula to meet the needs of all learners are: (i) *multiple means of representation* (e.g. print medium, Braille, video, audio, ICT, concrete materials, diagrams, simulations); (ii) *multiple means of engagement* (looking, listening, hands on, participating, discussing, individual, group, independent, collaborative, interacting, peer tutoring); and (iii) *multiple means of expression* (e.g. oral, written, demonstration, creation, illustration, performance). It is also suggested that digital formats and e-learning tend to be flexible enough to incorporate many of these features in ways that can adapt to individual differences among learners. Digital technology can build in many variations in modes of presentation, engagement and response, thus relieving the teacher of the massive burden of designing these alternate pathways in advance for lessons. UDL obviously has much in common with differentiated instruction, in the sense that barriers to learning are reduced by offering multiple pathways to achievement.

Unfortunately, up to this time UDL is a largely unfulfilled ideal: it remains a practice more written about than implemented. However, an increasing number of teachers are experimenting with ways of addressing individual differences and, for example, making more effective use of technology, multi-media study kits, peer tutoring, flexible grouping and tiered assignments. Similarly, designers of e-learning software are becoming increasingly skilled at producing motivating and interactive programs.

Online resources

- Details related to the goal of inclusion for all students in the new National Curriculum in England can be found online at: www.gov.uk/government/uploads/system/uploads/attachment_data/file/335133/PRIMARY_national_curriculum_220714.pdf.
- An article by Noella Piquette titled *What does inclusion and differentiation mean in a classroom?* is available online at: http://albertacouncilexceptionalchild.wordpress.com/2012/04/20/what-does-inclusion-and-differentiation-mean-in-a-classroom/.
- An article titled *Adapting the curriculum to meet the needs of diverse learners* (Susan Bashinski) is available at: http://littleescape.wordpress.com/2012/01/09/adapting-the-curriculum-to-meet-the-needs-of-diverse-learners/.
- Video clips illustrating ways of adapting subjects to address student diversity are available on the Australian Curriculum website at: www.australiancurriculum.edu.au/StudentDiversity/Illustrations-of-personalised-learning.
- Other practical suggestions for addressing student diversity, disability and giftedness in the classroom are provided by ACARA online at: www.australiancurriculum.edu.au/StudentDiversity/Student-diversity-advice.
- An online document titled *Differentiated instruction and implications for UDL implementation* (Tracey Hall, Nicole Strangman and Anne Meyer) can be accessed at: http://

aim.cast.org/learn/historyarchive/backgroundpapers/differentiated_instruction_
udl#.U_4WgxJ0xjo.

Further reading

Breaux, E. & Magee, M.B. (2013). *How the best teachers differentiate instruction.* London: Routledge.

Graham, L., Berman, J. & Bellert, A. (2015). *Sustainable learning: Inclusive practices for 21st century classrooms.* Melbourne: Cambridge University Press.

Heacox, D. (2012). *Differentiating instruction in the regular classroom: How to reach and teach all learners* (2nd edn). Minneapolis, MN: Free Spirit Publishing.

O'Meara, J. (2011). *RTI with differentiated instruction, Grades K-5.* Thousand Oaks, CA: Corwin Press.

Tomlinson, C.A. (2014). *The differentiated classroom: Responding to the needs of all learners* (2nd edn). Alexandria, VA: Association for Supervision and Curriculum Development.

Tomlinson, C.A. & Imbeau, M.B. (2014). *A differentiated approach to the Common Core.* Alexandria, VA: Association for Supervision and Curriculum Development.

Westwood, P. (2013). *Inclusive and adaptive teaching: Meeting the challenge of diversity in the classroom.* London: Routledge.

Chapter 15

Teaching methods for general and specific purposes

Growing concern about declining academic standards in several Western countries, as revealed for example in international and national surveys, has caused a number of experts to question the quality of teaching that occurs in many classrooms. There have been calls to increase the frequency and rigour with which classroom performance of teachers is evaluated, to ensure that the most effective teaching methods are being used. The adequacy of methodology courses for trainee teachers in pre-service teacher education institutions is also being queried, because the methods taught there are often not those that are regarded as 'evidence based' (Alper, 2014; Hammond, 2013; Leko *et al.*, 2012; Moats, 2014; Seidenberg, 2012).

For more than three decades, pre-service teacher education courses in the US, Britain, New Zealand and Australia have tended to advocate teaching approaches that are almost entirely student-centred and based on constructivist learning theory. At the same time, university lecturers in methodology have often presented the view that direct teaching (formal instruction) is old fashioned and to be despised. Remarking on this situation, Seidenberg (2012, p. 10) observed in relation to teaching literacy: 'Prospective teachers are socialized into a set of outdated beliefs about children, learning, and reading. Some of these beliefs are flatly contradicted by systematic research.' Similarly, teacher education has been described as 'ranging from inadequate to appalling' (Keller, 2013). There is therefore an urgent need to present trainee teachers with the research evidence concerning the most effective teaching methods. These methods not only raise achievement standards generally but also reduce failure rates by addressing the needs of students with learning difficulties.

This chapter presents teachers with an overview of teaching methods. The chapter describes approaches ranging from those that are regarded as 'teacher directed' (or *instructive*) to those that are clearly more 'learner oriented' (or *constructive*). The strengths of each method are summarized, with reference to achieving particular types of learning objectives and their suitability for teaching students with learning difficulties or disabilities. But first it is relevant to describe a professional practice from Asia that is gradually being adopted in schools in the West – namely lesson study.

Lesson study as a professional activity

In some parts of the world (e.g. Japan, Singapore) teachers have been encouraged for many years to conduct teacher development sessions where one or more teachers observe and constructively critique a lesson conducted by a colleague. The aim is to identify aspects of the lesson that have worked well, and to collaborate on suggestions for changes that could enhance the lesson even more (Isoda *et al.*, 2007; Kikkawa & Bryer, 2013). The general aim is to make teaching of that subject or topic increasingly more effective.

Lesson study is an important way of improving teaching standards, but the practice is only spreading to Western countries fairly slowly. There are, however, signs that some states in the US are adopting the approach (Cerbin, 2011), and interest has also been aroused in the UK (Dudley, 2012). This could be one step in the right direction to address concerns over teaching standards.

Selecting teaching methods

There is no single method that is superior to all other methods for all purposes. One particular method of teaching cannot possibly be appropriate for all types of learning, or for all ages and abilities of students, so methods must be selected according to their suitability for a given purpose. There are many ways of approaching the complex task of teaching children with special needs. A teacher's decision to select a specific approach for use at a particular time must depend upon the nature of the lesson content to be taught, the learning objectives and the salient characteristics of the students in the group. Learning difficulties may be exacerbated if an inappropriate teaching approach is used.

Current evidence suggests that many problems associated with learning may be directly related to use of inappropriate methods of instruction (Farkota, 2005; Pletka, 2007). For example, informal methods for teaching the beginning stages of reading, writing and mathematics are unlikely to be successful with children who experience learning difficulties – yet in many countries these methods still remain the approach advocated by the education authorities. As indicated in other chapters, classroom research studies have shown that most children make significantly better progress when essential knowledge and skills are directly taught, and when they are given feedback from the teacher as they practice, rather than being expected to discover key concepts and skills through unstructured activity-based lessons (Kroesbergen *et al.*, 2004; Westwood, 2011).

Teacher-directed approaches

Expository teaching

Expository teaching (or *explicit instruction*) is a traditional method for presenting new information directly to learners in a form they can access and understand. Expository methods include demonstrating, lecturing, explaining, narrating, requiring students to read a textbook or manual, showing students an instructional video, or asking students to work through a computer program that presents new information. Expository teaching can be used across the curriculum when introducing a new topic to a class, when clarifying a concept, when providing important new information, when setting out the steps in a new procedure or process, and when consolidating or reviewing content at the end of a lesson or series of lessons.

No teacher would ever use expository teaching as his or her *only* approach; but the ability to teach curriculum content and skills explicitly when necessary should always be part of a teacher's classroom expertise. The most essential skill for a teacher to possess for expository teaching is the ability to explain things simply and clearly. This skill depends partly on the teacher's ability to appreciate a new topic from the perspective of a student learning it for the first time, partly on the ability to organize information into teachable and learnable units, and partly on the ability to express ideas in plain language that can be understood by the learners. It is also vital that the teacher knows how to motivate and involve the students actively within the lesson, and can establish a good working relationship with the students (Hill, 2014).

Expository teaching was once the most common approach used in classrooms around the world for teaching almost all subject matter, but it dropped out of favour with the coming of constructivist learning theories that advocated student-centred activity methods. It is pertinent to note that the countries still using expository teaching as a main approach for academic subjects (e.g. China, Korea and Japan) are also the countries that report the highest student achievement levels (Hollingsworth, 2013). It is fair to assume that this relationship is not a coincidence.

Expository teaching is not 'old fashioned', nor is it simply a 'transmission' approach that attempts to fill students with information. Good expository teaching involves a great deal of interaction with students. The approach can be greatly enhanced by the use of appropriate visual support that increases learner engagement such as interactive whiteboards, on-screen PowerPoint material, pictures, models, well-illustrated textbooks and web-based resources. Good expository teaching can also include elements of exploratory teaching within lessons if teachers use questioning effectively, and if content-related issues that arise during teacher-directed lessons are investigated. Hattie and Yates (2014) have indicated that explicit instruction can play a key role in helping students develop complex cognitive skills.

Although expository and explicit instruction has proved to be of great value to students with learning difficulties, it is important to consider the following points:

- when used as a whole-class method it does not easily take account of individual differences among learners such as their prior knowledge, language background, literacy skills, experience, attention span or motivation;
- if used too frequently, or without adequate active participation by students, expository teaching can lead to boredom and disengagement;
- expository methods usually require learners to have adequate linguistic and study skills – in particular, good listening and vocabulary skills, adequate reading comprehension and functional writing skills – and these prerequisites are often poorly developed in students with learning difficulties;
- students with learning difficulties often lack confidence and assertiveness, so they are unlikely ever to raise issues or ask the teacher questions during the lesson.

It would be rare indeed to find a primary or secondary teacher using expository teaching as their only approach. They realize that almost any lesson at any age level requires active participation and input from the students. During the course of a single lesson a teacher may switch several times between teacher-directed input and student-centred activity. The lesson may commence with explicit instruction and explanation, but then change quickly to student-centred activity with the teacher adopting a more supportive and facilitative role. Then in the final stage of the lesson there is a return to teacher direction in order to consolidate learning and check for understanding. During a single lesson in a classroom, the instructional techniques will generally reflect the skilful integration of appropriate amounts of expository teaching together with student-centred activity.

Interactive whole-class teaching

Interactive whole-class teaching embodies many of the elements of expository teaching but facilitates very high levels of active participation and high response rates from the students. The lesson operates using a two-way process in which the teacher explains, ask questions and challenges students' thinking, but also responds to questions and ideas contributed frequently by the students. The students offer their own suggestions, express their opinions, ask questions of the teacher and each other, explain their thinking or demonstrate their methods. However, interactive whole-class teaching does not simply comprise verbal exchanges between teacher and students. The teacher also makes effective use of instructional media to gain and hold students' attention (Hennessy & Warwick, 2010). And at all times, students are encouraged to ask questions of the teacher and of each other, as one way of becoming more active and autonomous learners (Cifone, 2013).

Teaching strategies often incorporated into interactive whole-class teaching with lower-ability students include *choral responding* (Cartledge *et al.*, 2009) and the use of *response cards* (Munro & Stephenson, 2009). Choral responding simply involves all (or several) students answering a question or repeating information together, rather than the traditional method of asking them to raise a hand and then calling upon one student. When response cards are used, the teacher provides all students in the class with a set of blank cards at the beginning of the session. At certain times during the lesson the teacher asks the students a particular question and each student immediately writes his or her response on the card and holds it up for the teacher to check. Both choral responding and response cards ensure a high rate of active participation by all students.

In Britain, interactive whole-class teaching has been advocated as one way for improving literacy and numeracy standards in primary schools. The approach is seen as much more productive than individual programming or unstructured group work. It is claimed that effective use of interactive whole-class teaching helps to close the learning gap that usually appears between higher achievers and lower achievers when individualized 'work at your own pace' methods are used.

Some points to consider concerning interactive whole-class teaching include:

- the teacher needs to be very skilled in drawing all students into discussion otherwise some students will not participate actively in the lesson;
- some teachers, particularly those who believe strongly in informal methods, appear to find this fast-paced, interactive approach difficult to implement and sustain;
- if the pace of the lesson is too brisk, students with learning difficulties tend to fall behind and opt out.

Direct instruction

Direct instruction is the term applied to all forms of active expository teaching that attempt to convey the curriculum to students in a reasonably structured and systematic manner. Direct instruction is characterized by precise learning objectives, clear demonstrations and explanations, modelling by the teacher, guided practice, corrective feedback and independent practice by the students. Teaching takes place at a brisk pace and learning is assessed regularly. Re-teaching and remediation are provided where necessary. Direct instruction of this type has proved to be very effective indeed in raising achievement levels in basic academic skills for all students, and is particularly beneficial for students with learning difficulties and those with intellectual disability (Mitchell, 2008).

The most highly structured and carefully designed model using direct instruction is associated most closely with the work of Engelmann and others at the University of Oregon (e.g. Engelmann, 1999). This highly teacher-directed form of curriculum delivery, based on behavioural learning principles, is usually referred to using the capitalized form *Direct Instruction* (DI). DI is a system for teaching basic academic skills such as reading, spelling and arithmetic through the provision of carefully sequenced and scripted lessons (Carnine *et al.*, 2006). DI was originally associated with the published programme called DISTAR (*Direct Instructional System for Teaching and Remediation*) for teaching basic skills to disadvantaged and at-risk children in the US, but DI programmes now include materials covering writing, spelling, comprehension, mathematics and problem solving for a much wider age and ability range. Some elements of DI are highly appropriate for teaching students at Tier 3 (intensive remediation) in the Response to Intervention model.

In a typical DI session, young children are taught in small groups based on ability. Usually, they are seated in a semi-circle facing the teacher, who gains and holds their attention and follows the teaching steps clearly set out in the script. The scripted presentation ensures that all steps in the planned teaching sequence are followed, and that all questions and instructions are clear. Lessons are designed so that there is a very high rate of responding by all children in the group. The teacher gives immediate feedback, correction and encouragement. Choral responding by the whole group is used as a strategy for motivating students and maximizing participation.

Since DI is highly effective, one would expect to find the method being widely used for teaching the foundation stages of academic skills; but this is not the case. While DI has enjoyed some popularity in special education settings, it has had rather limited impact in mainstream schools. It appears that mainstream primary and early childhood teachers prefer to use methods that encourage children to learn at their own rate and in their own way. These teachers shy away from methods that appear prescriptive and structured. It is also clear that most teacher education institutions in the past 20 years have tended to omit coverage of DI in their methodology courses; instead, devoting their full attention to methods that are child-centred and guided by constructivist learning theory.

The following points need to be considered when deciding to use DI:

- published DI programmes must be implemented exactly as the designer has prescribed; teachers must not pick and choose certain parts to be used and parts to omit;
- the fact that DI must be implemented on a daily basis, using small group instruction rather than a whole-class teaching can cause problems in scheduling and staffing;
- many teachers, particularly in Britain and Australia, react very negatively towards DI, claiming that it is too highly structured, too rapidly paced and allows no creativity on the part of teachers.

Student-centred approaches

Discovery learning

In discovery learning (DL) the emphasis is on students being active investigators rather than passive recipients of information delivered to them by a teacher, textbook or computer program. Discovery learning draws upon constructivist learning theory. In DL, students construct knowledge about a topic largely through their interactions with materials and by accessing whatever human and other resources they may require. In order to participate successfully in open discovery activities, learners must have adequate inductive reasoning ability to recognize principles or relationships emerging from their observations. In typical discovery situations in mathematics, science or social studies, examples and non-examples of specific concepts are available to the learners, and from these they must 'discover' the corresponding rule or relationship.

The two main forms of discovery learning are 'unstructured' (or 'open') discovery and 'guided' discovery. Unstructured discovery places learners in situations where they are given very little direction from the teacher and must decide for themselves the appropriate way to investigate a given topic or problem. At the end of the process, they must reach their own conclusions and develop conceptual understanding from their observations and data. This unstructured approach (often under the guise of 'problem-based learning') is sometimes used in secondary school science, mathematics and for topics in social studies, but the outcome is not always good, particularly for students with poor literacy skills, weak self-management and difficulties with inductive reasoning (Hattie & Yates, 2014). Often students with learning difficulties do not have a clear idea of what they are expected to do, and do not believe in their own ability to engage successfully with a problem by thinking in an active way. Jacobsen *et al.* (2009) reviewed research on the effectiveness of discovery learning and concluded that some students develop serious misconceptions and can become very confused and frustrated in unstructured discovery activities.

Guided discovery has a much tighter structure, and teachers have found that learning is more successful when skills required in the investigative process are explicitly taught and the students have the prerequisite understandings. The teacher sets clear objectives, provides initial explanation to help students begin the task efficiently, and may offer suggestions for a step-by-step procedure to find the target information or to solve the problem. The approach is also known as 'guided inquiry' when it combines a fair degree of teacher direction to enable the students to achieve the objectives (Torrington, 2013).

The major benefits of DL include the following:

- learners are actively involved in the process of learning and the topics studied are often intrinsically motivating;
- activities used in authentic discovery contexts are usually more meaningful than classroom exercises and textbook study;
- it is claimed (but is by no means certain) that learners are more likely to remember concepts if they discover them;
- DL builds on learners' prior knowledge and experience;
- DL encourages independence in learning because learners acquire new investigative skills that can be applied in many other contexts;
- DL can also foster positive group-working skills.

The following points must be considered when deciding to use DL:

- the approach can be very time-consuming, often taking much longer for concepts to be understood than would occur with direct teaching;
- DL relies on learners having adequate literacy, numeracy and independent study skills;
- students may learn little of value from discovery activities if they lack adequate prior knowledge for interpreting their discoveries accurately;
- 'activity' does not necessarily equate with 'learning' – learners may be actively involved but may still not understand or recognize underlying concepts, rules or principles;
- children with learning problems often have difficulty forming valid opinions, making predictions and drawing conclusions based on evidence;
- poor outcomes occur when teachers are not good at designing and managing discovery learning environments.

Project-based

The project approach has been used in primary and secondary schools for many years. It lends itself easily to curriculum areas such as social studies, environmental education, geography, history, civics, science, mathematics and the languages, enabling students to apply and extend their knowledge. Project work can help students integrate ideas and information from these different subjects. It has also been found that the collaborative activities that are typically involved in project work can enhance the working relationship between students and their teachers (Pieratt, 2011). Information technology can be fully utilized in project work, resulting in students learning both ICT skills and specific content knowledge simultaneously. The extended timeframe usually provided for project work allows students to plan carefully, revise and reflect more deeply upon their learning.

There are many potential benefits from project work:

- it is an inclusive approach in that all learners can participate to the best of their ability;
- projects promote meaningful learning, connecting new information to students' past experience and prior knowledge;
- the learning process involved in gathering data is valued, as well as the product;
- students are responsible for their own learning, thus increasing self-direction;
- undertaking a project encourages decision-making and allows for student choice;
- researching the topic helps develop deeper knowledge of subject matter;
- learners use higher-order thinking and conceptual skills, in addition to acquiring facts;
- information collection, analysis and presentation encourages various modes of communication and representation;
- preparing the project helps students apply and improve basic reading, writing and ICT skills;
- assessment is performance based;
- if undertaken with a partner or in a group, project work can increase team work and cooperative skills.

Important points to consider when using project-based learning include:

- some students lack adequate study skills for researching and collating information;
- how will students with learning difficulties be helped to participate successfully?
- when working on projects, some students may give the impression of productive involvement but may in fact be learning and contributing very little;
- when projects involve the production of posters, models, charts, recordings, photographs and written reports for display, there is a danger that these are actually 'window dressing' that hides a fairly shallow investigation and understanding of the topic;
- when different aspects of a topic are given to different group members to research, there is a danger that individual members never really gain an overall understanding of the whole topic.

Resource-based learning

Resource-based learning (RBL) is closely associated with project work and issues-based or problem-based learning, and is underpinned by constructivist learning principles. RBL is best suited to social studies, history, geography, science and environmental studies, and is potentially adaptable to students' different abilities. In RBL students use books, community publications, reports, online information and other resources to obtain information they must then analyse and critique before organizing it in an appropriate form for presentation. The use of realistic resources and tools in a meaningful context can make the learning more authentic (Herrington et al., 2014).

The main aim of RBL is to foster students' autonomy in learning by providing opportunities for them to work individually or collaboratively while applying relevant study skills to investigate authentic topics. Typically in RBL situations the teacher introduces an issue, topic or problem to be investigated through the use of relevant resources that are made available. The teacher and students together clarify the nature of the task and set goals for inquiry; then students work individually or in groups to carry out the necessary investigation over a series of lessons. In some cases, it may be necessary to pre-teach researching skills such as locating information, extracting relevant data, summarizing, locating websites and taking notes.

Some of the advantages claimed for RBL include:

- the method motivates students and encourages self-directed learning and reflection;
- students learn from their own active and creative processing of information using a range of authentic resources;
- RBL topics can stimulate higher-order thinking (problem solving, reasoning and critical evaluation);
- through the use of print and electronic media, students' independent study skills are strengthened and extended in ways that may easily generalize to other learning contexts;
- RBL can foster enthusiasm for learning and can increase academic engagement time.

Points to consider when using RBL are similar to those suggested for discovery learning, namely:

- RBL generally requires a resource-rich learning environment, including easy access to reference books and computers;
- effective engagement in RBL depends upon the students having adequate literacy, numeracy and independent study skills;
- care must be taken to guard against students using a copy-and-paste approach to recording and collating information, without fully understanding the material;
- students will learn little from RBL if they lack the prior knowledge necessary for interpreting new information;
- RBL demands motivation, initiative and self-management from the students;
- How will students with learning difficulties be helped to participate successfully?

Problem-based, inquiry-based and issues-based learning

These approaches have much in common with project-based and discovery learning. Rightly or wrongly, learning through problem solving is often believed to be a much more effective approach than traditional expository and didactic methods, particularly for older learners. The use of problem-based, inquiry-based or issues-based methods is widely recommended, and is considered particularly useful in programmes for gifted students (Hua *et al.*, 2014). Currently, problem-based learning (PBL) is still not widely used as the main approach in primary and lower secondary schools, but has become very popular in higher education.

In problem- and issues-based learning, students are presented with a real-life situation or issue that requires a solution or a decision leading to action. With older learners, the problems are often intentionally 'messy' (ill-defined) in the sense that not all of the information required for solution is provided in the problem, and there is no clear path or procedure to follow. At the same time as tackling the issue, students will acquire new investigative skills and insights by engaging in the process (Alayont, 2014).

The advantages of this approach are considered to be:

- learning objectives are authentic and can link school learning with the real world;
- the process of tackling problems and identifying, locating and using appropriate resources can be motivating for learners;
- participating in the approach involves the active construction of new knowledge;
- solving problems usually requires the integration of information and skills from different disciplines;
- learning achieved is likely to be retained and can be transferred to other situations;
- the method encourages self-direction in learning and prepares students to think critically and analytically;
- investigating problems or issues usually requires cooperation and teamwork and can thus enhance communication and collaborative skills.

Issues to consider when applying problem-based, inquiry-based and issues-based learning include:

- Is the problem or issue to be studied of genuine interest and significance to the students?
- Does the school have the appropriate resources to support and facilitate students' investigations?

- Do the students have adequate prior subject knowledge to make sense of the topic or content of the problem?
- Do the students possess the prerequisite independent study skills to engage successfully with the problem or issue?
- How can the problem or issue best be presented to arouse interest?
- How much direction and input from the teacher will be required?
- How will students with learning difficulties be helped to participate successfully?

Situated learning

Using authentic tasks and contexts as the medium for teaching information, skills and strategies is also the basis of the approach known as 'situated learning'. Situated teaching and learning take place in a physical and social setting that is functionally identical to where the knowledge and skills will be applied in real life – for example, a workshop, the supermarket, airport, on a bus, in the kitchen (Northern Illinois University, 2014). Within that setting, a range of instructional methods may be used, including direct teaching, practice with feedback, problem solving and enquiry. Situated learning is an attempt to combat criticism that much of the teaching that goes on in schools is artificial because it is not presented in a real-life context, and often learners do not recognize the social and functional value of what they are taught. This fact has always been recognized in special schools – and special schools can perhaps be credited with the original concept of situated learning in the form of reality-based and experiential curricula.

The advantages of situated learning include:

- learning opportunities are provided in real or simulated contexts in which new knowledge or skills can be acquired for immediate use;
- experts or mentors are available to provide learners with support;
- instructional scaffolding and direct coaching are provided as necessary;
- situated learning represents a motivating and active approach to learning;
- students are more likely to become confident and independent thinkers;
- learning is likely to generalize more easily to new contexts;
- collaboration among learners can be encouraged.

Issues to consider when providing situated learning in school contexts include:

- the task of arranging and maintaining frequent real-life learning situations (often off campus) adds considerably to teachers' workload;
- technical expertise is often required for developing or assembling resources;
- some teachers are not confident in teaching in unusual settings and without clear lesson structures;
- class size can be a major obstacle to working off campus.

Computer-based instruction (CBI) and computer-aided learning (CAL)

There are at least a dozen different terms currently in circulation related to the use of computers for educational purposes. In most cases the differences in meaning are almost negligible. For the purposes of this chapter the preferred terms are *computer-based instruction* (CBI) and *computer-aided learning* (CAL).

Computer-based instruction is the broad term applied to all forms of instruction where a computer is used to present curriculum content. Usually the student responds on screen to material with embedded questions or problems. The computer often monitors the learning that takes place as the student works through the material, and may provide corrective feedback. CBI involves the use of pre-designed programmes that embody the basic principles of effective instruction – clear presentation of information, careful sequencing of steps, practice, feedback and application (Hattie & Yates, 2014). These programmes normally contain text, graphics, sound and video and are very effective in gaining and holding students' attention and participation. A CBI programme often provides direct links to other web-based resources. Computer presentations can greatly increase students' access to information and can, for example, provide visualizations of complex or remote situations that would not otherwise be available. CBI can be used as a starting point for studying a new topic independently, or later for extension and application work once a topic has been introduced by other methods.

Computer-aided learning is the term usually applied to the planned use of the computer to supplement or reinforce other forms of teaching. Often CAL programmes provide additional practice exercises or problems, or may present additional examples that enrich the content taught during face-to-face lessons. Corrective feedback to the learner is always a feature of CAL, and usually the programme does not move ahead until the student has mastered the current content. According to Hattie and Yates (2014) use of a computer to supplement traditional teaching produces stronger results than using computer-based instruction as a total alternative.

CAL has proved useful for students with learning difficulties and disabilities, and they frequently display a positive attitude towards using the computer. In the case of students with behaviour problems or with ADHD, working at a computer can improve on-task engagement. Students with learning difficulties usually require more time and direction than others in the early stages in order to develop confidence and competence in basic computer skills (Schwonke *et al.*, 2013; Smith *et al.*, 2013).

The use of CBI and CAL in the classroom has increased very rapidly in the past decade (Armstrong, 2014). But it should also be noted that while the overall impact of CBI and CAL on students' academic achievement is positive, the effect size is only around 0.3–0.4 (a modest effect) (Karich *et al.*, 2014). The main advantages of the approaches are most often seen in terms of students' increased motivation and self-esteem.

CBI and CAI have the following benefits:

- mode of presentation ensures that learners make active, self-initiated responses and are in charge of the learning situation;
- software can be matched to students' ability level and rate of learning, and is therefore one way of differentiating instruction;
- learners usually gain immediate knowledge of results after every response, so reinforcement and corrective feedback can be provided immediately;
- students move towards greater independence and self-regulation in learning;
- CBI and CAL provide a private method of making errors and self-correcting;
- learners can engage in extra practice and overlearning to master basic skills;
- most (but not all) students enjoy working at a computer more than using textbooks and print resources;

- students can extend their computer competencies (now regarded as essential life skills);
- teaching subjects such as science, social studies, mathematics, environmental education and the arts can be enhanced by documentary or simulation programs and by giving access to Internet resources.

Issues to consider in relation to CBI or CAL:

- students with literacy problems may have difficulty comprehending verbal information on the screen;
- some students lack prerequisite computer skills;
- there may be a shortage of computers in the school, or computers are only available in a computer lab at limited times each week;
- technical failures occur resulting in lost time and frustration;
- a few students actually prefer group interactions with peers and teacher, rather than using technology.

E-learning

The term e-learning covers all forms of online and web-based teaching and learning that occur through the electronic medium of information and communication technology (ICT). To some extent, CBI and CAL approaches are also included under the general category of 'e-learning'.

E-teaching can be delivered not only through conventional computer apps, but also via web-based learning resources accessible through the Internet, and by using hand-held devices (Rodriguez *et al.*, 2014). These and many other forms of technology and media can enrich the quality of educational programmes, and can greatly enhance students' motivation and participation (Borup *et al.*, 2013; Cumming & Strnadova, 2012; Naslund & Gardelli, 2013). However, e-learning and the effective use of technology in general still relies entirely on a teacher's pedagogical skills to determine how, when and where to integrate it effectively into the curriculum (Hattie & Yates, 2014; Murcia, 2014). The term *blended teaching* is often used to describe contexts in which face-to-face instruction is combined with use of web-based and resource-based study (Safar & Alkhezzi, 2013).

E-learning is being incorporated increasingly into the education of students with special needs (Carnahan & Fulton, 2013; Smith *et al.*, 2013). Combining e-learning and CAL with other forms of teaching has proved to be an effective approach with students with a variety of special needs (vision impairment, ADHD, intellectual disability, autism, dyslexia) (Cumming & Strnadova, 2012; Freire *et al.*, 2010; Izzo *et al.*, 2009; Schwonke *et al.*, 2013).

The current desire to move away from the traditional model of teaching to a more technology and e-based approach can be seen, for example, in the notion of the 'flipped classroom' (Douch, 2014). 'Flipped' in this context means a reversal of the conventional sequence where the teacher first presents new information through a formal lesson, and then students work on related class exercises and homework. In the flipped classroom each new curriculum topic is not introduced first by the teacher; instead the students study the topic by themselves at home, or with a partner in a designated room at school using books, e-learning resources and video lessons. Back in the classroom the students then use the knowledge they have gained to engage in work that requires them to apply what they know. The teacher monitors their work and acts as tutor when students require help or direction. The amount of help given depends on the individual student's ability and rate of progress. The teacher's role is to consolidate concepts and skills the students have acquired, regularly assess their progress and provide feedback. The approach has been suggested as particularly appropriate for academically gifted learners (Siegle, 2014).

Over the past decade the concepts of a 'cyber school' and 'virtual classroom' have also been introduced (Carnahan & Fulton, 2013; Dean, 2014; Warden *et al.*, 2013). This concept involves a learning situation where teaching interactions take place at distance and online, without the need for students' physical attendance in a classroom. This occurs through online presentation sessions, online feedback, and real time interaction between students and teacher – for example through chatroom messages, emails, discussion and questioning (Schwartzman, 2013). The initial programmed sessions from the teacher can embody multimedia presentations that cover the essential topic content. Online sessions can also be timetabled to enable students to communicate and work together on certain topics. At the moment, however, typical web-based e-teaching is not well geared to the needs of students with significant learning difficulties (Carnahan & Fulton, 2013).

Online resources

- A slide presentation on the value of lesson study for teachers is available at: www. slideshare.net/terri.science/lesson-study-science-pd-1.
- A paper discussing interactive whole-class teaching of mathematics from the National Foundation for Educational Research [UK] can be found online at: www. nfer.ac.uk/nfer/PRE_PDF_Files/02_28_05.pdf.
- The Special Education Resources for General Educators (SERGE) website provides basic information on selecting methods for SEN students, together with links to sources on related issues: http://serge.ccsso.org/question_2_1.html.
- Information on problem-based learning can be found at: www.studygs.net/pbl. htm.
- Comments on the effectiveness of Direct Instruction (DI) can be located at: www. jefflindsay.com/EducData.shtml.
- The theory underpinning discovery learning is explained at: www.learningtheories. com/discovery-learning-bruner.html.
- A helpful explanation of CBI and CAL can be located online at: www.studynet2. herts.ac.uk/ptl/common/LTDU.nsf/Teaching+Documents/04739C2AEC9B471B 8025729F00330361/$FILE/whatiscal.pdf.
- An overview of the advantages and disadvantages of e-learning can be found at: www.dso.iastate.edu/asc/academic/elearner/advantage.html.

Further reading

Archer, A.L. & Hughes, C.A. (2010). *Explicit instruction: Effective and efficient teaching*. New York: Guilford Press.

Bartalo, D.B. (2012). *Closing the teaching gap*. Thousand Oaks, CA: Corwin Press.

Burden, J. & Byrd, D.M. (2013) *Methods for effective teaching* (6th edn). Boston, MA: Pearson.

Coe, R., Aloisi, C., Higgins, S. & Major, L.E. (2014). *What makes great teaching? Review of the underpinning research*. London: The Sutton Trust.

Freeman, C., O'Malley, K. & Eveleigh, F. (2014). *Australian teachers and the learning environment*. Melbourne: Australian Council for Educational Research.

Masters, G. (2015). Essential teaching practices: Do they exist? *Teacher Magazine*, January Issue 2015. Melbourne: Australian Council for Educational Research.

International Association for the Evaluation of Educational Achievement. (2014). *Preparing for life in a digital age*. New York: Springer International.

Kauchak, D. & Eggen, P. (2012) *Learning and teaching: Research-based methods* (6th edn). Boston, MA: Pearson.

Knight, J. (2013). *High impact instruction*. Thousand Oaks, CA: Corwin Press.

Rice, K. (2012). *Making the move to K-12 online teaching: Research-based strategies and practices*. Boston, MA: Pearson.

References

Aasen, G. & Naerland, T. (2014). Enhancing activity by means of tactile symbols. *Journal of Intellectual Disabilities, 18,* 1: 61–75.

Abar, B. & Loken, E. (2010). Self-regulated learning and self-directed study in a pre-college sample. *Learning and Individual Differences, 20,* 1: 25–29.

Abrams, F. (2010). *Learning to fail: How society lets young people down.* London: Routledge.

ACARA (Australian Curriculum Assessment and Reporting Authority). (2013a). *Student diversity and the Australian Curriculum.* Sydney: ACARA.

ACARA (Australian Curriculum Assessment and Reporting Authority). (2013b). *Personalised learning.* Online teacher guidance materials, accessed 15 December 2014 at: www.australian-curriculum.edu.au/StudentDiversity/Students-with-disability-personalised-learning.

ACARA (Australian Curriculum Assessment and Reporting Authority). (2014a). *Review of the Australian Curriculum.* Sydney: ACARA.

ACARA (Australian Curriculum Assessment and Reporting Authority). (2014b). *Australian Curriculum: Mathematics.* Sydney: ACARA.

ACER (Australian Council for Educational Research). (2013). *Literacy and numeracy intervention in the early years: A report to the NSW Ministerial Advisory Group on Literacy and Numeracy.* Melbourne: ACER.

Adani, A., Eskay, M. & Onu, V. (2012). Effects of self-instruction strategy on the achievement in algebra of students with learning difficulty in mathematics. *US-China Education Review, A12:* 1006–1021.

Adetoro, N. (2012). Alternative format preferences among secondary school visually impaired students in Nigeria. *Journal of Librarianship and Information Sciences, 44,* 2: 90–96.

Alayont, F. (2014). Using problem-based pre-class activities to prepare students for in-class learning. *Primus, 24,* 2: 138–148.

Alberto, P.A. & Troutman, A.C. (2012). *Applied behavior analysis for teachers* (9th edn). Upper Saddle River, NJ: Pearson-Merrill.

Alderson, E. (2014). *Supporting people with intellectual disability to express appropriate sexual behaviour.* Perth: People First Programme.

Allen, K.E. & Cowdrey, G.E. (2014). *The exceptional child: Inclusion in early childhood education* (8th edn). Clifton Park, NY: Wadsworth-Cengage.

Allington, R.L. (2012). *What really matters for struggling readers?* (3rd edn). New York: Pearson.

Alper, S.L. (2014). First steps to education reform. *The Education Digest, 79,* 5: 47–51.

Alter, C. & Vlasak, E. (2014). Back to school meets Positive Behavioural Interventions and Supports (PBIS). *The Exceptional Parent,* May 2014 issue (n.p.).

Amato, S., Hong, S. & Rosenblum, L.P. (2013). The abacus: Instruction by teachers of students with visual impairments. *Journal of Visual Impairment and Blindness, 107,* 4: 262–272.

Andrews, P. (2013). Finnish mathematics teaching from a reform perspective: A video-based case study. *Comparative Education Review, 57,* 2: 189–211.

AngloInfo. (2014). *Special needs education in Australia.* Accessed 15 December 2014 at: http://australia.angloinfo.com/family/schooling-education/special-needs/.

APA (American Psychiatric Association). (2013). *Diagnostic and statistical manual of mental disorders* (5th edn) (*DSM-5*). Arlington, VA: American Psychiatric Association.

Apel, K., Brimo, D., Diehm, E. & Apel, L. (2013). Morphological Awareness Intervention with kindergartners and first- and second-grade students from low socioeconomic status homes: A feasibility study. *Language, Speech and Hearing Services in Schools, 44,* 2: 161–173.

Armstrong, A. (2014). Technology in the classroom: It's not a matter of 'if,' but when and how. *The Education Digest, 79,* 5: 39–43.

Ashcroft, W., Argiro, S. & Keohane, J. (2010). *Success strategies for teaching kids with autism.* Waco, TX: Prufrock Press.

Assouline, S.G., Nicpon, M.F. & Whiteman, C. (2010). Cognitive and psychosocial characteristics of gifted students with written language disability. *Gifted Child Quarterly, 54,* 2: 102–115.

ATL (Association of Teachers and Lecturers). (2014). *Disruptive behaviour in schools and colleges rises, alongside increase in children with behavioural and mental health problems.* Accessed 29 August 2014 at: www.atl.org.uk/media-office/media-archive/.

Ayres, K.M., Douglas, K.H., Lowrey, K.A. & Sievers, C. (2011). 'I can identify Saturn but I can't brush my teeth': What happens when the curricular focus for students with severe disabilities shifts. *Education and Training in Autism and Developmental Disabilities, 46,* 1: 11–21.

Azano, A. (2013). The CLEAR Curriculum Model. In C.M. Callahan & H.L. Hertberg-Davis (Eds), *Foundations of gifted education* (pp. 301–314). New York: Routledge.

Badge, K. (2013). Relationship Development Intervention: Information on current Australian websites. *Special Education Perspectives, 22,* 1: 29–34.

Baecher, L., Farnsworth, T. & Ediger, A. (2014). The challenge of planning language objectives in content-based ESL instruction. *Language Teaching Research, 18,* 1: 118–136.

Bardin, J.A. & Lewis, S. (2008). A survey of the academic engagement of students with visual impairments in general education classes. *Journal of Visual Impairment and Blindness, 102,* 8: 472–479.

Baroody, A., Eiland, M. & Thompson, B. (2009). Fostering at-risk preschoolers' number sense. *Early Education and Development, 20,* 1: 80–128.

Barth, A., Roberts, G., Vaughn, S., Fletcher, J. & Stuebing, K. (2013). Effects of a response-based, tiered framework for intervening with struggling readers in middle school. *Reading Research Quarterly, 48,* 3: 237–254.

Bates, J. & Munday, S. (2005). *Able, gifted and talented.* London: Continuum.

Bayat, N. (2014). The effect of the process writing approach on writing success and anxiety. *Educational Sciences: Theory and Practice, 14,* 3: 1133–1141.

Beal-Alvarez, J.S. & Huston, S.G. (2014). Emerging evidence for instructional practice: Repeated viewings of sign language models. *Communication Disorders Quarterly, 35,* 2: 93–102.

Beane, A.L. (2008). *Protect your child from bullying.* San Francisco, CA: Jossey-Bass.

Bellert, A. (2009). Narrowing the gap: A report on the *QuickSmart* mathematics intervention. *Australian Journal of Learning Difficulties, 14,* 2: 171–183.

Bender, W.N. (2007). *Learning disabilities: Characteristics, identification and teaching strategies* (6th edn). Boston, MA: Pearson-Allyn & Bacon.

Bennett, K.D. (2013). Improving vocational skills of students with disabilities: Applications of covert audio coaching. *Teaching Exceptional Children, 46,* 2: 60–68.

Berninger, V.W., Lee, Y.-L., Abbott, R.D. & Breznitz, Z. (2013). Teaching children with dyslexia to spell in a reading-writers' workshop. *Annals of Dyslexia, 63,* 1: 1–24.

Best, S.J., Heller, K.W. & Bigge, J.L. (2010). *Teaching individuals with physical or multiple disabilities* (6th edn). Upper Saddle River, NJ: Pearson-Merrill.

Betts, G. (1985). *The Autonomous Learner Model for the gifted and talented.* Greeley, CO: ALPS Publishing.

Birsh, J.R. (2011). *Multisensory teaching of basic language skills* (3rd edn). Baltimore, NJ: Brookes.

Bissex, G. (1980). *GYNS AT WRK: A child learns to write and read.* Cambridge, MA: Harvard University Press.

Bixler, J. (2009). *Negotiating literacy learning: Exploring the challenges and achievements of struggling readers.* Boston, MA: Pearson-Allyn & Bacon.

Boden, L.J., Swain-Bradway, J., Sprague, J.R. & Swoszowski, N.C. (2013). Voices from the field: Stakeholder perspectives on PBIS implementation in alternative educational settings. *Education and Treatment of Children, 36,* 3: 31–47.

Booth, S. (2013). When school is hard. *Scholastic Parent and Child, 21,* 3: 20–24.

Borup, J., Graham, C.R. & Davies, R.S. (2013). The nature of adolescent learning interactions in a virtual high school setting. *Journal of Computer Assisted Learning, 29,* 2: 153–167.

Bowen, J. (2010). Visual impairment and its impact on self-esteem. *British Journal of Visual Impairment, 28,* 1: 47–56.

Boyer, S.L., Edmondson, D.R., Artis, A.B. & Fleming, D. (2014). Self-directed learning: A tool for lifelong learning. *Journal of Marketing Education, 36,* 1: 20–32.

Brissiaud, R. & Sander, E. (2010). Arithmetic word problem solving: A situation strategy first framework. *Developmental Science, 13,* 1: 92–107.

Bromley, K. (2013). Using smartphones to supplement classroom reading. *Reading Teacher, 66,* 4: 340–344.

Browder, D., Ahlgrim-Delzell, L., Spooner, F., Mims, P.J. & Baker, J.N. (2009). Using time delay to teach literacy to students with severe developmental disabilities. *Exceptional Children, 75,* 3: 343–365.

Brown, C.M., Packer, T.L. & Passmore, A. (2013). Adequacy of the regular early education classroom environment for students with visual impairment. *Journal of Special Education, 46,* 4: 223–232.

Brown, G. & Colmar, S. (2009). Historical and current perspectives on the necessary and sufficient components for effective classroom instruction. *Special Education Perspectives, 18,* 1: 47–60.

Brugelmann, H. & Brinkmann, E. (2013). *Combining structure and openness in the initial literacy curriculum: A language experience approach.* Accessed 16 December 2014 at: www.academia.edu/4274824/Combining_structure_and_openness_in_the_initial_literacy_curriculum.

Buckingham, J. (2014). Why Jaydon can't read: A forum on fixing literacy. *Learning Difficulties Australia Bulletin, 46,* 1/2: 14–18.

Buckingham, J., Beaman-Wheldall, R. & Wheldall, K. (2012). A randomised control trial of a MultiLit small group intervention for older low-progress readers. *Effective Education, 4,* 1: 1–26.

Buckley, S. (2013). Deconstructing maths anxiety: Helping students to develop a positive attitude towards learning maths. *ACER Occasional Essay,* issued July 2013, pp. 1–3.

Buckley, S. & Reid, K. (2013). *Learning and fearing mathematics: Insights from psychology and neuroscience.* Paper delivered at ACER Conference 'How the Brain Learns: What lessons are there for teaching?' Melbourne, Victoria, 4–6 August 2013.

Caldwell, P. (2013). *Listening with all our senses.* Hove: Pavilion Publishing.

Carlon, S., Carter, M. & Stephenson, J. (2011). An internet survey of treatments by Australian parents of children with autism spectrum disorders. *Special Education Perspectives, 20,* 1: 40–57.

Carnahan, C. & Fulton, L. (2013). Virtually forgotten: Special education students in cyber schools. *TechTrends: Linking Research and Practice to Improve Learning, 57,* 4: 46–52.

Carnine, D.W., Silbert, J., Kameenui, E.J., Tarver, S.G. & Jongjohann, K. (2006). *Teaching struggling and at-risk readers: A direct instruction approach.* Upper Saddle River, NJ: Pearson-Merrill-Prentice Hall.

Carter, E.W., Brock, M.E. & Trainor, A.A. (2014). Transition assessment and planning for youth with severe intellectual and developmental disabilities. *Journal of Special Education, 47,* 4: 245–255.

Cartledge, G., Gardner, R. & Ford, D.Y. (2009). *Diverse learners with exceptionalities.* Upper Saddle River, NJ: Merrill.

Casey, J.E. (2012). A model to guide the conceptualization, assessment and diagnosis of nonverbal learning disorder. *Canadian Journal of School Psychology, 27,* 1: 35–57.

Cawthorn, S. & Leppo, R. (2013). Assessment accommodations on tests of academic achievement for students who are deaf or hard of hearing: A qualitative meta-analysis of the research literature. *American Annals of the Deaf, 158,* 3: 363–385.

CCSS (Common Core State Standards Initiative: US). (2014a). *English Language Arts Standards.* Accessed 16 December 2014 at: www.corestandards.org/ELA-Literacy/W/introduction/.

CCSS (Common Core State Standards Initiative: US). (2014b). *Core Standards for Mathematical Practice.* Accessed 16 December 2014 at: www.corestandards.org/Math/Practice/.

Cekaite, A. (2009). Collaborative corrections with spelling control: Digital resources and peer assistance. *International Journal of Computer-supported Collaborative Learning, 4,* 3: 319–341.

Cerbin, B. (2011). *Lesson study: Using classroom inquiry to improve teaching and learning in higher education.* Sterling, VA: Stylus Publishing.

Chambers, B., Slavin, R.E., Madden, N., Abrami, P.C., Tucker, B., Chueng, A. & Gifford, R. (2008). Technology infusion in Success for All: Reading outcomes for First Graders. *Elementary School Journal, 109,* 1: 1–15.

Chan, C., Chang, M.L., Westwood, P.S. & Yuen, M.T. (2002). Teaching adaptively: How easy is 'differentiation' in practice? A perspective from Hong Kong. *Asian-Pacific Educational Researcher, 11,* 1: 27–58.

Checker, L.J., Remine, M.D. & Brown, P.M. (2009). Deaf and hearing impaired children in regional and rural areas: Parent views on education services. *Deafness and Education International, 11,* 1: 21–38.

Chien, C.W. (2013). Using Raphael's QAR as differentiated instruction with picture books. *English Teaching Forum, 51,* 3: 20–27.

Chodkiewicz, A.R. & Boyle, C. (2014). Exploring the contribution of attribution retraining to student perceptions and the learning process. *Educational Psychology in Practice, 30,* 1: 78–87.

Christensen-Sandfort, R.J. & Whinney, S.B. (2013). Impact of milieu teaching on communication skills of young children with autism spectrum disorder. *Topics in Early Childhood Special Education, 32,* 4: 211–222.

Cifone, M.V. (2013). Questioning and learning: How do we recognize children's questions? *Curriculum and Teaching Dialogue, 15,* 1: 41–56.

Clark, B. (2012). *Growing up gifted* (8th edn). Upper Saddle River, NJ: Pearson-Merrill-Prentice Hall.

Colangelo, N. & Assouline, S. (2009). Acceleration: Meeting the academic and social needs of students. In T. Balchin, B. Hymer & D.J. Matthews (Eds), *The Routledge international companion to gifted education* (pp. 194–202). London: Routledge.

Colbert, T. (2013). Common allergies in kids. *HealthLine.* Accessed 15 December 2014 at: www.healthline.com/health-slideshow/common-childrens-allergies.

Coleman, L.J. & Cross, T.L. (2014). Is being gifted a social handicap? *Journal for the Education of the Gifted, 37,* 1: 5–17.

Colin, S., Leybaert, J., Ecalle, J. & Magnan, A. (2013). The development of word recognition, sentence comprehension, word spelling, and vocabulary in children with deafness: A longitudinal study. *Research in Developmental Disabilities: A Multidisciplinary Journal, 34,* 5: 1781–1793.

Colmar, S. (2014). A parent-based book reading intervention for disadvantaged children with language difficulties. *Child Language Teaching and Therapy, 30,* 1: 79–90.

Connor, C.M., Alberto, P.A., Compton, D.L. & O'Connor, R.E. (2014). *Improving reading outcomes for students with or at risk for reading disabilities: A synthesis of the contributions from the Institute of Education Sciences Research Centers. National Center for Special Education Research 2014–3000.* (ERIC document ED544759).

Conroy, M., Marchand, T. & Webster, M. (2009). *Motivating primary students to write using Writers' Workshop.* Action Research Project for MA Degree: Saint Xavier University, Chicago, Illinois.

Cooney, K. & Hay, I. (2005). Internet-based literacy development for middle school students with reading difficulties. *Literacy Learning: The Middle Years*, *13*, 1: 36–44.

Cooper, P., Kakos, M. & Jacobs, B. (2013). Best practice models and outcomes in the education of children with social, emotional and behavioural difficulties. *CAISE Review*, 1: 20–39.

Cordewener, K.A., Bosman, A.M. & Verhoeven, L. (2012). Characteristics of early spelling of children with Specific Language Impairment. *Journal of Communication Disorders*, *45*, 3: 212–222.

Cotugno, A.J. (2009). Social competence and social skills training and intervention for children with autism spectrum disorders. *Journal of Autism and Developmental Disorders*, *39*, 9: 1268–1277.

Court, D. & Givon, S. (2007). Group intervention: Improving social skills of adolescents with learning disabilities. In K.L. Freiberg (Ed.), *Educating exceptional children* (17th edn, pp. 63–67). Dubuque, IA: McGraw Hill-Duskin.

Cross, T.L. & Coleman, L.J. (2014). School-based conception of giftedness. *Journal for the Education of the Gifted*, *37*, 1: 94–103.

Crotty, G., Doody, O. & Lyons, R. (2014). Aggressive behaviour and its prevalence within five typologies. *Journal of Intellectual Disabilities*, *18*, 1: 76–89.

Crowe, K. (2012). Hearing loss in children: An overview for educators. *Special Education Perspectives*, *21*, 2: 23–39.

Cullen-Powell, L., Barlow, J. & Bagh, J. (2005). The Self-discovery Programme for children with special educational needs in mainstream primary and secondary schools. *Emotional and Behavioural Difficulties*, *10*, 3: 189–201.

Cumming, T. & Strnadova, I. (2012). The iPad as a pedagogical tool in special education: Promises and possibilities. *Special Education Perspectives*, *21*, 1: 34–46.

Cupples, L., Ching, T.Y.C., Crowe, K., Day, J. & Seeto, M. (2014). Predictors of early reading skill in 5-year-old children with hearing loss who use spoken language. *Reading Research Quarterly*, *49*, 1: 85–104.

Daraganova, G. & Ainley, J. (2012). Children's numeracy skills. In *Growing up in Australia: Longitudinal Study of Australian Children* [Annual Report, pp. 79–89]. Australian Institute of Family Studies, Canberra, Commonwealth of Australia.

Datchuk, S.M. & Kubina, R.M. (2013). A review of teaching sentence-level writing skills to students with writing difficulties and learning disabilities. *Remedial and Special Education*, *34*, 3: 180–192.

Davies, A. (2006). *Teaching THRASS*. Chester: THRASS UK.

Dawes, M. (2014). *Improving low-attaining pupils' calculation ability during KS3*. London: National Center for Excellence in Mathematics Teaching.

DCSF (Department for Children, Schools and Families: UK). (2009). *Special Educational Needs in England: January 2009*. Accessed 18 December 2014 at: www.dcsf.gov.uk/rsgatDB/SFR/s000852/SFR14_2009.pdf.

De Bartoli, L. (2014). Boys, girls and mathematics. *Snapshots* [ACER online magazine], *4*: 1–5.

Dean, M. (2014). *What is a virtual classroom?* Accessed 16 December 2014 at: www.ehow.com/about_5476106_virtual-classroom.html.

Delisle, J.R. (2006). *Parenting gifted kids*. Waco, TX: Prufrock Press.

Dennis, M. (2012). *Attention in spina bifida: Findings from the SANDI Project*. Paper delivered at the Second World Congress on Spina Bifida Research and Care, Las Vegas, 11–14 March 2012.

DeRosier, M.E. (Ed.). (2014). *Social skills assessment through games*. Cary, NC: Interchange Press.

DES (Department of Education and Science: UK). (1978). *Special Educational Needs: Report of the Committee of Enquiry into the Education of Handicapped Children and Young People (The Warnock Report)*. London: HMSO.

Dettmer, P., Knackendoffel, A. & Thurston, L. (2013). *Consultation, collaboration and teamwork for students with special needs* (7th edn). Boston, MA: Pearson.

Devonshire, V. & Fluck, M. (2010). Spelling development: Fine-tuning strategy-use and capitalizing on the connections between words. *Learning and Instruction*, 20: 361–371.

DfE (Department for Education: UK). (2011). *Support and aspiration: A new approach to special educational needs and disability*. London: Department for Education.

DfE (Department for Education: UK). (2012). *Year 1 Phonics screening check: Technical Report*. London: Standards and Testing Agency.

DfE (Department for Education: UK). (2013a). *Children with Special Needs 2013: Statistical Analysis*. London: Department for Education.

DfE (Department for Education: UK). (2013b). *Special Educational Needs (SEN) Code of Practice – 0 to 25 years*. London: Department for Education.

DfE (Department for Education: UK). (2013c). *Including all learners*. Accessed 16 December 2014 at: http://webarchive.nationalarchives.gov.uk/20130903160926/www.education.gov.uk/schools/teachingandlearning/curriculum/b00199686/inclusion/needs.

DfE (Department for Education: UK). (2013d). *The National Curriculum in England*. Accessed 16 December 2014 at: www.gov.uk/government/uploads/system/uploads/attachment_data/file/335133/PRIMARY_national_curriculum_220714.pdf.

DfE (Department for Education: UK). (2014a). *Performance – P Scale – attainment targets for pupils with special educational needs*. London: Government Publications.

DfE (Department for Education: UK). (2014b). *Behaviour and discipline in schools: Advice for head teachers and school staff*. London: Department for Education.

DfE (Department for Education: UK). (2014c). *Phonics products and self-assessment process*. Accessed 18 December 2014 at: www.education.gov.uk/schools/teachingandlearning/phonics/b00198579/phonics-products-and-the-self-assessment-process.

DfE (Department for Education: UK). (2014d) *Statutory guidance for National curriculum in England: Mathematics programmes of study*. Accessed 16 December 2014 at: www.gov.uk/government/publications/national-curriculum-in-england-mathematics-programmes-of-study/national-curriculum-in-england-mathematics-programmes-of-study.

DfES (Department for Education and Skills: UK). (2004). *Removing barriers to achievement*. Annersley: DfES Publications.

DHS (Department of Health Services, State of Victoria). (2014). *Sex education: Young people with intellectual disabilities*. Melbourne: Better Health Channel.

Diaz, I. (2010). *The effect of morphological instruction in improving the spelling, vocabulary, and reading comprehension of high school English language learners (ELLs)*. ProQuest LLC, PhD Dissertation, TUI University. (ERIC Document ED514872).

Dixon, R. & Englemann, S. (2006). *Spelling Through Morphographs*. Desoto, TX: SRA-McGraw Hill.

Doabler, C. & Fien, H. (2013). Explicit mathematics instruction: What teachers can do for teaching students with mathematics difficulties. *Intervention in School and Clinic*, 48, 5: 276–285.

Doabler, C., Nelson, N., Kosty, D., Fien, H., Baker, S., Smolkowski, K. & Clarke, B. (2014). Examining teachers' use of evidence-based practices during core mathematics instruction. *Assessment for Effective Intervention*, 39, 2: 99–111.

Dodd, J.L. & Gorey, M. (2014). AAC intervention as an immersion model. *Communication Disorders Quarterly*, 35, 2: 103–107.

Douch, A. (2014). Teaching methods: Flipped learning. *Teacher Magazine Online*, July issue (n.p.). Melbourne: Australian Council for Educational Research.

Dowker, A. (2005). Early identification and intervention for students with mathematics difficulties. *Journal of Learning Disabilities*, 38, 4: 324–332.

Dowsett, C., Shogren, K.A., Little, T. & Kennedy, W. (2014). Autonomy, psychological empowerment and self-realization: Exploring data on self-determination from NLTS2. *Exceptional Children*, 80, 2: 221–239.

Dudley, P. (2012). Lesson Study development in England: From school networks to national policy. *International Journal for Lesson and Learning Studies*, 1, 1: 85–100.

Duke University Talent Identification Program. (2014). *The Renzulli Learning System.* Accessed 16 December 2014 at: http://tip.duke.edu/node/850.

Dunlop, T. (2013). Why it works: You can't just PBIS someone. *The Education Digest, 79,* 4: 38–40.

Dymond, S.K. & Orelove, P. (2001). What constitutes effective curriculum for students with severe disabilities? *Exceptionality, 9,* 3: 109–122.

Ebbles, S. (2014). Effectiveness of intervention for grammar in school-aged children with primary language impairments: A review of the evidence. *Child Language Teaching and Therapy, 30,* 1: 7–40.

Ehri, L., Dreyer, L., Flugman, B. & Gross, A. (2007). Reading Rescue: An effective tutoring intervention model for first-grade struggling readers. *American Educational Research Journal, 44:* 414–448.

Ehri, L.C. (2014). Orthographic mapping in the acquisition of sight word reading, spelling memory, and vocabulary learning. *Scientific Studies of Reading, 18,* 1: 5–21.

Elliott, J. (2014). The dyslexia debate: Some key myths. *Learning Disabilities Australia Bulletin, 46,* 1–2: 4–6.

Engel, M., Claessen, A. & Finch, M.A. (2013). Teaching children what they already know? The misalignment between mathematics instructional content and students' knowledge in kindergarten. *Educational Evaluation and Policy Analysis, 35,* 2: 157–178.

Engelmann, S. (1999). The benefits of direct instruction: Affirmative action for at-risk students. *Educational Leadership, 57,* 1: 77–79.

Ennis, R.P. & Jolivette, K. (2014). Existing research and future directions for self-regulated strategy development with students with and at risk for emotional and behavioral disorders. *Journal of Special Education, 48,* 1: 32–45.

European Agency for Development of Special Needs Education. (2013). *Complete National Overview: United Kingdom (England).* Accessed 16 December 2014 at: www.european-agency.org/country-information.

Farkota, R. (2005). Basic math problems: The brutal reality! *Learning Difficulties Australia Bulletin, 37,* 3: 10–11.

Farkota, R. (2013). *Evidence based learning in the classroom: Direct instruction at work.* Workshop on direct instruction held at Treacy Conference Centre, Melbourne, 23 March 2013.

Farmer, T. (2011). *Supporting Early Adolescent Learning and Social Success – Project SEAL.* Institute of Education Sciences. Accessed 16 December 2014 at: www.ies.ed.gov/funding/grantsearch/details.asp?ID=1097.

Feuerborn, L. & Chinn, D. (2012). Teacher perceptions of student needs and implications for positive behavior supports. *Behavioral Disorders, 37,* 4: 219–232.

Fielding-Barnsley, R. (2010). Australian pre-service teachers' knowledge of phonemic awareness and phonics in the process of learning to read. *Australian Journal of Learning Difficulties, 15:* 99–110.

Flood, J., Lapp, D. & Fisher, D. (2005). Neurological Impress Method Plus. *Reading Psychology, 26:* 147–160.

Foster, L., McDuffie-Landrum, K., Oh, S. & Azano, A. (2011). *The CLEAR Curriculum: An integration of three gifted models.* Accessed 16 December 2014 at: http://nrcgtuva.org/presentations/CEC2011.pdf.

Fountas, I.C. & Pinnell, G.S. (2013). Guided Reading: The romance and the reality. *Reading Teacher, 66,* 4: 268–284.

Freire, A.P., Linhalis, F., Bianchini, S.L., Fortes, R. & Pimentel, M.C. (2010). Revealing the whiteboard to blind students: An inclusive approach to provide mediation in synchronous E-learning activities. *Computers and Education, 54,* 4: 866–876.

French, L.R. & Shore, B.M. (2009). A reconsideration of the widely held conviction that gifted students prefer to work alone. In T. Balchin, B. Hymer & D.J. Matthews (Eds), *The Routledge international companion to gifted education* (pp. 176–182). London: Routledge.

Frey, J. R., Elliott, S.N. & Kaiser, A.P. (2014). Social skills intervention planning for preschoolers: Using the SSiS-Rating Scales to identify target behaviors valued by parents and teachers. *Assessment for Effective Intervention, 39*, 3: 182–192.

Friend, M. & Bursuck, W.D. (2011). *Including students with special needs: A practical guide for classroom teachers* (6th edn). Upper Saddle River, NJ: Pearson Educational.

Gagné, F. (2009). Talent development as seen through the differentiated model of giftedness and talent. In T. Balchin, B. Hymer & D.J. Matthews (Eds), *The Routledge international companion to gifted education* (pp. 32–41). London: Routledge.

Gargiulo, R.M. (2009). *Special education in contemporary society* (3rd edn). Los Angeles, CA: Sage.

Gargiulo, R.M. & Metcalf, D. (2010). *Teaching in today's inclusive classrooms: A Universal Design for Learning approach*. Belmont, CA: Wadsworth.

Garvik, M., Idsoe, T. & Bru, E. (2014). Effectiveness study of a CBT-based adolescent coping with depression course. *Emotional and Behavioural Difficulties, 19*, 2: 195–209.

Geake, J. (2009). Neural interconnectivity and intellectual creativity: Giftedness, savants and learning styles. In T. Balchin, B. Hymer & D.J. Matthews (Eds), *The Routledge international companion to gifted education* (pp. 10–17). London: Routledge.

Genlott, A.A. & Grönlund, A. (2013). Improving literacy skills through learning reading by writing: The iWTR method presented and tested. *Computers & Education, 67*: 98–104.

Gibson, L. (2009). The effects of a computer-assisted reading program on the word reading fluency and comprehension of at-risk urban 1st Grade students. PhD thesis, Ohio State University. Accessed 16 December 2014 at: http://etd.ohiolink.edu/view.cgi?acc_num=osu1249578049.

Gillingham, A. & Stillman, B. (1960). *Remedial teaching for children with specific disability in reading, spelling and penmanship*. Cambridge, MA: Educators Publishing Service.

Gilman, B. (2008). *Challenging highly gifted learners*. Waco, TX: Prufrock Press.

Gladwell, M. (2008). *Outliers: The story of success*. London: Penguin Books.

Glass, K. (2011). *Differentiated tools, strategies, and assessments for social studies, writing, reading, and science classrooms*. Session presented at the Idaho Statewide Title 1 Conference (April), Boise, ID. Accessed 16 December 2014 at: www.sde.idaho.gov/site/title_one/conference11/pres/Idaho%20DI%202011%20PPt%20Kathy%20Glass.pdf.

Gobel, S.M., Watson, S.E., Lervåg, A. & Hulme, C. (2014). Children's arithmetic development: It is number knowledge, not approximate number sense that counts. *Psychological Science, 25*, 3: 789–798.

Goodwin, A., Lipsky, M. & Ahn, S. (2012). Word Detectives: Using units of meaning to support literacy. *Reading Teacher, 65*, 7: 461–470.

Goos, M. (2012). Digital technologies in the Australian Curriculum: Mathematics – a lost opportunity? In B. Atweh, M. Goos, R. Jorgensen & D. Siemon (Eds), *Engaging the Australian National Curriculum: Mathematics – Perspectives from the field* (pp. 135–152). Online Publication: Mathematics Education Research Group of Australasia.

Gov.UK. (2006). *Education and Inspections Act 2006*. National Archives. Accessed 16 December at: www.legislation.gov.uk/ukpga/2006/40/section/89.

Gov.UK. (2013a). *Children with special needs (SEN)*. Accessed 16 December at: www.gov.uk/children-with-special-educational-needs/overview.

Gov.UK. (2013b). *Persistent pupil absence falls by one third*. Press release accessed 16 December 2014 at: www.gov.uk/government/news/persistent-pupil-absence-falls-by-a-third.

Gov.UK. (2013c). *Evidence Paper: The importance of phonics*. Accessed 16 December 2014 at: www.education.gov.uk/schools/teachingandlearning/pedagogy/a00197709/phonics-screening-year-1.

Gov.UK. (2014a). *Improving the quality of teaching and leadership*. Accessed 16 December at: www.gov.uk/government/policies/improving-the-quality-of-teaching-and-leadership/activity.

Gov.UK. (2014b). *National Curriculum in England: English programmes of study*. Accessed 16

December at: www.gov.uk/government/publications/national-curriculum-in-england-english-programmes-of-study.

Graff, H.J., Evmenova, A.S., Behrmann, M.M., Mastropieri, M.A. & Baker, P.H. (2011). Effects of video adaptations on comprehension of students with intellectual and developmental disabilities. *Journal of Special Education Technology, 26*, 2: 39–55.

Graham, L. & Pegg, J. (2010). Hard data to support the effectiveness of QuickSmart numeracy. *Learning Difficulties Australia Bulletin, 42*, 1: 11–13.

Graham, S. (2008). *The power of word processing for the student writer.* Wisconsin Rapids, WI: Renaissance Learning.

Grant, M. (2014). *The effects of a systematic synthetic phonics programme on reading, writing and spelling: Longitudinal study from Reception to Year 2.* Accessed 16 December at: www.rrf.org.uk/pdf/Grant%20Follow-Up%20Studies%20-%20May%202014.pdf.

Grennan, S. & Kilham, C. (2011). Using social scripts and visual cues to initiate play in a preschooler with autism. *Special Education Perspectives, 20*, 1: 8–28.

Gross, M. (2004). *Exceptionally gifted children.* London: RoutledgeFalmer.

Groth-Marnat, G. (2009). *Handbook of psychological assessment* (5th edn). Hoboken, NJ: Wiley.

Gustafson, S., Samuelsson, C., Johansson, E. & Wallmann, J. (2013). How simple is the simple view of reading? *Scandinavian Journal of Educational Research, 57*, 3: 292–308.

Haggerty, N.K., Black, R.S. & Smith, G.J. (2005). Increasing self-managed coping skills through social stories and apron storytelling. *Teaching Exceptional Children, 37*, 4: 40–47.

Hamblet, E.C. (2014). Nine strategies to improve transition planning for students with disabilities. *Teaching Exceptional Children, 46*, 3: 53–63.

Hammond, L. (2013). From the President. *Learning Difficulties Australia Bulletin, 45*, 1: 1–3.

Hampshire, P.K. & Hourcade, J.J. (2014). Teaching play skills to children with autism using visually structured tasks. *Teaching Exceptional Children, 46*, 3: 26–32.

Hansen, B.D. & Wills, H.P. (2014). The effects of goal setting, contingent reward, and instruction on writing skills. *Journal of Applied Behavior Analysis, 47*, 1: 171–175.

Harris, R.S., Wang, Y., Oetting, T.L. & Spychala, H. (2013). The effectiveness of a phonics-based early intervention for deaf and hard of hearing preschool children and its possible impact on reading skills in elementary school: A case study. *American Annals of the Deaf, 158*, 2. 107–121.

Hattie, J. (2012). *Visible learning for teachers.* London: Routledge.

Hattie, J. & Yates, G.C.R. (2014). *Visible learning and the science of how we learn.* London: Routledge.

Heller, K.W. & Bigge, J.L. (2010). Augmentative and alternative communication. In S.J. Best, K.W. Heller & J.L. Bigge (Eds), *Teaching individuals with physical or multiple disabilities* (6th edn). Upper Saddle River, NJ: Pearson-Merrill.

Helms, K.T. & Libertz, D. (2014). When service members with traumatic brain injury become students: Methods to advance learning. *Adult Learning, 25*, 1: 11–19.

Henley, M. (2010). *Classroom management: A proactive approach* (2nd edn). Upper Saddle River, NJ: Merrill.

Hennessy, S. & Warwick, P. (2010). Editorial: Research into teaching with whole class Interactive technologies. *Technology, Pedagogy and Education, 19*, 2: 127–131.

Hepplewhite, D. (2011). *Phonics International.* Newbury: Phonics Intl. Ltd.

Herrington, J., Parker, J. & Boase-Jelinek, D. (2014). Connected authentic learning: Reflection and intentional learning. *Australian Journal of Education, 58*, 1: 23–35.

Hertberg-Davis, H. (2009). Myth 7: Differentiation in the regular classroom is equivalent to gifted programs and is sufficient. *Gifted Child Quarterly, 53*, 4: 251–253.

Hetzroni, O.E. & Shrieber, B. (2004). Word processing as an assistive technology tool for enhancing academic outcomes of students with writing disabilities in the general classroom. *Journal of Learning Disabilities, 37*, 2: 143–154.

Heward, W.L. (2012). *Exceptional children: An introduction to special education* (10th edn). Upper Saddle River, NJ: Pearson.

Hewitt, D. (2012). *Intensive interaction*. London: Sage.

Hill, L.H. (2014). Graduate students' perspectives on effective teaching. *Adult Learning, 25*, 2: 57–65.

Hodgson, J. (2013). Classroom activities. *English Teaching Forum, 51*, 3: 46–52.

Hoff, K.E. & Ervin, R.A. (2013). Extending self-management strategies: The use of a classwide approach. *Psychology in the Schools, 50*, 2: 151–164.

Hollingsworth, H. (2013). Challenges and opportunities for neuroscience: How to explain the connection between socio-cultural practices and cognition? Paper delivered at ACER Conference 'How the Brain Learns: What lessons are there for teaching?' Melbourne, Victoria, 6 August 2013.

Hoover, W.A. & Gough, P.B. (1990). The simple view of reading. *Reading and Writing, 2*: 127–160.

Houghton, C. (2014). Capturing the pupil voice of secondary gifted and talented students who had attended an enrichment programme in their infant school. *Gifted Education International, 30*, 1: 33–46.

House of Commons [UK]. (2014). *Children and Families Act: Section 20.1*. Accessed 16 December 2014 at: www.legislation.gov.uk/ukpga/2014/6/part/3/crossheading/special-educational-needs-etc/enacted.

Houston, T.K. & Stredler-Brown, A. (2012). A model of early intervention for children with hearing loss provided through telepractice. *Volta Review, 112*, 3: 283–297.

Howard, V.F., Williams, B.F. & Lepper, C. (2010). *Very young children with special needs* (4th edn). Boston, MA: Pearson Education.

Howlin, P., Magiati, I. & Charman, T. (2009). Systematic review of early intensive behavioural interventions for children with autism. *American Journal on Intellectual and Developmental Disabilities, 114*, 1: 23–41.

Hua, O., Shore, B.M. & Makarova, E. (2014). Inquiry-based instruction within a community of practice for gifted-ADHD college students. *Gifted Education International, 30*, 1: 74–86.

Hughes, L.A., Banks, P. & Terras, M.M. (2013). Secondary school transition for children with special needs: A literature review. *Support for Learning, 28*, 1: 24–34.

Hutchison, A. & Woodward, L. (2014). A planning cycle for integrating digital technology into literacy instruction. *Reading Teacher, 67*, 6: 455–464.

ICLI (International Communications Learning Institute). (2014). *Sound/Visual Phonics*. Accessed 20 January 2014 at: www.SD-1817.ORG/.

IES (Institute of Education Sciences: US). (2009a). *Assisting students struggling with reading: Response to Intervention (RTI) and multi-tier intervention in the primary grades*. Accessed 16 December at: http://ies.ed.gov/ncee/wwc/pdf/practiceguides/rti_reading_pg_021809.pdf.

IES (Institute of Education Sciences: US). (2009b). *Success for All*. What Works Clearinghouse online document. Accessed 16 December 2014 at: www.eric.ed.gov/ERICDocs/data/ericdocs2sql/content_storage_01/0000019b/80/44/d4/ec.pdf.

IES (Institute of Education Sciences: US). (2013). *What Works Clearinghouse Intervention Report: Reading Recovery*. Accessed 16 December 2014 at: http://ies.ed.gov/ncee/wwc/intervention-Report.aspx?sid=420.

Imray, P. & Hinchcliffe, V. (2012). Not fit for purpose: A call for separate and distinct pedagogies as part of a national framework for those with severe and profound learning difficulties. *Support for Learning, 27*, 4: 150–157.

Inclusive Technology. (2014). *Alternative and augmentative communication (AAC)*. Accessed 16 December 2014 at: www.inclusive.co.uk/articles/alternative-and-augmentative-communication-aac-a280.

Isoda, M., Stephens, M., Ohara, Y. & Miyakawa, T. (Eds). (2007). *Japanese lesson study in mathematics*. Singapore: World Scientific Publishing.

Iversen, S., Tunmer, W. & Chapman, J.W. (2005). The effects of varying group size on the Reading Recovery approach to preventive early intervention. *Journal of Learning Disabilities, 38*, 5: 456–472.

Izzo, M.V., Yurick, A. & McArrell, B. (2009). Supported E-text: Effects of text-to-speech on access and achievement for high school students with disabilities. *Journal of Special Education Technology, 24,* 3: 9–20.

Jacobsen, D.A., Eggen, P. & Kauchak, D. (2009). *Methods for teaching: Promoting student learning in K-12 classrooms* (8th edn). Upper Saddle River, NJ: Pearson-Merrill.

James, J. & Steimle, A. (2014). Problem solvers: Jesse's train. *Teaching Children Mathematics, 20,* 6: 346–349.

Jarrold, C. & Brock, J. (2012). Short-term and working memory in mental retardation. In J.A. Burack, R.M. Hodapp, G. Iarocci & E. Zigler (Eds), *Handbook of intellectual disability and development* (2nd edn, pp. 109–124). Oxford: Oxford University Press.

Jenkins, A., Oakes, W., Booker, B. & Lane, K.L. (2013). Three-tiered models of prevention: Teacher efficacy and burnout. *Education and Treatment of Children, 36,* 4: 95–127.

Jiang, Y.-H. & Associates. (2013). Detection of clinically relevant genetic variants in autism spectrum disorder by whole-genome sequencing. *American Journal of Human Genetics, 93,* 2: 249–263.

Jimenez, B.A. & Kemmery, M. (2013). Building the early numeracy skills of students with moderate intellectual disability. *Education and Training in Autism and Developmental Disabilities, 48,* 4: 479–490.

Jimenez, B.A., Lo, Y. & Saunders, A.F. (2014). The additive effects of scripted lessons plus guided notes on science quiz scores of students with intellectual disability and autism. *Journal of Special Education, 47,* 4: 231–244.

Joseph, L.M. & Konrad, M. (2009). Teaching students with intellectual or developmental disabilities to write: A review of the literature. *Research in Developmental Disabilities: A Multidisciplinary Journal, 30,* 1: 1–19.

Jung, M., Hartman, P. Smith, T. & Wallace, S. (2013). The effectiveness of teaching number relationships in preschool. *International Journal of Instruction, 6,* 1: 165–178.

Jung, S. & Sainato, D.M. (2013).Teaching play skills to young children with autism. *Journal of Intellectual and Developmental Disability, 38,* 1: 74–90.

Karemaker, A., Pitchford, N.J. & O'Malley, C. (2010). Enhanced recognition of written words and enjoyment of reading in struggling beginning readers through Whole-Word Multimedia software. *Computers and Education, 54,* 1: 199–208.

Karich, A.C., Burns, M.K. & Maki, K.E. (2014). Updated meta-analysis of learner control with educational technology. *Review of Educational Research, 84,* 3: 392–410.

Kast, M., Baschera, G., Gross, M., Jancke, L. & Meyer, M. (2011). Computer-based learning of spelling skills in children with and without dyslexia. *Annals of Dyslexia, 61,* 2: 177–200.

Kats-Gold, I. & Priel, B. (2009). Emotion, understanding and social skills among boys at risk of attention deficit hyperactivity disorder. *Psychology in the Schools, 46,* 7: 658–678.

Kauffman, J.M., Landrum, T.J., Mock, D.R., Sayeski, B. & Sayeski, K.L. (2005). Diverse knowledge and skills require a diversity of instructional groups: A position statement. *Remedial and Special Education, 26,* 1: 2–6.

Keller, B. (2013). Teacher training 'from inadequate to appalling'. *The Age* [newspaper; Melbourne]. 8 November 2013.

Kelly, J.R. & Shogren, K.A. (2014). The impact of teaching self-determination skills on on-task and off-task behaviours of students with emotional and behavioral disorders. *Journal of Emotional and Behavioural Disorders, 22,* 1: 27–40.

Kemper, M.J., Verhoeven, L. & Bosman, A.M.T. (2012). Implicit and explicit instruction of spelling rules. *Learning and Individual Differences, 22,* 6: 639–649.

Kettler, T. (2014). Critical thinking skills among elementary school students: Comparing identified gifted and general education student performance. *Gifted Child Quarterly, 58,* 2: 127–136.

Kikkawa, Y. & Bryer, F. (2013). Working together: Insights from a special education unit in Japan. *Special Education Perspectives, 22,* 1: 35–47.

Kirk, S., Gallagher, J., Coleman, M.R. & Anastasiou, N. (2012). *Educating exceptional children* (13th edn). Belmont, CA: Wadsworth-Cengage.

Koegel, R.L. & Koegel, L.K. (2006). *Pivotal response treatments for autism: Communication, social and academic development*. Baltimore, MD: Brookes.

Kolkman, M.E., Kroesbergen, E.H. & Leseman, P.M. (2013). Early numerical development and the role of non-symbolic and symbolic skills. *Learning and Instruction, 25*: 95–103.

Konings, K., Wiers, R., Wiel, M. & Schmidt, H. (2005). Problem-based learning as a valuable educational method for physically disabled teenagers? The discrepancy between theory and practice. *Journal of Developmental and Physical Disabilities, 17*, 2: 107–117.

Konrad, M. & Joseph, L.M. (2014). Cover-Copy-Compare: A method for enhancing evidence-based instruction. *Intervention in School and Clinic, 49*, 4: 203–210.

Krashen, S. (2014). The common core. *Knowledge Quest, 42*, 3: 36–43.

Krawec, J.L. (2014). Problem representation and mathematical problem-solving of students of varying math ability. *Journal of Learning Disabilities, 47*, 2: 103–115.

Kroesbergen, E.H., Van Luit, J.E.H. & Maas, C.J.M. (2004). Effectiveness of constructivist mathematics instruction for low-achieving students in The Netherlands. *Elementary School Journal, 104*, 3: 233–251.

Lam, J. & Tjaden, K. (2013). Intelligibility of clear speech: Effects of instruction. *Journal of Speech, Language and Hearing Research, 56*, 5: 1429–1440.

Landers, E., Alter, P. & Walker, J.N. (2013). Teachers' perceptions of students' challenging behaviour and the impact of teacher demographics. *Education and Treatment of Children, 36*, 4: 51–70.

Landis, D., Umolu, J. & Mancha, S. (2010). The power of Language Experience for cross-cultural reading and writing. *Reading Teacher, 63*, 7: 580–589.

Landis, R.N. & Reschly, A.L. (2013). Reexamining gifted underachievement and dropout through the lens of student engagement. *Journal for the Education of the Gifted, 36*, 2: 220–246.

Landstedt, E. & Persson, S. (2014). Bullying, cyber bullying and mental health in young people. *Scandinavian Journal of Public Health, 42*, 2: 1–7.

Lane, K.L., Kalberg, J.R. & Menzies, H.M. (2013). *Developing school-wide programs to prevent and manage problem behaviors* (e-book). New York: Guilford Press.

Larson, T.A., Normand, M.P., Morley, A.J. & Miller, B.G. (2013). A functional analysis of moderate-to-vigorous physical activity in young children. *Journal of Applied Behavior Analysis, 46*, 1: 199–207.

Latterell, C.M. (2005). *Math wars: A guide for parents and teachers*. Westport, CT: Praeger.

LDA (Learning Disabilities Association of America). (2014). *Defining learning disabilities*. Accessed 16 December 2014 at: http://ldaamerica.org/support/new-to-ld/.

Leko, M.M., Brownell, M.T., Sindelar, P.T. & Murphy, K. (2012). Promoting special education pre-service teachers' expertise. *Focus on Exceptional Children, 44*, 7: 1–16.

Letterland International. (2014). *Letterland Phonics*. Leatherhead, Surrey: Letterland International.

Levin, J. & Nolan, J.F. (2013). *Principles of classroom management* (7th edn). Upper Saddle River, NJ: Pearson Educational.

Levy, S.E. & Hyman, S.L. (2005). Novel treatments for autistic spectrum disorders, *Mental Retardation and Developmental Disabilities Research Reviews, 11*, 2: 131–142.

Liboiron, N. & Soto, G. (2006). Shared story book reading with a student who uses alternative and augmentative communication: A description of scaffolding procedures. *Child Language Teaching and Therapy, 21*, 1: 69–95.

Ling, D. & Ling, A. (1978). *Aural habilitation: The foundations of verbal learning in hearing impaired children*. Washington, DC: Alexander Graham Bell Association.

Lloyd, S. & Lib, S. (2000). *The phonics handbook: Jolly Phonics*. Chigwell: Jolly Learning Ltd.

Lonigan, C.J. & Shanahan, T. (2008). *Developing early literacy: Report of the National Early Literacy Panel (Executive Summary)*. Washington, DC: National Institute for Literacy.

Lovaas, O.I. & Smith, T. (2003). Early and intensive behavioral interventions in autism. In A.E. Kazdin & J.R. Weisz (Eds), *Evidence-based psychotherapies for children and adolescents* (pp. 325–340). New York: Guilford Press.

Ludlow, B. (2014). Intensifying intervention: Kicking it up a notch. *Teaching Exceptional Children*, *46*, 4: 4.

Lussier, C.M., Swanson, H.L. & Orosco, M.J. (2014). The effects of mathematics strategy instruction for children with serious problem-solving difficulties. *Exceptional Children*, *80*, 2: 149–170.

Lyndon, H. (1989). 'I did it my way': An introduction to Old Way–New Way. *Australasian Journal of Special Education*, *13*: 32–37.

Lyons, W. & Thompson, S.A. (2012). Guided Reading in inclusive middle-years classrooms. *Intervention in School and Clinic*, *47*, 3: 158–166.

Maccini, P. & Gagon, J. (2006). Mathematics instructional practices and assessment accommodations made by secondary special and general educators. *Exceptional Children*, *72*: 217–235.

MacConville, R. & Palmer, J. (2007). Including pupils with hearing impairment. In R. MacConville (Ed.), *Looking at inclusion: Listening to the voices of young people* (pp. 99–126). London: Paul Chapman.

MacConville, R. & Rhys-Davies, L. (2007). Including pupils with visual impairment. In R. MacConville (Ed.), *Looking at inclusion: Listening to the voices of young people* (pp. 39–55). London: Paul Chapman.

Malekoff, A. (2014). *Group work with adolescents*. New York: Guilford Press.

Mandelberg, J., Frankel, F., Cunningham, T., Gorospe, C. & Laugeson, E.A. (2014). Long-term outcomes from a parent-assisted social skills intervention for high-functioning children with autism spectrum disorders. *Autism*, *18*, 3: 255–263.

Mannix, D. (2009). *Social skills activities for secondary students with special needs* (2nd edn). San Francisco, CA: Jossey-Bass.

Manti, E., Scholte, E.M. & Van Bercklaer-Onnes, I.A. (2013). Exploration of teaching strategies that stimulate the growth of academic skills of children with ASD in special education schools. *European Journal of Special Needs Education*, *28*, 1: 64–77.

Martin, A.J. (2014). Academic buoyancy and academic outcomes: Towards a further understanding of students with Attention-Deficit/Hyperactivity Disorder (ADHD), students without ADHD, and academic buoyancy itself. *British Journal of Educational Psychology*, *84*, 1: 86–107.

Mason, L.H., Benedek-Wood, E. & Valasa, L. (2009). Teaching low-achieving students to self-regulate persuasive quick write responses. *Journal of Adolescent and Adult Literacy*, *54*, 4: 303–312.

Masters, G. (2014). *Is school reform working?* Research Development Occasional Paper. Melbourne: Australian Council for Educational Research.

Mayfield, K.H., Glenn, I.M. & Vollmer, T.R. (2008). Teaching spelling through prompting and review procedures using computer-based instruction. *Journal of Behavioral Education*, *17*, 3: 303–312.

Mayton, M.R., Carter, S.L., Zhang, J. & Wheeler, J.J. (2014). Intrusiveness of behavioral treatments for children with autism and developmental disabilities: An initial investigation. *Education and Training in Autism and Developmental Disabilities*, *49*, 1: 92–101.

Mazurek, M.O. (2014). Loneliness, friendship and well-being in adults with autism spectrum disorders. *Autism*, *18*, 3: 223–232.

McDonnell, J. (2010). Employment training. In J. McDonnell & M.L. Hardman (Eds), *Successful transition program* (2nd edn, pp. 241–256). Thousand Oaks, CA: Sage.

McDougall, M., Evans, D. & Spandagou, I. (2009). Teaching phonics and sight words to Year 1 through the medium of 'working with words' and 'games'. *Special Education Perspectives*, *18*, 1: 35–46.

McInerney, D.M. & McInerney, V. (2013). *Educational psychology: Constructing learning* (6th edn). Frenchs Forest, NSW: Pearson Australia.

McMaster, K.L., Fuchs, D. & Fuchs, L.S. (2006). Research on peer-assisted learning strategies: The promise and the limitations of peer-mediated instruction. *Reading and Writing Quarterly*, *22*, 1: 5–25.

McMullan, J. & Keeney, S. (2014). A review of the literature on the social and environmental factors which influence children (aged 3–5 years) to be obese or overweight and the accuracy of parental perceptions. *Health Education Journal, 73*, 2: 159–165.

McMurray, S., Drysdale, J. & Jordan, G. (2009). Motor processing difficulties: Guidance for teachers in mainstream classrooms. *Support for Learning, 24*, 3: 119–125.

Meadow, K.P. (2005). Early manual communication in relation to the deaf child's intellectual, social and communicative functioning. *Journal of Deaf Studies and Deaf Education, 10*, 4: 321–329.

Menard, S. & Grotpeter, J. (2014). Evaluation of 'Bully-Proofing Your School' as an elementary school anti-bullying intervention. *Journal of School Violence, 13*, 2: 188–209.

Mercer, C.D., Mercer, A.R. & Pullen, P.C. (2011). *Students with learning disabilities* (8th edn). Upper Saddle River, NJ: Pearson.

Mesibov, G.B., Shea, V. & Schopler, E. (2005). *The TEACCH approach to autism spectrum disorders*. New York: Kluwer Academic-Plenum.

Milburn, T.F., Girolametto, L., Weitzman, E. & Greenberg, J. (2014). Enhancing preschoolers' ability to facilitate conversations during shared book reading. *Journal of Early Childhood Literacy, 14*, 1: 105–140.

Miller, S.P. (2009). *Validated practices for teaching students with diverse needs and abilities* (2nd edn). Upper Saddle River, NJ: Pearson Education.

Mitchell, D. (2008) *What really works in special and inclusive education: Using evidence-based teaching strategies*. London: Routledge.

Moats, L. (2014). What teachers don't know and why they aren't learning it: Addressing the need for content and pedagogy in teacher education. *Australian Journal of Learning Difficulties, 19*, 2: 75–91.

Moats, L.C. (2009). Teaching spelling to students with language and learning disabilities. In G.A. Troia (Ed.), *Instruction and assessment for struggling writers: Evidence-based practices* (pp. 269–289). New York: Guilford Press.

Mockler, K. (2014). Establishing and maintaining high expectations for deaf/blind students using a team approach. *Odyssey: New Directions in Deaf Education, 15*: 50–53.

Moldavsky, M., Pass, S. & Sayal, K. (2014). Primary school teachers' attitudes about children with attention deficit/hyperactivity disorder and the role of pharmacological treatment. *Clinical Child Psychology and Psychiatry, 19*, 2: 202–216.

Montague, M. & Dietz, S. (2009). Evaluating the evidence base for cognitive strategy instruction and mathematical problem solving. *Exceptional Children, 75*, 3: 285–303.

Montgomery, D. (2008). Cohort analysis of writing in Year 7 following two, four and seven years of the National Literacy Strategy. *Support for Learning, 23*, 1: 3–11.

Montgomery, D. (2009). Special educational needs and dual exceptionality. In T. Balchin, B. Hymer & D.J. Matthews (Eds), *The Routledge international companion to gifted education* (pp. 218–225). London: Routledge.

Montgomery, D. (2012). The contribution of handwriting and spelling remediation to overcoming dyslexia. In T. Wydell (Ed.), *Dyslexia: A comprehensive and international approach* (pp. 109–146). Manhattan, NY: InTech.

Mooney, P., Ryan, J.B., Uhing, B.M., Reid, R. & Epstein, M.H. (2005). A review of self-management interventions targeting academic outcomes for students with emotional and behavioral disorders. *Journal of Behavioral Education, 14*, 3: 203–221.

Moore, W. (2014). What's working in the West – and why aren't we there yet? *Learning Difficulties Australia Bulletin, 46*, 1/2: 29–32.

Moscardini, L. (2009). Tools or crutches? Apparatus as a sense-making aid in mathematics teaching with children with moderate learning difficulties. *Support for Learning, 24*, 1: 35–41.

Mueller, V. & Hurtig, R. (2010). Technology-enhanced shared reading with deaf and hard-of-hearing children: the role of a fluent signing narrator. *Journal of Deaf Studies and Deaf Education, 15*, 1: 72–101.

Munro, D.W. & Stephenson, J. (2009). Response cards: An effective strategy for increasing student participation, achievement and on-task behaviour. *Special Education Perspectives, 18,* 1: 16–34.

Murcia, K. (2014). Interactive and multimodal pedagogy: A case study of how teachers and students use interactive whiteboard technology in primary science. *Australian Journal of Education, 58,* 1: 74–88.

Murray, B. & Steinen, M. (2011). Word mapping: How understanding spellings improves spelling power. *Intervention in School and Clinic, 46,* 5: 299–304.

Myhill, D. & Watson, A. (2014). The role of grammar in the writing curriculum: A review of the literature. *Child Language Teaching and Therapy, 30,* 1: 41–62.

NAEYC (National Association for the Education of Young Children). (2014). Framework for Response to Intervention in early childhood: Description and implications. *Communication Disorders Quarterly, 35,* 2: 108–119.

NAGC-CEC (National Association for Gifted Children–Council for Exceptional Children). (2013). *Teacher preparation standards in gifted and talented education.* Washington, DC: National Association for Gifted Children.

Narang, S. & Gupta, R.K. (2014). The effect of multimodal remedial techniques on the spelling ability of learning disabled children. *International Journal of Special Education, 29,* 2: 84–91.

Naslund, R. & Gardelli, A. (2013). 'I know, I can, I will try': Youths and adults with intellectual disabilities in Sweden using information and communication technology in their everyday life. *Disability & Society, 28,* 1: 28–40.

National Association for Gifted Children. (2003). *Ability grouping.* Washington, DC: The Association.

National Dissemination Center for Children with Disabilities [US]. (2010). *Intellectual Disability* (formerly *Mental Retardation*). Accessed 18 December 2014 at: www.nichcy.org/Disabilities/Specific/pages/IntellectualDisability.aspx.

National Foundation for Educational Research. (2013). *Evaluation of the Phonics Screening Check: First interim report.* Windsor: DfE/NFER.

NCES (National Center for Education Statistics: US). (2013). *Students with disabilities.* Washington, DC: Institute for Education Sciences.

NCETM (National Center for Excellence in Teaching of Mathematics: US). (2014). *Learning maths outside the classroom in a special educational needs environment.* Accessed 16 December 2014 at: www.ncetm.org.uk/resources/29014.

NCSE (National Council for Special Education: UK). (2011). *Access to the curriculum for pupils with a variety of special educational needs in mainstream classes.* Trim, Co. Meath: NCSE.

NCSiMERRA (National Centre of Science, Information and Communication Technology, and Mathematics Education for Rural and Regional Australia). (2009). *QuickSmart Intervention Research Program Data 2001–2008: Full Report.* Armidale, NSW: University of New England.

Nelson, N.W. (2013). Syntax development in the school-age years: Implications for assessment and intervention. *Perspectives on Language and Literacy, 39,* 3: 9–17.

New Zealand Government. (2014). *How special education works.* Wellington: Ministry of Education.

Nguyen, L.T.C. & Gu, Y. (2013). Strategy-based instruction: A learner-focused approach to developing learner autonomy. *Language Teaching Research, 17,* 1: 9–30.

Nields, A.N. (2014). *Preservice teachers' knowledge and perception of effective behavior management strategies.* ProQuest UMI Dissertations online.

Nijs, S. & Maes, B. (2014). Social peer interactions in persons with profound intellectual and multiple disabilities: A literature review. *Education and Training in Autism and Developmental Disabilities, 49,* 1: 153–165.

Noll, B.L. & Lenhart, L.A. (2014). Meeting first-year challenges in reading instruction. *Reading Teacher, 67,* 4: 264–268.

Nordahl, J., Beran, T. & Dittrick, C.J. (2013). Psychological impact of cyber-bullying: Implications for school counsellors. *Canadian Journal of Counselling and Psychotherapy, 47,* 3: 383–402.

Northern Illinois University. (2014). *Situated learning*. Accessed 16 December 2014 at: www.niu. edu/facdev/resources/guide/strategies/situated_learning.pdf.

Nowicki, E.A. (2012). Intergroup evaluations and norms about learning ability. *Social Development, 21*, 1: 130–149.

Nowicki, E.A., Brown, J. & Stepien, M. (2014). Children's structural conceptualizations of their beliefs on the causes of learning difficulties. *Journal of Mixed Methods Research, 8*, 1: 69–82.

OECD (Organisation for Economic Co-operation and Development). (2006). *Starting Strong II: Early childhood and care*. Paris: OECD.

OECD (Organisation for Economic Co-operation and Development). (2007). *Students with disabilities, learning difficulties and disadvantages: Policies, statistics, and indicators*. Paris: OECD.

OECD (Organisation for Economic Co-operation and Development). (2013). *OECD Skills Outlook 2013: First results from survey of adults*. Paris: OECD.

OfSTED (Office for Standards in Education: UK). (2010). *Special education needs and disability review*. London: Office for Standards in Education.

OfSTED (Office for Standards in Education: UK). (2013a). *The most able students: Are they doing as well as they should be in our non-selective secondary schools?* London: OfSTED.

OfSTED (Office for Standards in Education: UK). (2013b). *School inspection handbook*. London: OfSTED.

Oliver, R.M., Hollo, A. & Wehby, J.H. (2014). Unidentified language deficits in children with emotional and behavioral disorders: A meta-analysis. *Exceptional Children, 80*, 2: 169–187.

Ouelette, G., Senechal, M. & Haley, A. (2013). Guiding children's invented spelling: A gateway into literacy learning. *Journal of Experimental Education, 81*, 2: 261–279.

Pajares, F. & Urdan, T. (Eds). (2006). *Self-efficacy beliefs of adolescents*. Greenwich, CT: Information Age Publishing.

Pandya, A.A. & Jogsan, Y.A. (2013). Personality and locus of control among school children. *Educational Research and Reviews, 8*, 22: 2193–2196.

Papen, U., Watson, K. & Marriot, N. (2012). *The phonological influences on children's spelling*. Department of Linguistics and English Language, University of Lancaster. Accessed 16 December 2014 at: www.lancs.ac.uk/fss/linguistics/staff/kevin/spelling.htm.

Pappano, L. (2014). Changing the face of math. *The Education Digest, 79*, 6: 10–12.

Parsons, S.A. & Vaughn, M. (2013). A multiple case study of two teachers' instructional adaptations. *Alberta Journal of Educational Research, 59*, 2: 299–318.

Pawelski, C.E. (2007). Conductive education. In A.M. Bursztyn (Ed.), *The Praeger handbook of special education* (pp. 84–88). Westport, CT: Praeger.

Pearn, C. (2014). Reducing mathematics anxiety. *Teacher Magazine online*, 17 July 2014. Accessed 16 December 2014 at: http://teacher.acer.edu.au/article/reducing-mathematics-anxiety.

Pelatti, C.Y., Pentimonti, J.M. & Justice, L.M. (2014). Methodological review of the quality of Reach Out and Read: Does it work? *Clinical Pediatrics, 53*, 4: 343–350.

Pentimonti, J.M. & Justice, L.M. (2010). Teachers' use of scaffolding strategies during read alouds in the preschool classroom. *Early Childhood Education Journal, 37*, 4: 241–248.

Petersen, L. (2014). *Special Educational Needs Update*. Tamworth: NASEN.

Peterson, J.M. & Hittie, M.M. (2010). *Inclusive teaching: The journey toward effective schools for all learners* (2nd edn). Boston, MA: Pearson-Merrill.

Peterson, P.E., Woessmann, L., Hanushek, E.A. & Lastra-Anadon, C.X. (2011). *Globally challenged: Are U.S. students ready to compete?* PEPG Report No. 11–03. Cambridge, MA: Harvard Kennedy School.

Peterson, S. (2014). *Supporting struggling writers. What works? Research into Practice Monograph 49*. Government of Ontario Canada. Accessed 16 December 2014 at: www.edu.gov.on.ca/eng/literacynumeracy/inspire/research/WW_StrugglingWriters.pdf.

Peterson, S. & Portier, C. (2014). Grade One peer and teacher feedback on student writing. *Education 3–13, 42*, 3: 237–257.

Petscher, Y., Kershaw, S., Koon, S. & Foorman, B.R. (2014). *Testing the importance of individual growth curves in predicting performance on a high-stakes reading comprehension test in Florida* (REL 2014–006). Washington, DC: US Department of Education, Institute of Education Sciences.

Petscher, Y., Wanzek, J. & Otaiba, S.A. (2014). Oral reading fluency development for children with emotional disturbance or learning disabilities. *Exceptional Children, 80*, 2: 187–215.

Piaget, J. (1963). *Origins of intelligence in children.* New York: Norton.

Pieratt, J.R. (2011). *Teacher-student relationships in project based learning: A case study of High Tech Middle North County.* Online Proquest Dissertation and Theses.

Pletka, B. (2007). *Educating the Net generation.* Santa Monica, CA: Santa Monica Press.

Poduska, J.M. & Kurki, A. (2014). Guided by theory, informed by practice: Training and support for the Good Behavior Game, a classroom-based behavior management strategy. *Journal of Emotional and Behavioral Disorders, 22*, 2: 83–94.

Polkinghorne, J. (2004). Electronic literacy: Part 1 and Part 2. *Australian Journal of Learning Disabilities, 9*, 2: 24–27.

Pollard, M. (2004). *Sound Check Spelling 1 & 2.* Melbourne: Learning Logic & ACER Press.

Pooley, E. (2014). Motor skills: What's normal and what's not? *Today's Parent, 31*, 1: 28–30.

Porter, N. (2012). *Gifted education in the United States.* Accessed 16 December 2014 at: www.childresearch.net/projects/special/2012_01.html.

Powell, S.R. & Fuchs, L.S. (2012). Early numerical competencies and students with mathematics difficulties. *Focus on Exceptional Children, 44*, 5: 1–17.

Prizant, B.M., Wetherby, A.M., Rubin, E., Laurent, A. & Rydell, P. (2006). *The SCERTS Manual: A comprehensive educational approach for children with autism spectrum disorders.* Baltimore, MD: Brookes.

Prosser, B. & Reid, R. (2013). The DSM-5 changes and ADHD: More than a tweak of terms. *Australian and New Zealand Journal of Psychiatry, 47*, 12: 1196–1197.

Rabbidge, M. & Lorenzutti, N. (2013). Teaching story without struggle: Using graded readers and their audio packs in the EFL classroom. *English Teaching Forum, 51*, 3: 28–35.

Ravenscroft, J. (2012). Visual impairment and mainstream education: Beyond mere awareness raising. In L. Peer & G. Reid (Eds), *Special educational needs: A guide for inclusive practice* (pp. 196–210). London: Sage.

Reed, D.K. (2012). *Why teach spelling?* Portsmouth, NH: Center on Instruction/RMC Research Corporation. Accessed 16 December 2014 at: www.centeroninstruction.org/files/Why%20Teach%20Spelling.pdf.

Reed, M., Peternel, G., Olszewski-Kubilius, P. & Lee, S.Y. (2009). Project EXCITE: Implications for educators of gifted minority students. *Teaching for High Potential*, Spring Issue: 4–6.

Regan, K.S. & Martin, P.J. (2014). Cultivating self-regulation for students with mild disabilities. *Intervention in School and Clinic, 49*, 3: 164–173.

Reid, D.H. & Green, C.W. (2006). Preference-based teaching: Helping students with severe disabilities enjoy learning without problem behavior. *Teaching Exceptional Children Plus* (Article 2), 2: 3.

Renzulli, J.S. (1976). The enrichment triad model: A guide for developing defensible programs for the gifted and talented. *Gifted Child Quarterly, 20*: 303–326.

Renzulli, J.S. (2005). The three-ring conception of giftedness: A developmental model for promoting creative productivity. In R.J. Sternberg & J.E. Davidson (Eds), *Conceptions of giftedness* (2nd edn, pp. 246–279). New York: Cambridge University Press.

Renzulli, J.S. & Reis, S.M. (1997) *The Schoolwide Enrichment Model: A how-to guide for educational excellence.* Mansfield Center, CT: Creative Learning Press.

Reynolds, M., Wheldall, K. & Madelaine, A. (2007). Meeting Initial Needs in Literacy (MINILIT): A ramp to MULTILIT for younger low-progress readers. *Australian Journal of Learning Disabilities, 12*, 2: 67–72.

Reynolds, T., Zupanick, C.E. & Dombeck, M. (2014). *Onset and prevalence of intellectual disabilities.* Pecan Valley Centers Behavioral and Developmental Healthcare. Accessed 16 December 2014 at: www.pvmhmr.org/poc/view_doc.php?type=doc&id=10329&cn=208.

Rhodes, C. (2014). Do social stories help to decrease disruptive behaviour in children with autism spectrum disorders? A review of the published literature. *Journal of Intellectual Disabilities, 18*, 1: 35–50.

Rimm, S.B. & Lovance, K.J. (2004). The use of subject and grade skipping for the prevention and reversal of underachievement. In L. Brody (Ed.), *Grouping and acceleration practices in gifted education* (pp. 33–45). Thousand Oaks, CA: Corwin Press.

Ring, J., Barefoot, L.C., Avrit, K.J., Brown, S.A. & Black, J.L. (2013). Reading fluency instruction for students at risk for reading failure. *Remedial and Special Education, 34*, 2: 102–112.

Ritchey, K.D. & Coker, D.L. (2014). Identifying writing difficulties in first grade: An investigation of writing and reading measures. *Learning Disabilities Research & Practice, 29*, 2: 54–65.

Rivera, C.J. & Baker, J.N. (2013). Teaching students with intellectual disability to solve for X. *Teaching Exceptional Children, 46*, 2: 14–20.

Roberts, D. (2012). *Spelling With Imagery (SWIM)*. Accessed 16 December 2014 at: www.psych-online.co.uk/p3s.html.

Robertson, L. (2009). *Literacy and deafness*. San Diego, CA: Plural Publishing.

Rodriguez, C.D., Strnadova, I. & Cumming, T. (2014). Using iPads with students with disabilities: Lessons learned from students, teachers and parents. *Intervention in School and Clinic, 49*, 4: 244–250.

Rogers, B. (2014). Calm the classroom storm. *Teacher Magazine Online*, August issue. Accessed 16 December 2014: at http://teacher.acer.edu.au/article/calm-the-classroom-storm.

Rogers, S. & Ozonoff, S. (2014). Intervention in 6-month-olds with autism ameliorates symptoms, alleviates developmental delay. News Bulletin from University of California Davis Health Center, 8 September 2014. Accessed 16 December at: www.ucdmc.ucdavis.edu/publish/news/newsroom/9182.

Rose, J. (2009). *Identifying and teaching children and young people with dyslexia and literacy difficulties*. Nottingham: DCSF Publications. Accessed 1 September 2014 at: http://publications.teachernet.gov.uk/default.aspx?PageFunction=productdetails&PageMode=publications&ProductId=DCSF-00659-2009&.

Rosenberg, M.S., Westling, D.L. & McLeskey, J. (2013). *Primary characteristics of students with intellectual disability*. Accessed 16 December 2014 at: www.education.com/reference/article/characteristics-intellectual-disabilities/.

Rosenshine, B. & Meister, C. (1994). Reciprocal teaching: A review of research. *Review of Educational Research, 64*, 4: 479–530.

Rosenthal, J. & Ehri, L.C. (2011). Pronouncing new words aloud during the silent reading of text enhances fifth graders' memory for vocabulary words and their spellings. *Reading and Writing: An Interdisciplinary Journal, 24*, 8: 921–950.

Rowe, K. (2006). Effective teaching practices for students with and without learning difficulties. *Australian Journal of Learning Disabilities, 11*, 3: 99–115.

Russell, J. & Cohn, R. (2012). *Snoezelen*. Stoughton, WI: Books on Demand.

Sabielny, L.M. & Cannella-Malone, H.I. (2014). Comparison of prompting strategies on the acquisition of daily living skills. *Education and Training in Autism and Developmental Disabilities, 49*, 1: 145–152.

Safar, A.H. & Alkhezzi, F.A. (2013). Beyond computer literacy: Technology integration and curriculum transformation. *College Student Journal, 47*, 4: 614–627.

Salend, S.J. (2011). *Creating inclusive classrooms: Effective and reflective practices for all students* (7th edn). Upper Saddle River, NJ: Pearson.

Salisbury, R. (Ed.). (2008). *Teaching pupils with visual impairment*. London: Routledge.

Salmon, N. (2013). 'We just stick together': How disabled teens negotiate stigma to create lasting friendship. *Journal of Intellectual Disability Research, 57*, 4: 347–358.

Sanchez, M., Magnan, A. & Ecalle, J. (2012). Knowledge about word structure in beginning readers: What specific links are there with word reading and spelling? *European Journal of Psychology of Education, 27*, 3: 299–317.

Sanetti, L.M.H., Maggin, D.M., Ruberto, L.M. & Fallon, L. (2012). Training paraeducators to implement a group contingency protocol: Direct and collateral effects. *Behavioral Disorders, 38,* 1: 18–28.

Scharer, P.L. & Zutell, J. (2003). The development of spelling. In N. Hall, J. Larson & J. Marsh (Eds), *Handbook of early childhood literacy.* London: Sage.

Scheffler, R.M., Brown, T.T., Fulton, B.D., Hinshaw, S.P., Levine, P. & Stone, S. (2009). Positive association between attention deficit-hyperactivity disorder medication use and academic achievement during elementary school. *Pediatrics, 123,* 5: 1273–1279.

Schefkind, S., James, L.W. & Pizur-Barnekow, K.A. (2014). Online survey examining practitioners' perceived preparedness in the early identification of autism. *American Journal of Occupational Therapy, 68,* 1: 13–23.

Scheidecker, B., Hendrickson, J.M., Carson, R., Woods-Groves, S. & Mendenhall, J. (2013). UI REACH: A postsecondary program serving students with autism and intellectual disabilities. *Education and Treatment of Children, 36,* 4: 169–188.

Schwartzman, R. (2013). Reviving a digital dinosaur: Text-only synchronous online chats and peer tutoring in communication centers. *College Student Journal, 47,* 4: 653–668.

Schwonke, R., Ertelt, A., Orieno, C., Renkl, A., Aleven, V. & Salden, R.J. (2013). Metacognitive support promotes an effective use of instructional resources in intelligent tutoring. *Learning and Instruction, 23:* 136–150.

Scott, C.M. & Balthazar, C. (2013). The role of complex sentence knowledge in children with reading and writing difficulties. *Perspectives on Language and Literacy, 39,* 3: 18–33.

Scott, J.G., Moore, S.E., Sly, P.D. & Norman, R.E. (2014). Bullying in children and adolescents: A modifiable risk factor for mental illness. *Australian and New Zealand Journal of Psychiatry, 48,* 3: 209–212.

Scottish Government. (2013). *Report: Children and young people's experience of, and views on, issues related to implementation of the United Nations Convention on the Rights of the Child.* Edinburgh: Government of Scotland.

Seidenberg, M.S. (2012). Politics [of reading] makes strange bedfellows. *Perspectives on Language and Literacy, 20:* 9–11.

Serry, T., Rose, M. & Liamputtong, P. (2014). Reading Recovery teachers discuss Reading Recovery: A qualitative investigation. *Australian Journal of Learning Difficulties, 19,* 1: 61–73.

Shepherd, T.L. (2010). *Working with students with emotional and behavior disorders.* Upper Saddle River, NJ: Pearson Education.

Siegle, D. (2014). Technology: Differentiating instruction by flipping the classroom. *Gifted Child Today, 37,* 1: 51–55.

Slavin, R., Lake, C. & Groff, C. (2009). Effective programs in middle and high school mathematics: A best-evidence synthesis. *Review of Educational Research, 72,* 2: 839–911.

Slavin, R. & Madden, N.A. (2012). *Success for All: Summary of research on achievement outcomes.* Accessed 16 December 2014 at: www.successforall.org/SuccessForAll/media/PDFs/Summary_of_Research_September_2012.pdf.

Slavin, R.E. & Madden, N.A. (2013). Success for All at 27: New developments in whole-school reform. *Journal of Education for Students Placed at Risk, 18,* 3–4: 169–176.

Slavin, R., Madden, N.A., Chambers, B. and Haxby, B. (2009). *Two million children: Success for All* (2nd edn). Thousand Oaks, CA: Corwin Press.

Smith, B., Spooner, F. & Wood, C.L. (2013). Using embedded computer-assisted explicit instruction to teach science to students with autism spectrum disorder. *Research in Autism Spectrum Disorders, 7,* 3: 433–443.

Smith, D.D. & Tyler, N.C. (2010). *Introduction to special education: Making a difference* (7th edn). Upper Saddle River, NJ: Pearson Educational.

Smithers, A. & Robinson, P. (2012). *Educating the highly able: The Sutton Trust Report.* London: The Sutton Trust.

Sood, S. & Jitendra, A.K. (2013). An exploratory study of a number sense program to develop kindergarten students' number proficiency. *Journal of Learning Disabilities*, *46*, 4: 328–346.

Southwell, P. (2012). The psycho-social challenge of adapting to visual impairment. *British Journal of Visual Impairment*, *30*, 2: 108–114.

Stahmer, A.C. (2014). Effective strategies by any other name. *Autism*, *18*, 3: 211–212.

Staudt, D.H. (2009). Intensive word study and repeated reading improves reading skills for two students with learning disabilities. *Reading Teacher*, *63*, 2: 142–151.

Stockall, N. & Dennis, L.R. (2014). Using pivotal response training and technology to engage preschoolers with autism in conversations. *Intervention in School and Clinic*, *49*, 4: 195–202.

Strassman, B.K. & Schirmer, B. (2013). Teaching writing to deaf students: Does research offer evidence for practice? *Remedial and Special Education*, *34*, 3: 166–179.

Sulak, T.N. (2014). Using CBM to identify advanced learners in the general education classroom. *Gifted Child Today*, *37*, 1: 25–31.

Sullivan, A.L. & Sadeh, S.S (2014). Is there evidence to support the use of social skills interventions for students with emotional disabilities? *Journal of Applied School Psychology*, *30*, 2: 107–131.

Sullivan, A.M., Johnson, B., Owens, L. & Conway, R. (2014). Punish them or engage them? Teachers' views of unproductive behaviour in the classroom. *Australian Journal of Teacher Education*, *39*, 6: 43–56.

Sumner, E., Connelly, V. & Barnett, A.L. (2013). Children with dyslexia are slow writers because they pause more often and not because they are slow at handwriting execution. *Reading and Writing: An Interdisciplinary Journal*, *26*, 6: 991–1008.

Supalo, C.A., Mallouck, T., Rankel, L., Amorosi, C. & Graybill, C. (2008). Low cost laboratory adaptations for pre-college students who are blind or visually impaired. *Journal of Chemical Education*, *85*, 2: 243–247.

Swain, K., Bertini, T. & Coffey, D. (2010). The effects of folding-in of basic mathematical facts for students with disabilities. *Learning Disabilities: A Multidisciplinary Journal*, *16*, 1: 23–29.

Swanson, H.L. (2000). What instruction works for students with learning disabilities? In R. Gersten, E. Schiller & S. Vaughn (Eds), *Contemporary special education research* (pp. 1–30). Mahwah, NJ: Erlbaum.

Szymanski, C., Lutz, L., Shahan, C. & Gala, N. (2013). *Critical needs of students who are deaf or hard of hearing: A public input summary*. Washington, DC: Laurent Clerc National Deaf Education Center.

Tanguay, P.B. (2010). *Nonverbal learning disorder: Common characteristics*. Accessed 16 December 2014 at: www.nldontheweb.org/nldentrylevelreading/nldcharacteristics.html.

TeacherNet. (2010). *Quality Standards in Education: Support Services for Children and Young People with Visual Impairment*. Accessed 18 December 2014 at: www.teachernet.gov.uk/_doc/6576/quality%20standards%20-%20visual%20impair.htm.

Templeton, S.R., Bear, D.R., Invernizzi, M.A., Johnston, F.R., Flanigan, K., Townsend, D.R., Helman, L. & Hayes, L. (2015). *Vocabulary their way: Word study with middle and secondary students* (2nd edn). Boston, MA: Pearson.

TES Connect. (2014). *SEN and the National Curriculum: The DfE's advice*. Accessed 16 December 2014 at: http://community.tes.co.uk/national_curriculum_2014/b/sen_and_the_new_national_curriculum/archive/2014/01/06/sen-and-the-national-curriculum-the-dfe-39-s-advice.aspx.

Tetley, D. & Jones, C. (2014). Pre-service teachers' knowledge of language concepts: Relationships to field experiences. *Australian Journal of Learning Difficulties*, *19*, 1: 17–32.

Thompson, D. (2013). Obese children more likely to have asthma. *Health Day News Online*. Accessed 16 December 2014 at: http://consumer.healthday.com/respitory-and-allergy-information-2/asthma-news-47/asthma-and-obesity-679009.html.

Thornton, J. (2013). The 4E Wiki Writing Model: Redefining collaboration for technological relevance. *Curriculum and Teaching Dialogue*, *15*, 2: 49–62.

Toland, M.D., Bottge, B.A., Ma, X., Gassaway, L. & Butler, M. (2014). Detecting and correcting fractions computation error patterns. *Exceptional Children*, *80*, 2: 237–255.

Tomlinson, C.A., Kaplan, S.N., Purcell, J.H., Leppien, J.H., Burns, D.E., Renzulli, J.S., Imbeau, M.B. & Strickland, C.A. (2008). *The Parallel Curriculum* (2nd edn). Thousand Oaks, CA: Corwin Press.

Torgerson, C., Brooks, G. & Hall, J. (2006). *A systematic review of the research literature on the use of phonics in the teaching of reading and spelling. Research Report 711.* London: Department for Education and Skills.

Torrington, J. (2013). Using guided inquiry in a Year 3 classroom. *Access, 27,* 4: 22–24.

Tout, D. (2014a). Lessons from PISA. *Teacher,* June issue (n.p.). Melbourne: Australian Council for Educational Research.

Tout, D. (2014b). Buried or not? What's happened to numeracy? *RD Research Developments.* Australian Council for Educational Research, July issue online.

Tracey, L., Chambers, B., Slavin, R.E., Hanley, P. & Cheung, A. (2014). Success for All in England: Results from the third year of a national evaluation. *SAGE Open, 4,* 3.

Treiman, R., Stothard, S. & Snowling, M.J. (2013). Instruction matters: Spelling of vowels by children in England and the US. *Reading & Writing: An Interdisciplinary Journal, 26,* 3: 473–487.

Trezek, B.J., Wang, Y. & Paul, P.V. (2010). *Reading and deafness: Theory, research and practice.* Clifton Park, NY: Delmar.

Tunmer, W.E., Chapman, J.W., Greaney, K.T., Prochnow, J.E. & Arrow, A.W. (2013a). Reading Recovery and the failure of the New Zealand national literacy strategy. *LDA Bulletin, 45,* 3: 13–17.

Tunmer, W.E., Chapman, J.W., Greaney, K.T., Prochnow, J.E. & Arrow, A.W. (2013b). Report: *Why the New Zealand national literacy strategy has failed, and what can be done about it.* Palmerston North, NZ: Massey University Institute of Education.

Turnbull, A., Turnbull, R., Wehmeyer, M.L. & Shogren, K.A. (2012). *Exceptional lives* (7th edn). Upper Saddle River, NJ: Pearson.

Ullman, E. (2014). Helping children to help themselves. *Tech and Learning, 34,* 6: 36–37.

University of Kansas. (2014). *Learning strategies.* Center for Research on Learning. Accessed 16 December 2014 at: www.ku-crl.org/sim/strategies.shtml.

University of Washington. (2012). *Working together: Computers and people with learning disabilities.* Accessed 16 December 2014 at: www.washington.edu/doit/Brochures/Technology/atpwld. html.

US Department of Education. (2004). *Individuals with Disabilities Education Improvement Act, Public Law 108–446:108th Congress.* Accessed 16 December 2014 at: http://idea.ed.gov/download/statute.html.

US Department of Education. (2014). *Digest of education statistics.* Washington, DC: Institute of Educational Sciences.

VanNess, A.R., Murnen, T.J. & Bertelsen, C.D. (2013). Let me tell you a secret: Kindergartners can write! *Reading Teacher, 66,* 7: 574–585.

VanTassel-Baska, J. (2014). Curriculum issues: Artful inquiry – the use of questions in working with the gifted. *Gifted Child Today, 37,* 1: 48–50.

Vaughn, S. & Wanzek, J. (2014). Intensive interventions in reading for students with reading disabilities: Meaningful impacts. *Learning Disabilities Research & Practice, 29,* 2: 46–53.

Vesay, J.P. & Gischlar, K.L. (2013). The Big 5: Teacher knowledge and skill acquisition in early literacy. *Reading Horizons, 52,* 3: 281–293.

Virues-Ortaga, J., Julio, F.M. & Pastor-Barriuso, R. (2013). The TEACCH program for children and adults with autism: A meta-analysis of intervention studies. *Clinical Psychology Review, 33,* 8: 940–953.

Vogl, K. & Preckel, F. (2014). Full-time ability grouping of gifted students: Impacts on social self-concept and school-related attitudes. *Gifted Child Quarterly, 58,* 1: 51–68.

Walcott, C.M., Marett, K. & Hessel, A.B. (2014). Effectiveness of a computer-assisted intervention for young children with attention and reading problems. *Journal of Applied School Psychology, 30,* 2: 83–106.

Wang, C., Berry, B. & Swearer, S.M. (2013). The critical role of school climate in effective bullying prevention. *Theory into Practice, 52,* 4: 296–302.

Wang, C.H., Shannon, D.M. & Ross, M.E. (2013). Students' characteristics, self-regulated learning, technology self-efficacy, and course outcomes in online learning. *Distance Education, 34,* 3: 302–323.

Wang, P. & Spillane, A. (2009). Evidence-based social skills interventions for children with autism: A meta-analysis. *Education and Training in Developmental Disabilities, 44,* 3: 318–342.

Warden, C.A., Stanworth, J., Ren, J.B. & Warden, A.R. (2013). Synchronous learning best practices: An action research study. *Computers and Education, 63:* 197–207.

Waters, H.S. & Schneider, W. (Eds). (2010). *Metacognition, strategy use and instruction.* New York: Guilford Press.

Wehmeyer, M.L. & Abery, B.H. (2013). Self-determination and choice. *Intellectual and Developmental Disabilities, 51,* 5: 399–411.

Wehmeyer, M.L. & Field, S.L. (2007). *Self-determination: Instructional and assessment strategies.* Thousand Oaks, CA; Corwin Press.

Weierink, L., Vermeulen, R.J. & Boyd, R.N. (2013). Brain structure and executive functions in children with cerebral palsy: A systematic review. *Research in Developmental Disabilities: A Multidisciplinary Journal, 34,* 5: 1678–1688.

Wendling, B.J. & Mather, N. (2009). *Essentials of evidence-based academic interventions.* Hoboken, NJ: Wiley.

Wendon, L. (2014). *Letterland phonics teacher's guide.* Epsom: Letterland International.

Wendt, J.L. (2013). Combating the crisis in adolescent literacy: Exploring literacy in secondary classrooms. *American Secondary Education, 41,* 2: 38–49.

Wery, J. & Thomson, M.M. (2013). Motivational strategies to enhance effective learning in teaching struggling students. *Support for Learning, 28,* 3: 103–108.

Westwood, P. (2011). The problem with problems: Potential difficulties in using problem-based learning as the core method for teaching mathematics in the primary years. *Australian Journal of Learning Difficulties, 16,* 1: 5–18.

Westwood, P. (2013). *Inclusive and adaptive teaching: Meeting the challenge of diversity in the classroom.* London: Routledge.

Westwood, P. (2014). *Teaching spelling: Exploring commonsense strategies and best practices.* London: Routledge.

What Works Clearinghouse. (2014). *Spelling Mastery: Intervention report.* Princeton, NJ: WWC.

Wheeler, J.J. & Richey, D.D. (2013). *Behavior management* (3rd edn). Columbus, OH: Pearson-Prentice Hall.

Wheldall, K. (2013). Small bangs for big bucks: The long-term efficacy of Reading Recovery. *LDA Bulletin, 45,* 2: 19–20.

William, R.T., Swanlund, A., Miller, S., Konstantopoulos, S., Eno, J., van der Ploeg, A. & Meyers, C. (2014). Measuring instructional differentiation in a large-scale experiment. *Educational and Psychological Measurement, 74,* 2: 263–279.

Williams, A. (2013). A teacher's perspective of dyscalculia: Who counts? *Australian Journal of Learning Difficulties, 18,* 1: 1–16.

Willings, C. (2013). *Transition planning.* Accessed 16 December 2014 at: www.teachingvisually-impaired.com/transition-planning.html.

Windman, V. (2013). Assistive technology 2.0: Special Tech. *Tech and Learning, 33,* 9: 19–21.

Wolter, J.A. & Dilworth, V. (2014). The effects of a multi-linguistic morphological awareness approach for improving language and literacy. *Journal of Learning Disabilities, 47,* 1: 76–85.

Wolter, J.A. & Green, L. (2013). Morphological awareness intervention in school-age children with language and literacy deficits: A case study. *Topics in Language Disorders, 33,* 1: 27–41.

Wood, S. (2010). Best practices in counselling the gifted in schools: What's really happening? *Gifted Child Quarterly, 54,* 1: 42–58.

Woolf, A.M. (2013). Social and emotional aspects of learning: Teaching and learning or playing and learning? *Pastoral Care in Education*, *31*, 1: 28–42.

Woolley, G. (2014). *Developing literacy in the primary classroom*. London: Sage.

Wright, C., Shelton, D. & Wright, M. (2009). A contemporary review of the assessment and treatment of ADHD. *Australian Journal of Learning Difficulties*, *14*, 2: 199–214.

Wright, E.R. & O'Dell, R.S. (2013). The need for effective writing instruction. *Australian Journal of Learning Difficulties*, *18*, 1: 87–101.

Wright, R. (2003). Mathematics Recovery: A program of intervention in early number learning. *Australian Journal of Learning Disabilities*, *8*, 4: 6–11.

Wright, S., Fugett, A. & Caputa, F. (2013). Using E-readers and Internet resources to support comprehension. *Educational Technology & Society*, *16*, 1: 367–379.

Zheng, X., Flynn, L.J. & Swanson, H.L. (2013). Experimental intervention studies on word problem solving and math disabilities: A selective analysis of the literature. *Learning Disabilities Quarterly*, *36*, 2: 97–111.

Index

Main entries are in bold

ability grouping 53, **54**, 113, 151, 159
absences from school 7, 34, 35, 80
academic buoyancy 82
acceleration for gifted **54–5**, 159
accommodations 40: within curriculum 10,
    168–9; for testing 48, **166–7**
activity-based learning 147, 173, 177
adaptive approach: classroom environment 28,
    29, 33, 38, 39, 71, 75, 76, 161, 162;
    adapting curriculum 151, **163–4**; adapting
    instruction 6, 39, 161, **165–6**; adapting
    teaching materials 14, 40, 162, **163–4** (*see
    also* differentiation)
adaptive functioning **13**
ADHD (*see* attention deficit hyperactivity
    disorder)
aggression 18, 25, 32, 75, **79–80**, 91
albinism 36
algorithms 147, 155, 157
allergies 5, **35**, 82
analytic phonics 96
anaphylactic shock 35
applied behaviour analysis (ABA) **21**, **23**, 25, **75**
Asperger syndrome **22**
assessment 6, 20, 22, 48, 63, **106**, 136, **151–2**,
    166, 177
assistive technology 28, **29**, 162, 168: for
    hearing impairment **46–7**; for physical
    disability 28, **29**; for vision impairment **39**
asthma 5, **34–5**
ataxia 29
athetosis 29
attendance at school 7, 34, 35, 72, 80
attention as a prerequisite for learning 25, 32,
    39, **82**, 101, **116**, 174, 175, 181: in autism
    25; as a problem in cerebral palsy 29; in
    intellectual disability 13, **15–16**, 21;
    selective attention 25; in spina bifida 31
attention deficit hyperactivity disorder
    (ADHD) 4, 14, 53, **82–3**, 85, 107, 182;
    interventions for 68, **82–3**

attention-seeking behaviour 69, **74**
attribution retraining **65**
auditory skills in spelling **136–7**
augmentative and alternative communication
    16, 24, 30, **33**, 105, 162
Australian Curriculum 2, 4, 12, **161**, 169;
    mathematics 151, 156, **160**; writing 122
autism spectrum disorders 20, 21–4, 182;
    defined and described 5, **22**; interventions
    for **23–6**, 71, 75; parent involvement 24, 26
automaticity 16, 113, 120, 122: in decoding
    96, 98, 109; in number skills **148**, 150, 154;
    in reading **101**, 109; in spelling 138; in
    word recognition 99, **101**; in writing 122
Autonomous Learner Model **58**, **59**
avoidance strategies 9, 65, 110, 123, 165

basic sight vocabulary 44, **99**, 111, 115 (*see also*
    sight vocabulary)
behavioural learning principles 21, 43, 77, **175**
behaviour contracts **78**
behaviour: management of **69–73**; policies
    concerning **70**, 72, 73, 78, 81; prevention
    70; problems with 21, 69, 70, 74, 85; rules
    for **73**; school team approach **72**
behaviour modification 21, **23**, **74–5**, 83, 85
behaviour problems 21, 69, 70, 74, 85 (*see also*
    emotional or behavioural disorders)
behaviour support teams **72**
blended teaching **182**
blending sounds 95, 109, 113 (*see also* phonics)
blind students 5, 36, **37–9**, 40, 168
booster classes 109
Braille **38**, 162
brain imaging (fMRI) 29, 44, 149
brain injury **32**, 82
bullying 70, 72, **80–1**, 87 (*see also* cyber
    bullying)

calculators 39, 150, 152, **156**, 158, 164
cerebral palsy 5, 28, **29–30**, 35, 36

challenging behaviours 18, 21, 23, 71, 72, 75
childhood obesity **34**
Children and Families Act (UK) 12
Children's Friendship Training 26
choral responding **174**, 175
Circle of Friends **87–8**, **92**
Circle Time **87**
classroom management **69–80**
Classwide Peer Tutoring (CWPT) **87**
CLEAR Curriculum Model **59**
cloze procedure **118**, 119
cluster groups 53, 56
cochlear implants **46–7**
Code of Practice (SEN) **6**
cognitive approaches in autism 23
cognitive behaviour modification (CBM)
    67–8, **75–6**, **79–80**, 85
cognitive control 62
cognitive impairment **5**, **13**: effects of **13–16**,
    34, 61, 81, 85
cognitive load 123, 125
cognitive strategies 16, **65**, 103, 123, 162 (*see
    also* strategy training)
Common Core State Standards (US) 2: for
    mathematics 148, 150, 156, **159**; for reading
    113; for writing 122
comprehension (*see* reading comprehension)
computational skills: numeracy **154–6**, 158
computer-aided instruction (CAI) 11, 159,
    164, 183
computer-aided communication 33
computer-assisted learning (CAL) 56, 83, 119,
    148, **180–1**
computer-based instruction (CBI) **180–1**, 183
concrete operational stage 15, 19, 152
conduct disorders 82
conductive education **30**, 35
conductive hearing loss **41–2**
conference approach to writing **125**
conflict resolution 72, 80
connectedness to school 72, 86
constant time delay **111**, 120
constructivist approach 171, 175, 176, 178: in
    literacy 112; in mathematics **147–8**, 155
cooperative learning 19, 54, 58, 66, **86–7**, 88,
    105, 125, 164, 178
copy-cover-compare spelling strategy **139**
corrective feedback (*see* feedback)
counting as a number skill 150, **153**
creativity **51**
cross-curricular math 149
cued speech 33, 42, 44, **45**
cues and prompts 19, 25, 63, 66, 130, 150,
    155, 162, 164, 166, 167
curriculum adaptation **15**, 151, **163–4**
curriculum compacting **55**
cyber bullying **81**

cyber school 183

daily living skills 14, 15
deaf students (*see* hearing impairment)
deaf-blind students 36
decoding skills for reading 9, 44, 94, **95–8**,
    106, 109, 112, 114 (*see also* phonics)
deficit model **8**
descriptive praise **64**, 76, 88, 126, 166
developmental coordination disorder 10
developmental delay 5, 63, 154
diabetes 5, 34, 36
diagnostic approach in mathematics **151–2**
*Diagnostic and Statistical Manual of Mental
    Disorders* (DSM-5) 1, 5, 8, 9, 10, 13, 22, 23,
    82
diagnostic assessment: number skills **151–2**;
    reading 94, 102–3; spelling **136**, 142, 145
dictation: within spelling programme **142**
differentiation 6, 59, 102, 108, 110, 148, 159,
    161–5, 181: of assessment methods 48,
    166–7; of curriculum content 151, **163–4**;
    for gifted students 50, **54**, 159, 163, 165; of
    homework 165; of objectives for learning
    168; of output (products) from students 34,
    165, 168; of reading assignments **103**; of
    teaching method 6, 39, 161, **165–6**; of
    teaching resources 162, **163–4**
direct instruction **174–5** (*see also* direct
    teaching)
direct teaching 7, 8, **11**, 66, 110, 134, **148**,
    153, 162, 171, 172, 183
disabilities: accommodations for 166, **168–9**;
    defined **3**; mainstream inclusion of **161**, 163
    (*see also* severe and complex disabilities)
discipline plan **73**
discovery learning 147, **176–7**
discovery mathematics 147
discrete trial training 21, **25**
distractibility 8, **16**, 25, 165
disruptive behaviour 69, 72, **76–7**, 110
dyscalculia **149**, 159
dyslexia 5, **9**, 53, 182
dyspraxia 10

Early Intensive Behavioural Therapy (EIBT)
    25
early identification 9, 109: of autism 22; of
    gifted students **50**; of learning difficulties 9;
    of reading difficulties 109; of sensory
    impairment 42, 43; of social problems 86; of
    writing difficulties 122
early intervention 9, 17, 43: for autism **25–6**;
    in reading 93, 110, **115–16**; in vision
    impairment **37**
Education, Health and Care Plan (UK) **5–6**
e-learning 11, 55, 61, 115, 169, **181–2**

emotional or behavioural disorders **4**, 7, 9, 21, 52, 61, 70, 75, 80, 85, 86, 89
English as a second language (ESL) **53**, 98, 103, 117, 118, 138, 141, 142
enrichment for gifted **55–6**, 159
Enrichment Triad Model **57**, 59
epilepsy 29, **31**, 32, 34
evidence-based methods **1**, 6, 7, **11**, 75, **109**, 171
exceptional children **3**
executive functioning **62**
explicit instruction 8, **19**, 71, **94**, 112, 173, 176; in mathematics 148; in reading **94**, 96; in comprehension **101**
explaining: as a teaching tactic 63, 101, **173**, 174
expository teaching **172–3**
extension for gifted **55**, 159, 163, **166**
extrinsic motivation 28

feedback to learners 11, **16**, 32, 73, 91, 110, 119, 120, 124, 162, 166, 172, **181**
First Wave Teaching 6
flashcards 18, 99, 113, 115, 117, **140**
'flipped' classroom 182
fluency in reading 9, 44, **94**, 100, **101**, 109, 111, 113–14, 115, **118**
friendships 18, 22, **85**, 88, 89, **91**
full inclusion **15**

games: in mathematics 153; in reading 18, 97, 99, 115–16; for spelling 145
gender differences in mathematics 149
generalization of learning **16**, **17**, 43, **66–7**, 90, 102, 127, 151, 158, 178, 180 (*see also* transfer of learning)
gifted students 3–4, 10, **49–57**, 93, **165**, 179, 183: creativity **51**; defined **50**; differentiation for 54, 159, 163, 165, 169; identification of **49–50**, 52; with learning disabilities 10, **53**; mathematics **159**, 160; organizational options **53**; prevalence 49; teaching of **54–9**, 179 (*see also* talented students)
Good Behaviour Game **78**
grade skipping 53, **55**
graded reading books 19, **98**, 109, 118
graded worksheets 164 (*see also* tiered assignments)
grammar **122**, 124, 125, 126
group work 62, 91: importance of **88–9**; in mathematics **148–9**, 159; in reading 109, 110, 113, 118
grouping in class 72, 76, 148, 159, 162, 165, **175**
guided discovery **176**
guided practice 8, 11, 101, 110, 114, **128**, 131, 158, 162

guided reading **105–6**, 108, 111, 118
guided writing 124, **126**

handwriting 10, 30, **122**, 132, **138**, 146, 154
health problems 3–4, 5, 8, 34
hearing aids 42, 44, **46**, 48, 168
hearing impairment 5, 29, **41–5**, 138, 168; assessment of **42**, 46; and basic academic skills **44**; teaching methods for **47–8**, 105, 117, 118; types and degrees of 41–2
high achievers (*see* gifted students)
higher-order thinking 56, **177**, **178**
homework 11, 35, 106, 120, **165**, **166**
hydrocephalus **31**
hyperactivity **82**

ICT (information and communication technology) 81, 119, 169, 177, **182**
IEP (Individual Education Plan) **6**, 18, **163**, 168
Impress Method **119**
impulsivity 76, 82
incidental learning 138
inclusive education 13, 14, 15, 17, 36, 37, 43, 54, 62, 85–6; full inclusion 15
Individuals with Disabilities Education Act (US) (IDEA) **4**, **6**, 12
Infant Start **26**
inquiry-based learning **179–80**
intellectual disability: defined and discussed 4–5, **13**, 30, 71; effects of **13–16**, 34, 61, 81, 85; inclusion of students with 13, **14–15**, 91; parental involvement 20; teaching principles and methods **19–21**, 79, 116, 151, 152; transition issues 14, **20**
intellectually gifted students **49**, **56** (*see also* gifted students)
Intensive Interaction Method **20**
interactive whole-class teaching 148, **174**
interventions: for autism **23–6**; for behaviour **71–8**; for mathematics **154–9**; for reading **109–11**; for spelling **143–6**; for writing **127–9** (*see also* early intervention)
invented spelling 95, 134, **135**, 137
issues-based approach **179–80**

Jolly Phonics 97, 108

Kansas Strategic Instruction Model (SIM) 67

language delay **16–17**, 43
language disorders 41, 95, 117, 141
language in deaf students **43**
language-based learning disability **7**, **9**
Language-Experience Approach **116–17**, 120
learned helplessness 8, 93, 157
learning centers 56, 164

learning contracts **55**, 164
learning difficulties **7–8**, 61, 65, 85, 98, 101,
    126, 171, 173, 174, 177, 181: causes 7;
    defined and discussed **3**, 7; general **7–8**;
    specific **8** (*see also* learning disabilities)
learning disabilities **4**, 7, **53**, 61, 67, 112, 141,
    149, 159; defined **8**
Learning Disabilities Association of America 8
lesson study **171–2**
letter clusters **137** (*see also* orthographic units)
Letterland 97
letter-to-sound correspondences **94**, **96–7**,
    109, 115, **118**, 135, **136**, 140 (*see also*
    phonics)
lip reading **45**
lists for spelling **142**
literacy hour 128
literacy skills **9**, 11, 14, 43, **93–107**, **109–20**,
    147, 171, 177, 182; and technology **119–29**,
    147 (*see also* reading; spelling; writing skills)
locus of control 64
look-and-say reading 96
look-cover-write-check: spelling 45, 137,
    139–40, 143
low vision 5, 36, 40
low vision aids **39**

manual communication (*see* sign language)
math anxiety 149
mathematically talented students **159**, 160
mathematics **147–59**: error patterns 151;
    learning difficulties 147, **149–50**, 153;
    problem solving 32, 65–6, 67, 147, 150,
    156; standards **147**; teaching of **148–50** (*see
    also* numeracy)
medication **29**, 31, **34**, **83**
memory 8, 17, 99, 101, 116–7: in intellectual
    disability 13, **16**; in spina bifida 31; in
    traumatic brain injury 32, 33
mental arithmetic 156
mental retardation (*see* intellectual disability)
methods of instruction (*see* teaching methods)
mentoring for gifted 53, 55, **56**
metacognition 23, **61**, **67**, 127, 157
mild intellectual disability **14**
milieu approach **17**, 43
mini lessons 125
mixed-ability teaching 54, 103, 161 (*see also*
    differentiation)
mnemonics 66, 101, 127, 138, 158
mobility training **37–8**
modelling: for problem solving **158**; for
    spelling 143; as a teaching strategy **19**, 43,
    63, **65–6**, 89, 91, **102**, 110, 117, 119, 124,
    162, 175; for writing 124, 128
moderate intellectual disability **14**
modifying the curriculum **15**, **55**, 151, **163–4**

Moon: tactile communication system for the
    blind **39**
morphemes 138, **141**
morphemic approach to spelling **140–1**, 145
morphology 136
motivation 8, 52, 54, 64, 93, 105, 117, 120,
    123, 124, 125, 149, 157, 175, 176, 181
motor coordination **10**, **30**, 32, 33–4, 37, 155,
    164, 167
MULTILIT **114–15**
multiple disabilities 5, 33
multisensory approaches **21**, 97, 109, **116**, 139
music therapy 23
myelomeningocele **31**

National Curriculum (UK) **161**, **169**:
    mathematics 151, 155, 156, **159**; writing 122
non-verbal communication 10
non-verbal learning disability 7, **10–11**, 91
number facts 111, 150; mastery of **154–5**
number sense **150**
number skills 31, 40, 148 (*see also*
    computation)
numeracy 11, 43, **147–59**, 175

obesity **34**
objectives for learning 6, 9, 17, 18, 20, 21, 24,
    55, 63, 116, 145, 150, **163**, **168**, 169, 171,
    172, 174, 176, 179
Old Way/New Way: spelling strategy **144–5**
online learning **183**
onset and rime 95, 144
operant conditioning 21
oralism **45**
oral language 9, 10, 16, 42, 43, 45, 80, 94, 135
oral reading fluency 9, **118**, 119
orientation training for vision impaired 38, 40
orthographic mapping **137**
orthographic memory 137
orthographic units 44, 97, 98–9, **136**, 142
overlearning 11, 115, 117, 145, 181

paired writing **129**
Parallel Curriculum Model **58**, 59
paraprofessionals (aides) 18, 30, 34, 89, **110**,
    113, 125, 162, 166
parental involvement **6**, **17**, **43**, 41, 162: in
    autism **24**; in behaviour change 70, 81; in
    homework 11, 165; in literacy 104, 110,
    120; in numeracy 155
patterned writing **130**
Pause-Prompt-Praise **110–11**
peer assistance 14, 40, 168
peer tutoring 66, 87, 111, 119, 120, 129, 150,
    169
pervasive developmental disorders (PDDs) 5
phonemic awareness 44, **95**, 114, 137

phonetic stage of spelling **135**, 140
phonics 9, 44, **94**, 95, **96**, 104, 107, 110, 112, 122, 137: teaching approach 44, 94, **96–9**, 107, 113, 118, **140** (*see also* synthetic phonics)
Phonics Screening Check (UK) 94, 96, 107
phonological awareness **9**, 94, **95**
physical disabilities **28–32**, 53, 153
pivotal response training 21, **25**
place value in numeracy 150, 153
policies: on bullying 70, 81; on discipline **70**, 72; on gifted students 50
Positive Behaviour Intervention and Support (PBIS) **71**, 83
positive behaviour support **71**, 83
positive reinforcement 71, 73 (*see also* reinforcement)
poverty: effects of 7, 53
practice: vital importance of 9, **11**, **16**, 19, 66, 105, 114, 148, 154
praise: descriptive 76, 126, 166; teachers' use of **64**, 110
preference-based teaching **21**, **25**
prior knowledge: role and importance of 7, 58, 101, 106, 173, 177, 179, **180**
problem-based learning 147, 176, **179–80**
problem-solving 51, 178: in mathematics 32, **65–6**, 67, 147, 150, 151, **152**, **156**
procedural knowledge 151
process approach to writing **124–5**
Program for International Student Assessment (PISA) 147
project-based learning **177**
prompting (*see* cues and prompts)
proofreading for spelling 136, **142**
protective behaviours **18**
P Scales 161
punishment **79**

quality of life **15**, 28, 38, 69
questioning as teaching tactic 11, 106, 128, **165**, **166**, 167, 173, **174**
QuickSmart **113–14**, 120, 150

Reach Out and Read 104
readability of text **101**, 103, 106, **107**, 110, 115, 164
reading **93–107**, **109–20**: comprehension 32, 67, 99, **100–2**; decoding skills 94, **96–8**; fluency **94**, 100, 101, 118, 122; letter knowledge 94, **96–7**, 109, 118, 135, 140; phonics 94, 95, **96**, 104, 107, 110, 112, 122, 137; reading aloud 104–5, **106**, 119; simple view of reading **94–5**; standards 96; teaching methods **104–7**, 172; technology and reading 115, **119**; word recognition 94, **99**, 109, 113, 114, 117, 122

reading comprehension 32, 67, 94, 99, 120, 164: difficulties with 100; improvement in **100–2**, 106, 113, 119; strategies 101, 113, 118, 175
reading disability (*see* dyslexia)
Reading Recovery® **111–12**, 115, 120
reality-based teaching **15**, **19**, 151, **180**
receptive language 7, 30, 135
reciprocal teaching **102**, 103
reinforcement: for behaviour change 63, 71, 73, **75**, **77**, 83; inappropriate use of 74; as a teaching tactic 11, 19, 20, **25**, 91, 97, 115, 125, 181
reluctant writers 123, 127, **128**
remedial teaching 32, 34, 35, 109, 175: mathematics 152, 155; spelling **143–4**
Renzulli's Learning System **57**, 59
repeated reading 113, **118–19**
repeated writing 137, 143, **144**
research-based methods (*see* evidence-based methods)
resource-based learning 163, **178**, 182
response cards **174**
response to intervention model (RtI) **6–7**, 93, 109, 120, 175
rewards (*see* reinforcement)
rote learning 139, 141, 147, 155
rules: for behaviour **73**; for spelling 138, **141**, 145

scaffolding as a teaching tactic 104, 114, 120, 151, 162, 180; for writing 124, 125, 134
SCERTS model **25–6**, 27
Schoolwide Enrichment Model **57**, 59
School-wide Positive Behaviour Support (SWPBS) **71**
segmentation of words **95**, 113, 139
selective attention **25**
self-correction 61, 66, 106, **111**, 127, 134, 135, 142, 157
self-determination **18**, **61–2**, 80
self-directed learning **61**, 177
self-efficacy 8, 28, 61, **64**
self-esteem 8, 34, 37, 53, 58, **79**, 80, 81, 93, 123, 157, 181
self-help skills for intellectually disabled 13, 163
self-injurious behaviour (SIB) 21
self-management 13, 18, 22, 23, **61**, 71, 83, 176, 179: defined **62**; importance of 55, **61–3**; teaching of 25, **63–4**
self-monitoring 18, 65, **67**, **75**, 100, 157
self-regulation 10, 14, **18**, **61**, 67, 80, 127, 143
self-talk 17, 66, **67**, 68, 114: for behaviour control 76, 80
sensori-neural hearing loss **42**, 46
sensory impairments 5, 14, **36–48** (*see also* hearing impairment; vision impairment)

sentence building 111, 116, **118**
sentence combining 130
severe and complex disabilities **14**, 33, 36, 163
shared-book approach **104–5**, 108, 118
shared writing **126**
sight vocabulary 44, **99**, 106, 109, 114, **115**, 117 (*see also* basic sight vocabulary)
sign language 16, 24, **33**, 42, **43**, **45**, 47, 105
simple view of reading **94–5**, 100
Simultaneous Oral Spelling (SOS) **143–4**
situated learning **180**
situation analysis **29**
skills-based approach: reading 94; writing **124**
Snoezelen **21**, **23**
social acceptance **85**
social adjustment: facilitating **86–8**
social development 69, 85: in autism **22**, 24; in intellectual disability **17–18**; in gifted 52; in vision impaired **37**
social communication disorder 23
social competence 82, **85**
social skills 10, 14, 81, **85**: training (coaching) of 10, **18**, 22, 71, **89–90**
social stories: for autism **26**; for behaviour change **78**, 90
spasticity 29
special educational needs: defined and discussed **3–4**, 62, 85, 87, 89, 93, 161, 162, **167**, **168**, 172, 182
special schools 14, **15**, 17, 20, 21, 25, 81, 151, 180
specific learning disability (SpLD) 4, **5**, 112, 141; in gifted learners 53; and social skills 10 (*see also* learning disabilities)
specific learning disorder **8**
speech therapy 17, 42, 43, 47
speech training 43
spelling 44, 95, 105, 109, 119–20, 122, 129, 132, 167; by analogy 136, 142; assessment of 136; dictation **142**; errors 123, 142, 144, 167; lists **142**; methods of instruction **134–41**, 175; rules 138, **141**, 145; stages of development **135–6**, 142; strategies 143
spina bifida 5, **31**
stereotypic behaviours **22**
strategy training 9, 11, 16, 63, 67, **103**, 114: for problem solving 66, **158**; for reading comprehension 94, **101–2**, 109, 114; for spelling 139, **143**; for writing 123, **126–7**
strategy-based instruction 11, **65–6**, 114 (*see also* strategy training)
structural materials for number work 150, **152–3**, 154, 156
student-centered methods 124, 171, 173, 175, **176–8**
study skills 10, 53, 56, 102, 173, 177, 178
Success for All **112–13**, 120

supportive classrooms 70, 80, **86–7**, 110, 128
support personnel 40, 43, 48, 110, 162
Sustained Silent Reading **107**
synthetic phonics **96**, 97, **113**

tactical ignoring 73, **76**
talented learners 4, **49**; defined **51**; fostering talents 56, 57; in mathematics **159** (*see also* gifted students)
task analysis **29**
TEACCH 24, 26
teacher training 50, 72, 93, 114, **115**; deficiencies in **1**, 93, 96, **171**, 175
teaching methods **171–83**: activity-based 147, 173, 177; constructivist 112, **147–8**, 155, 171, 175; explicit 8, **19**, **94**, 112, 148, 173; expository **172–3**; problem-based **179–80**; student-centered 171, 173, **176–8**; teacher-directed 171, 173
technology and reading 115, **119**
THRASS **97**
Tier 1 teaching 6, 12: for behaviour 71; for reading **93–4**, **104–5**
Tier 2 teaching methods 6: for behaviour 71; for reading **109–11**
Tier 3 intensive instruction 6, 175: for behaviour 71; for numeracy 150; for reading 109, **111–12**, 114
tiered assignments **163**, 169
tiered instruction 54
time out 73, 75, **77–8**
token reinforcement **77**
Total Communication Method (TC) **46**
transfer of learning 16, **17**, 43, 90, 113, 115, 124, 142, 176
transition from school 7, 9, 147: for students with intellectual disability 14; for students with specific learning disabilities **9–10**; for students with impaired vision **41**
traumatic brain injury 5, **32–3**, 35, 36
tutoring 6, 28, 64, 107, 109, **110**, 113, 114, **115–16**, 119, 155

underachievement 3, **50**, **52**
Universal Design for Learning (UDL) 162, **168–9**

VAKT (visual, auditory, kinaesthetic, tactile) **116** (*see also* multisensory approaches)
verbal cues 155
virtual classroom 183
vision impairment: assistive technology **39**; defined and discussed 5, 29, **36–9**, 164; social development in **37**; teaching methods for **39–40**
visiting teacher services 40, 48
visual approach in spelling **139–40**

visual cues 24, 33, 136, 158
visual imagery 33, 136, 139, **140**
visual memory 44, 45, 137
visual schedule for autistic students 24, 25
visual skills in spelling **137–8**
vocabulary controlled books 98 (*see also* graded
  reading books)

web-based teaching and learning 57, 119, 148,
  182
whole-class teaching **148**, 173, 174 (*see also*
  interactive whole-class teaching)
whole-language approach 94, 96, 112, 124, 134
word building activities **98**
word families 96, 105, 140, 142, 145
word processing 30, 117, 125, 129, 131,
  132–3

word recognition in reading 94, **99**, 104, 109,
  113, 114, 117, 122
Word Sorts 141, **145**
word study 96, 98–9, 109, **137–8**, 139, **141**,
  145
Word Walls **142**
work experience 20, 41
working memory 62, 158
worksheets 14, 40, 114
writing skills 109, **122–5**, 173: of deaf students
  44; difficulties with writing 67, **122–3**;
  handwriting **10**, 30, **122**; teaching
  approaches **124–7**
writing workshop 124, **125**

Young Autism Program (Lovaas) **25**, **27**

Commonsense Methods for Children with Special Educational Needs

This fully revised and updated seventh edition of *Commonsense Methods for Children with Special Educational Needs* continues to offer practical advice on evidence-based teaching methods and intervention strategies for helping children with a wide range of disabilities or difficulties. The advice the author provides is embedded within a clear theoretical context and draws on the latest international research and literature from the field. Coverage includes:

- learning difficulties and disabilities;
- students with autism spectrum disorders, intellectual disability, physical or health issues, and sensory impairments;
- gifted and talented students;
- developing social skills and self-management;
- behaviour management;
- teaching methods;
- literacy and numeracy;
- curriculum differentiation and adaptive teaching;
- computer-based instruction and e-learning.

Peter Westwood also provides additional information and advice on transition from school to employment for students with disabilities, lesson study, e-learning and computer-aided instruction, and reflects on the important changes made within the latest *Diagnostic and Statistical Manual of Mental Disorders (DSM-5)*.

Peter Westwood is an education consultant, editor and freelance education writer.

Other books by this author

Published by Routledge
Inclusive and adaptive teaching: Meeting the challenge of diversity in the classroom
Teaching spelling: Exploring commonsense strategies and best practices

Published by David Fulton
Learning and learning difficulties
Numeracy and learning difficulties
Reading and learning difficulties
Spelling: Approaches to teaching and assessment